Sustainable Olympic Design and Urban Development

This book explains how a modern Olympic Games can successfully develop a more sustainable design approach by learning from the lessons of the past and by taking account of the latest developments. The text focuses at two levels: one is at the strategic planning level of whether and how Olympic intervention can transform the host city into a more sustainable urban form; the other is on the measures applicable to individual Olympic projects which can be taken to reduce the resource usage and lower the environmental impacts during their procurement and maintenance. It offers an assessment tool that can be tailored to individual circumstance – a tool which emerges from the analysis of previous Summer Games' host cities and from techniques in environmental analysis and assessment.

The work demonstrates that with appropriate planning and design, Olympic urban development has the potential to leave positive environmental legacies to the host city and contribute to environmental sustainability. The environmental performance and effects of Olympic schemes can be judged, and hence improved, by applying appropriate evaluation systems to them. By these means, 'green' Olympic development can be pursued in a more meaningful and controllable way.

Adrian Pitts is Professor of Sustainable Architecture at Sheffield Hallam University.

Hanwen Liao is a Research Fellow in the School of Architecture and Construction at the University of Greenwich and a member of the Urban Renaissance Institute in London.

D1558565

Sustainable Olympic Design and Urban Development

Adrian Pitts and Hanwen Liao

Routledge
Taylor & Francis Group

LONDON AND NEW YORK

First published 2009
by Routledge
2 Park Square, Milton Park, Abingdon, OX14 4RN

Simultaneously published in the USA and Canada
by Routledge
270 Madison Avenue, New York, NY10016

Routledge is an imprint of the Taylor & Francis Group, an informa business

Typeset in Gill Sans by
Florence Production Ltd, Stoodleigh, Devon
Printed and bound in Great Britain by
MPG Books Group, UK

British Library Cataloguing in Publication Data
A catalogue record for this book is available from the British Library

Library of Congress Cataloging in Publication Data
  Pitts, Adrian C.
  Sustainable Olympic design and urban development/Adrian Pitts
  and Hanwen Liao.
       p. cm.
     Includes bibliographical references and index.
  1. Olympics – Environmental aspects.   2. City planning – Environmental
  aspects.   3. Sustainable development.   I. Liao, Hanwen.   II. Title.
  GV721.9.P58 2009
  711′.558 – dc22   2008048999

ISBN10: 0–415–46761–6 (hbk)
ISBN10: 0–415–46762–4 (pbk)

ISBN13: 978–0–415–46761–2 (hbk)
ISBN13: 978–0–415–46762–9 (pbk)

Contents

Illustrations

Figures

Tables

Acknowledgements

The authors wish to acknowledge the valued support and advice of their families, without which this text would not have been possible.

Hanwen Liao thanks the IOC Olympic Studies Centre for the award of a research grant that enabled him to carry out research in the archives of the Olympic Museum in Lausanne, and which supported some of the detailed research necessary for the text.

Illustrations have been prepared by the authors except for the following:

Figure 2.2 © IOC/Albert Meyer
Figure 4.2 © IOC
Figure 4.4 © IOC
Figure 4.6 © IOC/Lothar Rübelt
Figure 4.9 © IOC
Figure 4.10 © IOC/Lothar Rübelt.

Note: This text in no way attempts to associate itself with, nor is it endorsed by, the IOC or the London 2012 Games organisers.

The Olympic development scenario

PART I

Introduction

CHAPTER I

The Olympic dilemma

The first inclination of many readers might be to find the words 'sustainability' and 'Olympics' mutually exclusive. After all, the many thousands of kilometres travelled to attend the event, not only by the numerous athletes, but also by their coaching staff, Olympic officials, worldwide media representatives, sponsors and spectators, represents a significant use of resources and energy. This clearly has significant and consequent negative impacts on the environment and on sustainability. Although numerous commentators may express concern about such impacts, there does not yet appear to be any enthusiasm for cancelling or moderating the scale of the event. Indeed the expectations grow for each Games to be larger and more impressive than the last. The significance of the Games on the world stage is now such that abandoning it is inconceivable.

And yet, at the same time as many concerns are expressed, the hosting of a Games has often been seen as an opportunity for a city to enhance its sustainability (in the broadest sense of the word) and to initiate environmental improvements. Some of the variations in opinion and stance arise from the definitions attributed to the word 'sustainability', and to differences in its interpretation and exploitation.

This text takes a pragmatic view: that the hosting of Olympic Games in cities spread across the globe is likely to continue for some decades to come; but that there is significant opportunity both better to understand and also optimise those aspects of the Games associated with sustainability. Since many of the impacts of hosting the event are at urban and indeed regional scale, much of the description and analysis that follows relates to that scale. Component impacts, such as of sports venues and villages, are also included, but with a view to their incorporation in the larger picture. It must also be acknowledged that much research and development of recent years has already enabled the assessment for sustainability of individual building projects. This book therefore attempts to develop ideas that can work at the overarching, often urban, level. One of the outcomes is a proposal for an evaluation methodology that might be adapted for future events, or used as a guide to optimise sustainable design and development features. In arriving at that point it exposes much valuable material to aid understanding of the dilemma of bringing together sustainable development and the Olympics.

The structure of the discussion

The text is divided into three main sections. In Part 1 (Chapters 1 and 2) the Olympic development scenario is described in which the background to the evolution of the modern Olympic Games since 1896 is expounded, along with significant development that has impacted particularly in the urban context. In Part 2 (Chapters 3 to 6) discussion and explanation focuses on the historic development of the three major components of any Games: planning and integration at urban scale; the procurement of the major venues utilised; and the design and construction of the Olympic Village. Part 3 (Chapters 7 to 11) is concerned with current requirements for hosting an Olympic Games and how criteria and assessment may be used to enhance the sustainability of future events. An evaluation methodology is set out and part tested in relation to contemporary Games. The Games of London in 2012 and its organisers' attempts to produce sustainable outcomes are reviewed. Finally, conclusions and recommendations are offered for the future.

Sustainability and development

The Brundtland report (WCED, 1987) and the Rio Earth Summit (UNCED, 1992) demonstrated a global realisation that a more environmentally sound approach to human development was needed. This included conservation of limited natural resources, avoidance of ecosystem pollution, and reducing the production of greenhouse gases. These features are usually implicit within what is now known as sustainable development, although this can be a rather vague concept that may assume different interpretations.

Among the many definitions, two are often quoted. The first was provided by the Brundtland Commission Report itself, *Our Common Future*: 'Sustainable development is development that meets the needs of the current generation without compromising the ability of future generations to meet their own needs and aspirations' (WCED, 1987). The second comes from the International Union for the Conservation of Nature and Natural Resources (IUCN) in its 1991 joint report: 'Sustainable development is development that improves the quality of human life while living within the carrying capacity of supporting ecosystems' (IUCN, UNCP and WWF, 1991).

These definitions have two essential components: a respect for the natural environment and a concern for human well-being; though these two aspects may often be contradictory. Human activities undertaken in the socio-economic field improve the quality of life, but in doing so may result in negative impacts on the natural environment. On most occasions these impacts are inevitable consequences rather than deliberate acts. By combining these two issues, the concept of sustainability implies equilibrium between resource exploitation and resource conservation in the development process.

The 1992 Rio Earth Summit linked environmental sustainability with issues such as economic conditions and social justice. It is now generally held that sustainable development has three main components: economic sustainability, environmental sustainability and societal sustainability (or equity); and thus abbreviated to 'the three Es' (economics, environment and equity).

There are several points arising from these interpretations. First, the concept of sustainability changes the traditional view of the relationship between human development and the environment. For a long time, the task of urban planning and architectural design was to protect human activities from the robust natural environment. But now it has been realised that the climate and the environment itself also needs to be protected from human activities. Second, it indicates that a 'good' society cannot be achieved only through economic growth without consideration of environmental cost, nor should it unfairly reduce living standards in exchange for resources conservation. Instead, the societal, environmental and economic needs must be met in a balance with each other for a sustainable outcome over time. Third, as climate change and environment degradation are common phenomena faced by the whole human community, sustainable development has a global dimension. In fact, a small development activity occurring in one location can potentially impact upon a much wider spatial area. Hence when considering urban sustainability, it is necessary to think beyond urban areas themselves and in the sense of their wider repercussions on regional and global ecosystems. Finally, sustainable development pursues a harmony and balance between current and future generations, suggesting it is a dynamic inter-generational process of change rather than an ultimate destination. It also means that the concept and its principles are subject to adaptation with the evolution of human society and technology.

The built environment

Although advocacy of the principles of sustainable development implies a need to change many facets of conventional human lifestyle, it is widely recognised that the built environment is perhaps the most important component requiring adjustment. The built environment clearly represents a meaningful sub-set of the whole context of sustainable development (Brandon, 1998). Its production entails significant consumption of raw materials, manpower, energy and other natural resources, which consequently results in dynamic impacts on ecology and habitat. The built environment also determines the spatial organisation of a society and hence impacts upon daily life. The format, quality and distribution of building units, the land-use patterns and the structure of a city affect intrinsic energy needs and efficiency within which social and economic activities operate. On many occasions, luxurious lifestyles, profligate use of finite resources and over-dependence on motorised transportation make cities the prime energy consumer and the major cause of environmental degradation.

Major world cities can be problematic and are more important as the trend of urbanisation continues. At the end of the twentieth century, 47 per cent, or 2.8 billion of the world's population lived in cities, and this is set to increase by around 60 million people per year. By the middle of the twenty-first century, more than five billion, or 61 per cent, of the world's eight billion people will be urban dwellers (UNFPA, 2000).

The resource-profligate nature of the urban built environment in procurement and lifestyle, and the continuing urbanisation process, endow the sustainability debate with an urban focus. If world cities can be designed and managed in such a way that resource use and pollution are reduced, then a major contribution to the solution of the global problem in climate change and environment degradation can be achieved. In this context, the role of urban planners and architectural professionals is significant in leading the environmental movement towards better planning and design. Urban development entails the consumption of non-renewable resources, and is generally irreversible and not self-sufficient; it therefore impacts on the environment not only in the city but also from wherever its needs are resourced. Nevertheless, it should be noted that the natural environment and ecosystem has certain self-rehabilitation capabilities; for instance, to convert man-made carbon dioxide in the atmosphere back to oxygen through its flora, or to decompose landfill waste into mineral elements by soil bacterial action. Thus if the level of inputs and outputs of an urban system can be maintained to match the rate of the environmental self-rehabilitation, the overall system would still be theoretically sustained. If this scenario is not possible using current human technology, development should minimise the use of resources and reduce production of polluting outputs.

The rationale of sustainable development in the urban context can be understood as to encompass planning and design techniques to optimise architectural and urban forms and hence control the exploitation of the built environment on its surrounding natural environment. At the building level, a more sustainable building can be created by employing the latest environmental technology and techniques in the design and construction process. It is less easy at urban and regional level; a sustainable urban form is very unlikely to be established upon virgin soil; rather, it has to be adapted from an existing less-sustainable fabric. As Lombardi and Brandon (1997) pointed out, because human society and its activities are generally in a state of evolution, settlements should be regularly regenerated to meet new economic and social demands. In line with this observation, most mega-event strategies pursued by cities in the developed world aim to act as a stimulus to, and justification for, desirable urban transformation. The case in point here is the planning intervention driven by the preparation for the Olympic Games.

Environmentally sustainable Olympic urban development has two components. First, Olympic projects should be conceived to minimise, if not avoid entirely, the creation of negative consequences to the environment of the host society. Second, at a higher level, Olympic projects should be capitalised, through planning and design efforts, to address local environmental deficiencies and steer the city towards a more sustainable form. Hence, for Olympic urban planners, it is imperative to understand both which dynamics and mechanisms cause the environmental problems that an unsustainable urban context may confront, and the possible ways to avoid or remedy them through design initiatives.

Sustainable urban form

A considerable body of research has been carried out on sustainable urban forms as a response to increasing environmental problems. The general goal is that cities should be developed towards greater self-sufficiency in consuming finite resources. For a long time, the density and distribution of urban populations have been identified as key issues for optimising living–working patterns and reducing dependence on private motorised transport. Various forms of compact and mixed settlements have found favour in recent writings on urban studies, with the rationale of accommodating growth while minimising the use of undeveloped land by encouraging infill and 'brownfield' development (use of previously developed land), and high-density urban cores. Supporters of this theory believe that the trend towards low urban density and the separation of land-use contribute to urban sprawl. The consequences of which would be increased travel demands and energy consumption, causing pollution and congestion, and threatening the natural environment, the ecosystem and agriculture (Jenks et al., 1996; Jenks and Burgess, 2000; Breheny, 2001; EPA, 2001).

In 1990, the Commission of the European Communities took a lead in publishing its Green Paper on the urban environment in advocacy of urban concentration. This marked the beginning of the compact city idea being officially promoted by an influential policy-making body (CEC, 1990). Following this, a number of European countries adopted the idea as policy during the 1990s. In North America, a similar planning theory 'smart growth' has been promoted, though in Asian cities such as Tokyo and Hong Kong, the policy of urban concentration has already been active for decades. At the end of the 1990s, this urban compactness became a planning tendency and was widely welcomed as contemporary wisdom for sustainable development.

Even as the popularity of urban compactness reached its peak, it was widely recognised among the scientific community that the relationship between urban form and environmental improvement was not as simple and direct as portrayed. Debates existed over the feasibility and desirability of promoting compact forms of urban living in traditionally low-density areas; the viability of public transport in societies with high car ownership; and whether the integration of diverse activities at local level would reduce long-distance commuting (Owens, 1986; Banister, 1992; Breheny, 1996; Richardson et al., 2000). These debates suggest that a sustainable urban form cannot be described by a single formula to address the problems of all world cities. Nevertheless, some consensus in urban planning has been accumulated; themes that are generally agreed to support urban sustainability. The key points can be summarised as following:

- urban containment policies should continue to be adopted, and leap-frog expansion of urban mass into surrounding greenfield (undeveloped land) should be avoided;
- extreme compact cities are unnecessary, yet over-dispersed development should be avoided, and various forms of 'decentralised concentration' should be promoted;
- inner cities should be regenerated, and 'counter-urbanisation' activities need to be constrained;
- mixed-use development and employment–housing balance should be reinforced;
- public transportation and transit-orientated development should be fostered;
- vibrant and multi-functional centres of activity should be defined and nurtured;
- urban greening and public realm must be enhanced;
- redevelopment of obsolete estates should be encouraged, and dereliction discouraged;

- Combined Heat and Power (CHP) and District Heating (DH) systems should be encouraged in new and existing developments;
- community and public participation in the decision-making process must be engaged;
- assessment of the environmental impact of any specific proposals should be applied on an individual basis.

The purpose here in outlining these points is to serve as background, based upon which different types of Olympic intervention can be compared and examined in a more meaningful way. Most contemporary environmental problems have arisen from the excessive use of energy for transportation and building operation in current urban spatial arrangements. Substantial effort may be needed to reduce private car travel without compromising people's ability to meet their quality-of-life expectations. A society fulfilling all the above criteria may not be guaranteed energy saving and sustainability since personal choice will still have an effect, however at least it will provide the opportunity for change.

Olympic urban intervention

Olympic urban development impacts on the host city's built environment at different levels. At the building level, newly built and refurbished Olympic facilities endow the city with new examples; and at the same time may change the city's environment in terms of the building scale and size, materials usage, energy demands, water consumption and ecological value. These changes can be positive and inspirational. For instance, to apply passive thermal techniques to an existing sports arena may lead to both energy savings and improvement to comfort levels; and to establish a venue on a previously contaminated site using appropriate remedial measures and horticultural practice can improve the site's ecology. For each Games, the number of Olympic projects is limited, but considering their greater impacts on design fashion and technological understanding, their wider demonstration effects should not be underestimated.

At the neighbourhood level, Olympic projects may modify urban blocks with respect to building density, public utility provision, civic infrastructures, open spaces and urban landscape. By introducing new development, a declining community could be regenerated with socio-economic vigour, cultural identity and a more environmentally friendly spatial order. Olympic intervention may also result in the emergence of several highly concentrated urban nuclei in the host city as new centres of social engagement. At the urban and regional level, by tactically deploying newly defined Olympic urban centres in combination with new transportation infrastructure and urban parklands, Olympic intervention can revise a host city's overall urban form and structure, and reshape its development orientation in the long term.

Much early work on Olympic architecture for sustainable outcomes was focused on the building level of the problem. Yet success at the larger scale is often more important because it addresses more directly the urban deficiencies and the delivery of a holistically sustainable built environment. It has already been recognised for some time that urban sustainability should be considered at a large scale, as the

Charter of European Cities and Towns towards Sustainability (the Aalborg Charter) states:

> We are convinced that the city or town is both the largest unit capable of initially addressing the many urban, architectural, social, economic, political, natural resource and environmental imbalances damaging our modern world and the smallest scale at which problems can be meaningfully resolved in an integrated, holistic and sustainable fashion.
>
> (Aalborg Charter, 1994: 1)

This book, in devising the evaluation framework for Olympic urban intervention, places emphasis on issues with greater impact at the urban or regional level in the overall structure.

The structure of the Olympic Movement

Before embarking on the detailed discussions of the text, a few paragraphs to explain Games structure are valuable. After more than a century of development, the modern Olympic Movement has established an umbrella system encompassing several levels of function. The supreme authority is the 'International Olympic Committee' (IOC) domiciled in Lausanne, which controls the conduct of the Olympic celebration, recognises member organisations and selects host cities. The members of the IOC are elected from the sports realm and its member organisations. In addition to the IOC, the Olympic Movement also includes the 'International Federations' (IFs) for each Summer Olympic sport, the National Olympic Committees (NOCs), the 'Organising Committees of the Olympic Games' (OCOGs) and some other organisations and institutions recognised by the IOC.

The IFs administer each individual sport at world level and encompass sub-organisations administrating sports at national level. Under the supervision of the IOC, each IF maintains its independence and autonomy in controlling the develop-ment of respective sports and technical regulations regarding the competition facilities. The NOCs govern Olympic-related issues within their own countries and take charge of sending athletes to world sports events including the Olympic Games on behalf of their states. The OCOGs are the organisers of each Olympic Games and are responsible for the provision of the competition, and the supporting infrastructure (this is often delegated to a further body). The OCOG is a temporary organisation formed by the NOC of the host country upon the award of the Olympic Games and directly instructed by the IOC for the Games preparation and coordination. Although the organising committee actually organises and runs the event a further body, the Olympic Development Authority (ODA) is normally responsible for providing the infrastructure and settings within which the events take place.

The selection of the host city is voted on by IOC members seven years before the holding of the Olympic Games, following their study of the report by the IOC Evaluation Commission for candidate cities, and/or their own visits. The winning city is tied to a strict contract with the IOC; the cost of staging an Olympic Games is assumed entirely by the OCOG and the host city, sometimes subsidised by the national or local government. Since the Los Angeles Games in 1984, most Games have generated considerable revenue through sponsorship; television rights sales, licensed merchandising and ticketing. It is the privilege of the IOC to negotiate the television rights and sponsorship agreements, and distribute the income to its partners. Undoubtedly the IOC has a major role to play in fostering the notion and practice of sustainable Olympic Games, however the means to achieve it and the vigour, style, skill and understanding with which this is pursued, lies, as will be seen, with the host city and its supporters.

Olympic history and its urban context

The origins of the Olympics

The modern Olympics have inherited cultural and spiritual legacies from their Greek ancestors, but have also grown beyond being a mere sports celebration; they have developed an inclusive set of ideals, known as Olympism. There is a strict bidding procedure based on a detailed examination of candidate cities, ranging from economic vigour to environmental amenity. Many issues are dealt with during preparation for the Games, from marketing propaganda to the Olympic sites' delivery. All of these create a far greater impact on modern host cities than on older counterparts; and this impact is growing. This chapter provides an introduction to the Olympic Movement, its origins and development, and subsequent urban impacts. Some categorisation is provided as a basis for the future framework within which analysis of sustainability issues can occur.

The Olympic Games originated at the shrine of Olympia in ancient Greece as a ritual ceremony celebrated in honour of the god, Zeus. By 776BC the occasion had developed into a quadrennial sports event covering the whole Hellenic world. Originally the Games lasted only one day, but after 472BC it was extended to a five-day event including competitions for running, wrestling, boxing, equestrian sport, chariot racing and a pentathlon.

The ruins of Olympia were rediscovered in 1766 by Richard Chandler, and from 1875 to 1881 German archaeologists, under the direction of Curtius and Adler, excavated the sanctuary in detail. Discoveries revealed that ancient Olympia was crowned with sports premises beautifully planned and built for the pageants: the stadium, the palaestra, the gymnasium and the hippodrome. In the centre of the site rose the Olympieium, the temple that housed the monumental statue of Zeus, one of the Seven Wonders of the Ancient World. On this sacred site, the Olympic Games spanned a period of 1,170 years until abolished by the Roman emperor Theodosius in AD394.

The return of the Games in the modern era

Over several centuries, but particularly in the nineteenth, a series of athletic tournaments took place in a number of cities in Europe, and later North America. These were held under the banner of the 'Olympic Games' and have been well documented (De Coubertin, 1896). These Games left little impact in history but

Figure 2.1

The old Olympic Stadium in Athens refurbished for the 1896 Games

did evoke the aspiration of the Olympic spirit and tradition. The archaeological rediscovery of Olympia, along with other spectacular excavations in Greece and Asia Minor, coincided with a wave of philhellenism sweeping through the occidental world, and this paved the way for the resurrection of the Olympics on the international stage.

The nineteenth century also saw dramatic changes in people's understanding of, and attitudes towards, social affairs. Reforms occurred in many fields and the form of traditional education was criticised for its increasing incompatibility with the new conditions of scientific, industrial and social life (Sorbonne, 2000). Starting with ideas for education reform, French thinker and educationalist, Baron De Coubertin (1863–1937), proposed to revive the Olympic Games at the International Athletes Congress in 1894. De Coubertin believed that with the spirit of Olympism, an individual could 'restore the ancient harmony between the body and the mind, which the education system in the west had lost after the collapse of ancient culture'; and overcome 'physical weakness, intellectual dullness and moral degradation' (reported by Sorbonne, 2000). He also believed organised sport could be used as an agent of international unity and social equality (Essex and Chalkey, 1999). De Coubertin's perseverance led to the establishment of the International Olympic Committee (IOC) in 1894, and the first modern Olympiad in 1896 in Athens. He himself laid down the objectives and principles of the Olympic Movement, which remain even today as central concepts of the Games:

- to foster the goals of competitive sport;
- to provide a legacy of facilities that would stimulate athletic development which would not otherwise have been possible; and
- to raise the profile of the sports involved by providing better opportunities for training as well as sites for national and international competition.

(Hall, 1992)

A brief history of the modern Games

Since 1896, except during times of war, Olympiads have taken place every four years. Up to 2008, 26 Summer Olympiads had been staged in 22 different cities scattered in 18 countries. There is much published literature summarising the development of the Olympic Games with attempts at 'periodising' its history. Table 2.1 shows the Olympic chronology and provides examples of periodisation made by Essex and Chalkey (1999), Preuss (2000) and Varela (2002). The methods of division vary depending on the purpose and nature of the research, but they reveal the Games developing from small-scale sports events of modest influence, into colossal scale, high-profile global celebrations.

The first modern Olympics at Athens in 1896 was a successful and hopeful beginning, but the following two Games at Paris and St Louis were poorly organised and chaotic, being eclipsed by Universal Exhibitions. There were almost no meaningful settings built specifically for these Games.

Figure 2.2
De Coubertin (second from the left) and some members of the 1st International Olympic Committee in 1894 (source: IOC, Lausanne © IOC/ Albert Meyer)

Table 2.1 Olympic chronology and periodisation

Year/city	Essex and Chalkey: impact on urbanisation	Preuss: Olympic economics	Varela: Olympism	
1896 Athens	**Phase 1,** small scale, poorly organised and not necessarily involving any new development		**Phase 1,** 'foundation and folklore'	
1900 Paris				
1904 St Louis				
1908 London				1908
1912 Stockholm	**Phase 2,** small scale, better organised and involving construction of purpose-built sports facilities	**Phase 1,** suffering from financing problems, the macroeconomic impacts were given almost no attention	**Phase 2,** reinforcement of sports character, establishment of International Federations	
1920 Antwerp				
1924 Paris				
1928 Amsterdam				
1932 Los Angeles				
1936 Berlin	**Phase 3,** large scale, well organised and involving construction of purpose-built sports facilities with some impact on urban infrastructure			1936
1948 London			**Phase 3,** generalisation of mass media	
1952 Helsinki				
1956 Melbourne				
1960 Rome				1960
1964 Tokyo				
1968 Mexico City	**Phase 4,** large scale, well organised and involving construction of purpose-built sports facilities with significant impact on urban infrastructure		**Phase 4,** financial stability	
1972 Munich		**Phase 2,** sale of TV rights and sponsoring programme grew to a considerable extent, but Games still publicly financed		
1976 Montreal				
1980 Moscow				1980
1984 Los Angeles				
1988 Seoul		**Phase 3,** commencement of major commercialisation and the financial independence of the Olympic Movement	**Phase 5,** renovation of IOC management, Samaranch period	
1992 Barcelona				
1996 Atlanta				
2000 Sydney	(Games not held at time of authors' work)	**Phase 4,** further development of the trends of phase 3	**Phase 6,** new era of twenty-first century	2000
2004 Athens				
2008 Beijing				
2012 London				2012

Source (identified authors)

The fourth Games in London in 1908 proved to be a turning point in terms of preparation and management. For the first time, a sports venue was created especially for the Olympics: the White City Stadium. Although it was widely criticised for its over-inclusive configuration, the stadium marked the start of Olympic design and development. The 1912 Games at Stockholm featured technological innovations: electric timing devices and a photo finish; public address systems; and module-based artificial turf.

The First World War (1914–18) caused the cancellation of the 1916 Games and when the world's athletes re-gathered at Antwerp in 1920 to celebrate the arrival of peace, the five entwined rings flag was first introduced (symbolising the five continents united by Olympism). These were set on a white background representing the peace governing the Olympic spirit. Appearing at the same time was the athletes' oath, and also the Olympic motto 'Citius, Altius, Fortius' (Swifter, Higher, Stronger).

The following Games in Paris (1924) and Amsterdam (1928) saw the involvement of the mass media; besides newspapers, radio broadcasting appeared at the Paris Games, which subsequently attracted 1,000 journalists (Guttmann, 1992). In Amsterdam the first permanent giant scoreboard was erected in order to publish the results more quickly. The Los Angeles Games of 1932 continued the trend of expansion in developing Olympic venues: not only in that the 105,000-seat Memorial Coliseum was the largest Olympic Stadium yet built, but also in the birth of the first communal facilities for athletes: the Olympic Village. Los Angeles also modified the competition programme to 16 days, which has remained the approximate duration to the present day.

The 1936 Games in Berlin had an unwelcome political dimension driven by Hitler and the Nazis. Ritualism was further reinforced: for the first time the Olympic torch was relayed from Olympia to the host city, and television broadcasting made its experimental debut. Much new construction was involved in the process of preparation, leaving a much wider impact on the urban fabric than previous Games; the Berlin Games were large-scale, sumptuous and spectacular.

The Second World War (1939–45) brought a 12-year break until the London Games of 1948. Post-war austerity characterised the London Games, though total participants rose to a new high of over 4,000. The 1952 Games in Helsinki had the first Olympic 'theme park', foreshadowing the rise of the Olympic tourist industry. The Helsinki Games were also regarded as the last Games 'conducted in a spirit close to the original Olympic ideas', where amateurism and chauvinism had not been disturbed by professionalism, commercialism and political antagonism (Wilson, 1976: 64).

The 1956 Games at Melbourne were the first in the southern hemisphere; they were also the only Summer Games staged in two different countries; the equestrian events were held in Stockholm due to laws of quarantine in Australia. In Melbourne, the blossoming Olympic Movement met some setbacks due to the remote location of the host city and international conflicts: the invasion of Hungary by the USSR and the Suez Crisis caused several nations to withdraw. As a result, the number of participants dropped by nearly a half.

The 1960s growth of the world economy and technological progress marked the start of a move towards the gigantism of later Olympic events. From the 1960s onwards, Olympic urban development extended far from the provision of sports facilities to more comprehensive urban improvement schemes. In both Rome (1960) and Tokyo (1964) tremendous investment was made in upgrading public transportation systems, water supply infrastructure, urban road networks and street aesthetics. These developments seemed so extravagant at the time that they even led to calls for the Games to be cancelled (Essex and Chalkey, 1999). Television rights were sold for the first time at the Rome Games and this has now become a major income source for the IOC and the local organising committee. The Tokyo Games saw worldwide satellite broadcasts and the utilisation of the recently invented computer in the Games management system.

In contrast, the Games that followed had more negative characteristics: civic opposition (Mexico City – 1968); terrorist attack (Munich – 1972); long-term debt (Montreal – 1976); and international boycotts (Moscow – 1980 and Los Angeles –

1984). The Olympic Games came to be viewed as major investments with considerable risks. Although the scale of these Games (the number of participants, sports events and Olympic visitors) were still increasing, the number of cities interested in bidding for the Games was declining which, at the time, seemed to threaten the very future of the Olympic Movement.

The Montreal Games is notable for its effect on future Games. The 1976 Games had a poor economic outcome, resulting from over-ambitious construction plans interwoven with lax project management, a worsening economic situation, a period of global inflation, and local labour disputes. This resulted in an exceptional debt of CAN$1.5 billion (COJO'76, 1976), yet the financial failure of Montreal prompted economic reforms in later Games, such as the introduction of a global sponsorship programme and public–private-sector partnerships.

In contrast the Games in Los Angeles were a great commercial success and prompted a renaissance of the Olympic Movement. After Montreal's problems, Los Angeles had emerged as the only viable location for the 1984 Games, allowing the local organising committee to negotiate with the IOC for a more flexible operational strategy. This included the increase of television rights revenue, and the establishment of 'The Olympic Program' (TOP scheme), which guaranteed exclusive worldwide advertising/marketing opportunities. Substantial use of existing facilities avoided great capital expenditure and the creation of the Olympic volunteers' body reduced the salaried workforce. The Games were totally private-sector funded and generated a profit of US$225 million; greater than all previous Olympic Games combined. Inspired by the commercial achievements of the Los Angeles Games, many potential host cities developed renewed interest in staging the Olympics.

The 1988 Games in Seoul and the 1992 Games in Barcelona focused on urban transformation. Here developments emphasised the improvement of urban environment quality, especially the remediation of neglected areas rather than promotion of new greenfield development. The Chamsil area in Seoul and the seafront of Poblenou in Barcelona were transformed from declining neighbourhoods to thriving Olympic parklands and residential quarters. In addition, both Korean and Catalan organisers capitalised on the Olympics to showcase their history, culture and identity.

The Centennial Games of 1996 in Atlanta should have been a celebrated anniversary for the modern Olympic Movement but ended in some disappointment. The Atlanta organising committee self-consciously followed the successful Los Angeles model but perhaps failed to appreciate the difference in their existing facilities compared to those of Los Angeles. The lack of major investment in Atlanta's infrastructure, partly as a result of financial regulations, resulted in criticism of the transportation, logistics and security arrangements. The IOC President pronounced the Games in Atlanta a qualified success in his speech at the closing ceremony, rather than as the customary 'best Games ever'. He was also reported to have told a German newspaper that a totally privately funded Olympics would no longer be endorsed by the IOC (Essex and Chalkey, 1999).

The last Games of the twentieth century took place in Sydney in 2000 and prominently featured concerns for environmental sustainability issues. Under the influence of the IOC's new policy, Sydney had developed a set of 'green' guidelines to govern the development of Olympic facilities and the operation of the Games.

The Olympic precinct at Homebush Bay was intended to act as a benchmark for eco-sensitive design. A number of environmental organisations questioned the eventual outcome, but Sydney is still widely regarded as the greenest Games at the time of writing.

The Games returned to its birthplace, Athens, in 2004 and this perhaps represented the end of the evolutionary cycle of the modern Olympic Movement. Compared to 108 years earlier, the nature and magnitude of the Olympic Games had dramatically changed. There is also a worry that they may have become too large and too expensive to be staged in cities of moderate size such as Athens; further, the security costs have increased since the terrorist attack in New York on 11 September 2001 and London in July 2005, on the day after the award of the 2012 Games to the city. The IOC has signalled a desire to reduce the financial burden and complexity of future Olympic Games in case it becomes 'a victim of its own success' (IOC, 2002). Reform has also been called for in the IOC itself. In the wake of the bribery scandal associated with the Winter Games at Salt Lake City, an investigation made by BBC television released on the eve of the Athens Games also suggested corruption in the Olympic bidding process (BBC, 2005). The IOC leaders subsequently promised to take any initiatives necessary to safeguard Olympic values.

The 29th Summer Games (2008) held in Beijing marked a further highpoint in terms of size and impact on a scale that seems unlikely to be matched in the near future. The 2012 Games comes to London for the third time, with high expectations for exploitation of the sustainability agenda and a focus on legacy impacts. So in the early part of the twenty-first century, the Olympic Movement has entered a new era with new priorities and issues.

Olympic policy-makers and Olympic urban development

Since Olympic city urban development depends on the Olympic Games, it is also impacted upon by Olympic policy-makers; in particular, the IOC and its leaders. This was particularly the case in the early decades of the Olympic Movement, when the incipient Olympic physical settings needed to be defined with function and scale, architectural form and urban context, and steered in terms of evolution. Among all the Olympic form-givers, the most important figure is Pierre De Coubertin, whose idea and vision of creating a 'Modern Olympia' set the tone for much of the early modern Olympic built environment, and continues to impact on contemporary venue planning and design. The following sections help reveal some of the attitudes of De Coubertin and his successors in shaping urban design and development; the specific current requirements of the IOC for Olympic infrastructure and facilities are discussed in more detail later.

De Coubertin and his 'Modern Olympia'

As Cashman (1999) pointed out, the Olympic Movement's survival and strength has often arisen from the contribution of powerful and dominant individuals who have been passionate in their commitment to the Games. It was De Coubertin's aspiration that motivated the Games' revival in 1896; his tenacious faith in their value that sustained them through numerous early trials; and his dedication that helped promote them on a world stage. De Coubertin appealed to history in his pursuit of the Olympic ideal. He perceived the long-term prosperity of the ancient Olympic Games as deeply rooted in its unique festival form, a 'cult of human essence'; as well as a solid foundation of a physical setting, the holy city of Olympia. In a treatise published in the *Revue Olympique*, De Coubertin wrote that Olympia:

> drew its holiness from the feeling of patriotic piety that imbued the place, that saturated its atmosphere and enveloped its monuments ... A sort of seriousness, not necessarily austere, but one that allows for joy, must surround it so that, in the silence between competitions, it draws visitors as a place of pilgrimage, inspiring in them a respect for places devoted to noble memories and profound hopes.
>
> (De Coubertin, 1909a: 153)

De Coubertin realised that if the modern Games were to be more than a pure sports event, if they were to develop a philosophy, then the creation of new Olympias was paramount. At the 1906 advisory conference in Paris, De Coubertin convinced the IOC to organise an international architecture competition for 1910, to model the 'Modern Olympia'. His vision of the future Olympic setting was a city that 'harmoniously linked with athletics, literature and art', and 'closely collaborated of man and nature'. He wished the buildings to be closely linked and yet appear not crowded, and to be well laid out on the site to impress the visitor, but not a recreation of the ancient layout. As for the scale of the stadium, De Coubertin recommended plans for 800 to 1,200 contestants and no more than 10,000 spectators. In fact, he did not think spectators played an important role in transmission of Olympic values; he rather imagined the spectators to be other sportsmen. In a speech in Lausanne in 1928, De Coubertin even suggested that there were too many stadiums being built and of too large a size, and the result of local commercial interests. He also felt there were lessons to be taken from the over-inclusive layout of the White City Stadium for the London Games; in 1908 he wrote for the Olympic Review:

> It will be necessary to avoid attempting to copy the Olympic Games of London. The next Olympiads must not have exactly the same character; they must not be so comprehensive. There was altogether too much at London. The Games must be kept more purely athletic; they must be more dignified; more discreet; more in accordance with classic and artistic requirements; more intimate and above all, less expensive.
>
> (reported by Henry, 1948: 84)

When the neoclassical stadium was built for the Stockholm Games in 1912, De Coubertin applauded its eurhythmia without reservation. He wrote in his memoirs, 'The gothic stadium, with its pointed arches and towers, its technical perfection, its well-planned and methodical regulations, seem a model of its kind' (reported by Muller, 2000: 439).

It has been suggested that De Coubertin inherited his favour of Gothic aesthetics from the English philosopher John Ruskin (1819–1900), and he was unwilling to accept any design approach that might have sacrificed his lofty humanistic aim to functionalism or technocracy.

De Coubertin did not live long enough to see his Games widely translocated throughout the world, and if he had done, he might have been disappointed to see the over-lavish settings, astonishing construction costs, and unbridled leverage of Olympics for the satisfaction of local interests. From a contemporary point of view, much of his opinion about Olympic infrastructure seems rather conservative and ill-suited to modern requirements. However, De Coubertin's concept in establishing a 'Modern Olympia' contributed much to Olympic urban history, and it was De Coubertin himself who insisted that the Modern Olympia should be a periodical stage moving from one city to another instead of a permanent site. It is this movement that now makes it possible to capitalise Olympic preparation for urban transformation and sustainability.

The changing attitude of the IOC to urban design and development

Whereas De Coubertin spent much time encouraging trial-and-error design to reconcile the emerging Olympic needs, most of his successors seldom intervened to such depth in the engineering details of Olympic installations. An interesting example of how things changed is the correspondence between Lord Killanin (IOC president 1972–80) and Willi Daume (then German NOC president): Daume was entrusted by the IOC to make an inspection of Montreal in the run-up to the 1976 Games. In March 1973 he wrote to Killanin with doubts about the roof structure for the Olympic Stadium based on his own experience of Munich, and asked for support from the IOC to ensure the project could be finished smoothly. Killanin refused his request because it was 'a technical matter'; furthermore, Killanin reminded the inspector to 'be very careful not to be involved in architectural jealousies, especially in view of the controversial and expensive Munich roof' (Killanin, 1973). Even when, later, difficulties arose, the IOC tried to avoid any comment on the architectural features.

For later IOC leaders, more complex socio-economic and technological environments prevailed than in De Coubertin's time, and greater flexibility was allowed for local OCOGs to deal with their development objectives. Nevertheless, later IOC leaders have concentrated much of their attention on protecting the purity of the Games and not as an excuse for ambitious and expensive urban plans. Avery Brundage (IOC president 1952–72) criticised the huge investment at the Grenoble Winter Games of 1968: 'the French spent US$240 million in connection with these Grenoble Games and when you consider that this was for ten days of amateur sport, it seems to be somewhat out of proportion' (Espy, 1979: 136).

Similarly, commenting on the astonishing deficit of the Montreal Games, Killanin is reported to have said:

> Who forces the cities to take on excessive costs? They use the Olympic Games to develop their city and to create new sports facilities . . . Mexico City, Tokyo,

> Munich and also Montreal used the Games as an occasion to develop their cities. Sport is not guilty for this.
>
> (Huberty and Wange, 1976: 11–12)

It is understandable that in the late 1960s and 1970s when the Olympic Movement was at a low ebb, the IOC might take a more conservative attitude with urban development issues. However, during recent decades the IOC's attitude has undergone a major change. Driven by joining the global campaign for environmental sustainability, the IOC is now more willing to support positive urban transformations through Olympic preparations. The IOC and the UIA (International Union of Architects) organised conferences on Olympics and Architecture at Lausanne in 2001 and 2002; Balderstone (Director, IOC Sport and Environment Commission) addressed the 2001 meeting with:

> the Olympic Movement and the Games, is increasingly a catalyst for comprehensive and strong environmental plans and actions for a city, many of them non Olympic specific, particularly in regard to land rehabilitation and redevelopment. Cities see this as a requirement now, and, on top of that, recent Games have proven that action and influence is possible and practical – illustrating, as the Fundamental principles of the Olympic Charter put it, 'the educational value of good example'. So we can, through Agenda 21, through our proof, and our influence and profile, be a catalyst, impose our pace, and we are achieving that, because there are, now, effectively requirements.
>
> (Balderstone, 2001: 1–6)

Additionally, Felli (Director, IOC Department of Sports, Olympic Games and Relations with the IFs) expressly stated at the 2002 event:

> The Games are a big project which may change the image of a city. We also thought that they should speak of architecture – the key to the success of this new image of the city . . . We realised that the Games were more and more a catalyst for the development of the cities, not only for sport. You see some renovations of airports, new links and highways, new developments, new housing projects and a lot of city improvements . . . Cities like Barcelona changed completely because of the Games.
>
> (Felli, 2002: 15–19)

The IOC's support in effect provides the raison d'être of mass Olympic urban development, which could potentially impact on the criteria used for host city selection.

Olympic architecture and development

The prototypes of the modern stadium can be traced back to the Greek hippodromes and Roman amphitheatres. For many subsequent centuries, studies of ancient Greek arenas or Roman coliseums merely concentrated on the aesthetics: the proportion, ornament and classic orders of the façade rather than the spatial forms. The excavation of the Panathenaic Stadium and ancient Olympia around the 1870s led to an enthusiasm among design professions to search for appropriate architectural settings for modern sports events. Through a range of articles, conference speeches and design competition briefs published in the *Olympic Review*, De Coubertin (1906, 1907, 1908, 1909a, 1909b) influenced the initial form of Olympic facilities. His drawings and writings, along with the Organising Committees' Post-Game Reports, compose the most important research archives related to Olympic urbanisation from the Games' early period.

Research on Olympic urban development flourished after the Second World War along with the growth of the Olympic Movement, and was also influenced by Modernism nourished by Le Corbusier and the CIAM (International Congress for Modern Architecture). Cable (1982), Gordon (1983), Walker (1984), Brandizzi (1989), Melhuish (1999) and Sheard (2001) all studied, from different standpoints, the development of Olympic competition facilities and their architectural values as well as other modern sports arenas. Frenckell (1949), Schmidt (1971), Ortensi (1972), Robinson (1990), Abad (1996), Millet (1996), Munoz (1997) and Thomas (1999) elaborated the evolution and typology of Olympic Villages, and their significance to contemporary housing design for large-scale events. Colombo (1984), Kwaak (1988), Conde (1993), Essex and Chalkey (1999, 2003), Cashman (1999), Chalkey and Essex (2000), Andranovich *et al.* (2001), and McKay and Plumb (2001, 2003) have researched the impacts of the Olympic Games on the host city's urban policy, real estate market and regional planning strategy. A vast array of literature has reported that the gigantism of Olympic urbanisation has emerged as an agent of urban renewal, and can be used to 'fast-track' large urban projects.

With the more recent prominence of sustainability issues, the focus of Olympic urban research has shifted to environmental impact, long-term legacies and social equity. Meinel (2001), Synadinos (2001), Essex and Chalkey (2002), Cashman (2003), Hiller (2003), Searle (2003) and De Jesus (2004) discussed, from various perspectives, how to integrate sustainable development principles into the decision-making process. In particular, researchers, such as Somma (1993), Rurheiser (1996), Hamilton (2000) and Tejero (2001), have paid attention to the detrimental effects of Olympic urban activities on the local ecosystem, social segregation and the diversion of essential urban services to pay for Olympic-related infrastructure.

Following the adoption of environment as the third pillar of Olympism, the IOC (1993, 1999b, 1999c, 2004, 2005) produced a range of related, instructive documents for Olympic preparations. The International Federations of each sport and all Olympic organising authorities also released their own sustainable development strategies, assessment tools or regular auditing reports to guide the development and management of Olympic projects, after the Winter Games of Lillehammer in 1994.

This wealth of literature provides essential background information for this book; however, it also indicates gaps that must be addressed. First, most of the researchers have concentrated on individual Games, or have been isolated by the boundary of disciplines (e.g. architectural design, social affairs, real estate analysis, etc.). There is a lack of systematic approach to bring together the longitudinal (trans-Games) and latitudinal (between different disciplines) links of Olympic architecture and development. Second, most of the researchers so far have attempted theoretical analyses of what Olympic impacts could create for a host city, but failed to provide quantitative analysis on how the objectives should be achieved. Third, for those researchers from non-architectural fields, some of the outcomes need further interpretation before practical guidelines can be produced. This book attempts to address some of these gaps and omissions and contributes to a better understanding of the subject.

Definitions of Olympic urban development

Before entering into more detailed analysis it is necessary to define the concept and scope of 'Olympic urban development'. The purpose of these differentiations will be seen in relation to the evaluation framework used in later sections. Urban development is structured in a complex manner and is richly textured in its inter-weaving of a mixture of environmental, architectural, economic, social and cultural dimensions. The whole process encompasses the integration of different activities such as planning, design, implementation and management, ranging from the urban and regional scale down to that of individual buildings, and with the involvement of a variety of agents and decision makers from different fields.

Urban design and development clearly has a much broader connotation than the combination of activities involved in its processes (architectural design, building construction and town planning), which only reflect a part of its significance. The term 'Olympic urban development' is used here to refer to all the development that is incurred by staging the Summer Olympic Games. At regional and urban level it includes the impacts of decisions about the investment, scale, and the nature and distribution of Olympic-related projects in a broad strategic way. At neighbour-hood and community level it encompasses the planning of venues, the infrastructure and landscape provision within the Olympic precinct, and their articulation with other territories of the host society. At building and system level it embraces the design and construction of individual facilities and temporary installations for Olympic use. The objective is, in the short-term, to ensure the organisation of a successful Olympic Games; and in the long-term, to promote the host city's economic vitality, social equity and well-being, and consequently its environmental sustainability.

Olympic-incurred urban development

Since 'Olympic urban development' is a rather broad concept, it needs further interpretation to clarify which development can be classified as 'Olympic incurred'. Staging an Olympic Games creates a long and expensive commitment by a city and the preparation process involves intensive bidding, planning and implementation of urban development. Normally, the urban development unfolds over a consider-able period of time; typically it would last more than 10 years, starting before the launch of a serious bid, climaxing a year or so before the Games, and ending with the redevelopment of the Olympic facilities for post-Games use and moving or demolishing of unwanted structures. Of course, this sequence occurs only in the circumstances of a successful bid, whereas in fact, an Olympic bid is a difficult and uncertain undertaking and with uncertain outcomes and timescales.

Cities such as Barcelona and Sydney waited 30 or more years to get the Games; their Olympic urban developmental initiatives had therefore effectively spanned several decades. Barcelona made its first formal request to organise the 1924 Games; attempts were also made for the 1936 Games, the cancelled 1940 Games and the 1972 Games. While waiting for the years to pass, work had been undertaken on various Olympic facilities over that time (COOB'92, 1992). In Sydney, the Olympic bid can be dated back to the 1970s. The development on the government-owned land at Homebush Bay started as early as 1980 in building the States Sports Centre, although the whole site was only finalised 20 years later for the 2000 Games.

During the preparation for bidding phase, the normal development of a candidate or host city has to be continued with and, in most situations, the Olympics squeezes its way to the top of the urban agenda. As Hiller points out:

> The Olympics is in many ways an intrusion (though often a welcome one) in normal urban processes and urban decision-making. Cities are forced to rearrange their urban planning around what will help to win the bid as well as what will produce a successful Games event.
>
> (Hiller, 2003)

This Olympic dominance is especially intensive in those cities with insufficient existing facilities to host the Games and may thus cause suppression of other local development. Nevertheless, the execution of Olympic projects does not mean that all the concurrent urban developments in the host city are 'Olympic incurred'. For instance, improving the visual appearance of a city may assist in creating a favourable image during preparations, but it is not a necessity for the Games. In other cases, developments may have been planned long before the Olympic bid and would have emerged anyway in the fullness of time, irrespective of the event. These urban developments are not defined as 'Olympic incurred' development.

It has been chosen to define six different forms of potential development undertaken in a candidate/host city during the preparations for the bidding/staging of the Olympic Games. They are listed as follows:

a   development that would have been made in the city in the fullness of time even without the Olympic Games;
b   development that is planned in the city anyway but would otherwise be implemented at another time;
c   development that is not made in the city but would have been made without the Games;
d   development that would have been made in the city anyway but which has more investment because of the Games;
e   development that is made only because of the Games;
f   development that would have been made in the city anyway but which has less investment because of the Games.

The development type (a) is entirely independent of the Olympic preparation in which the Olympic impact is almost neutral or ineffectual. Development types (b), (d) and (e) are ones in which the Olympic impact is positive and promotional; they emerge either as essential facilities for staging of the Games, or are boosted to facilitate the city's host capability. Undoubtedly, this group complies exactly with the criteria of the 'Olympic incurred' development. In development types (c) and (f) the Olympic impact is rather negative and/or impeditive. They are either overshadowed or marginalised by the Games, as resources may focus elsewhere – these types are not dealt with in this study.

In its 2008 and 2012 Olympiad candidature manuals, the IOC identifies three kinds of facilities under the Organising Committee's budget. These are (a) competition facilities, (b) the Olympic Village and (c) the Main Press Centre (MPC) and International Broadcast Centre (IBC). All other projects incurred by the Games are considered outside the Organising Committee's budget although they should be disclosed. In IOC technical appraisals, the competition venues and the Olympic Village(s) are always listed as the chief concerns, outweighing other general infrastructure. Hence in this book and in line with the IOC, these two sorts of facility together with MPC and IBC are recognised as the core hierarchical elements that directly relate to Olympic urban development. Others are specified as 'indirect-Olympic-related' instead of 'non-Games-related' development to differentiate from Preuss's classification.

The 'direct-Olympic-related' developments include:

- competition venues and their temporary overlays;
- Olympic Village, official village and media village;
- MPC and IBC.

The 'indirect-Olympic-related' developments include:

- transport infrastructures (airport, port, road network, underground and light rail, etc.);
- visitor accommodation and facilities (social housing, hotel rooms, rentable dormitories, tourist centres, etc.);
- civic infrastructures (water and sewage system, waste disposal facilities, etc.);
- urban recreational facilities (cultural and entertainment premises, urban parklands and open spaces, etc.);
- other developments (telecommunication, office stock, commercial and retail stock, hospitals, power plants, etc.).

Summary

The impact of the Olympic Games on its host city is multi-dimensional, where urban issues are one of the most important. In terms of city impact several events stand out:

- the Games of London in 1908 with the first Olympic architecture – the White City Stadium;
- the Berlin Games of 1936 as a larger scale, hallmark event with significant intervention in the urban fabric of the host city;

- the Tokyo and Mexico City Games of the 1960s, both of which moved the Olympics from a Eurocentric to a global stage; Tokyo also incorporated major development of indirect-Olympic-related infrastructure;
- the 2000 Games in Sydney, remembered as the 'green Games', suggesting the increasing importance of environmental sustainability issues;
- the Beijing Games of 2008 in which scale and cost as well as urban intervention was at a level unlikely to be exceeded in the near future.

De Coubertin and the early Olympic policy-makers influenced greatly the settings of early Olympic infrastructure, and this influence continues to the present day: the concentrated venue approach, encouraged by the IOC, retains the imprint of De Coubertin's 'Modern Olympia'. But the changing attitude of the IOC in supporting urban sustainable development (even perhaps leading to some compromise of Olympic interests) has allowed Olympic preparation to address the host city's environmental problems and provide a new line of analysis, which will be examined in the following chapters.

Olympic design and development

PART II

Past and present

Urban development CHAPTER 3

Introduction

It is clear that environmentally friendly design of specific Olympic venues and buildings contributes to the overall green credentials of the Olympic Games; however, holistic Olympic masterplanning at the urban level can play an even more significant role in helping host cities to achieve broader and more lasting benefits. Historically Olympic urbanisation has taken different roles during different periods: during the 1950s it was combined with the needs of post-war urban restoration; during the 1960s and 1970s it supported urban expansion; during the 1980s and 1990s it stimulated inner-city regeneration; and in the most recent decade attention has turned to sustainable urban form. There is a constant intimacy between Olympic development and the evolution of host cities; an intimacy that steers the preparation for the Games. This chapter therefore examines the different ways that Olympic facilities have been integrated into the host cities' urban fabric. The focus is on the post-Second World War period when Olympic planning to stimulate and justify large-scale urban improvements became commonplace.

The discussion has four themes: to provide a panoramic view of Olympic urban practices and changes over time; to identify the influential factors that determined the ever-changing course of Olympic urban planning (and also their significance as an aid for contemporary decision-making); to examine various Olympic urban policies with reference to twentieth-century town planning concepts; and to evaluate, with the benefit of hindsight, Olympic urban legacies against their stated original intentions, and then to posit lessons for planning and design of future Olympic preparation.

The Olympic Games and cities

The interdependency of the Olympic Games and the host city is reflected in the Olympic Charter, according to which the Games are entrusted by the IOC to a city rather than a country. Rule 35 of the Charter further regulates that 'All sports competition must take place in the host city of the Olympic Games, unless the IOC Executive Board authorises the organisation of certain events in other cities, sites or venues situated in the same country' (IOC, 2007). This is particularly central with regard to the Summer Games; for the Olympic Winter Games, the IOC introduced an additional option into the Olympic Charter in 1991, in which a regional host of events is permitted in order to cope with geographic or topographic limitations of a host city. Although the IOC sets no rigid physical, economic or social criteria in selecting host cities, convention indicates that the Summer Games are preferably accommodated by large cities with more than three million inhabitants (Essex and Chalkey, 2002).

The modern Olympics have grown to the point that their size and complexity distinguish them from any other major sporting events. Contemporary Olympic Summer Games typically involve more than 15,000 athletes and officials, at least the same number of media representatives, and from 400,000 to a million out-of-city visitors. This means the host city experiences a huge increase in temporary population, which places great demands on civic infrastructure and accommodation. Only the world's largest cities have the required resources to cope with such challenges and sufficient population to sustain the viability of the facilities in the longer term. Moreover, the investment required, even for the bidding stage, and overall costs of the Games themselves, mean that only key cities with regional economic power can afford the financial commitment. This is highlighted by data contained in the 'GaWC inventory of world cities' produced by the Globalisation and World Cities Study Group in 1999. This inventory is based on size, population, scientific and cultural impacts, economic capacity, and role in the global network of large world cities. It shows that most cities that have acted as Olympic hosts were categorised as within the most influential 'world-class nexus' in the inventory (Taylor et al., 2002).

These factors have created geographic inequalities by excluding as potential hosts smaller cities and cities in the developing world, raising concerns within the IOC. In 2002 the Olympic Games Study Commission was appointed to evaluate a possible reduction in the number of events, participants, procedures and costs for future Games. It seems, however, that no matter the extent to which the Olympics may be moderated in the future, the Games will remain as high-profile events in promoting host cities on the world stage and attracting inward investment to these cities.

Olympic host cities are often among the world's largest and most cosmopolitan cities, and the evolution of these cities reflects the mainstream of urbanisation processes in a modern, democratic and industrialised society. This urbanisation process can be used as an important reference to understand the ways that Olympic facilities are integrated into different urban contexts.

History of Olympic urbanisation

Processes of Olympic urbanisation have now been developing for over a century. The result is that in various cities with often diverse urban patterns and cultural contexts, the Games have left very different legacies in the local environment. Some of the legacies continue to impact on the cities' development decades after the event. Three main elements can be observed when reviewing the history of Olympic urbanisation: the first is the expansion of the Olympic event itself and the consequent implications for infrastructure provision; the second concerns the discontinuities characterising the process of Olympic urbanism not only caused by the interval of each Olympiad but also by the unsynchronised socio-economic development cycles of host cities; the third is the connection between Olympic urban initiatives and the evolution of town planning concepts in the twentieth century.

Four historical phases are evident within which the host cities seem to have performed similar urban-scale activities in preparing for the Games. The first phase is that of the first decade of the Olympic revival corresponding to the three earliest and modestly scaled events with minimal urban intervention. The second phase covers the period between 1908 and 1928 when the event began to attract more international attention, with preparations in a planned manner and production of sport-specific venues. The debut of the first Olympic Village in 1932 marked the start of the third phase, lasting to 1956; this period witnessed substantial Olympic-related urban change with some renovation activities. In the fourth phase, since 1960, Olympic urbanisation extended far beyond the boundary of sports and associated facilities, to more comprehensive urban design. In this phase, cities were no longer passive 'containers' for Olympic performances; rather, the Olympics were used to trigger large-scale urban improvement and shaped planning policy.

The origins of Olympic urbanism (1896–1904)

The origin of Olympic urbanism can be traced back to De Coubertin's concept of creating a 'Modern Olympia', which paralleled other contemporary urban utopianism in the nineteenth and twentieth centuries, such as the 'phalanstère' of Charles Fourier (in the 1840s) and the 'international city' of Ernest Hebrand (in the 1910s), and which were inspired by various avant-garde design practices for urban-scale spectacles such as World Expositions at that time. Many of De Coubertin's principles can be seen to continue guiding modern Olympic urban decision-making; for instance, the term 'Modern Olympia' implies a site concentration approach, favoured by the IOC. De Coubertin's preference for a more pastoral setting (harmony between man and nature) has inspired the creation of scenic Olympic Parks in crowded urban contexts. Additionally, his insistence on the 'Modern Olympia' moving from one city to another to spread the Olympic spirit to the four corners of the earth made it possible to capitalise on Olympic preparation to create urban transformation.

However, during the first decade of the Olympic revival, the Games did not attract much public attention and were extremely financially constrained. Although Athens in 1896 did involve limited provision of new facilities, including the restoration of the 2,000-year-old Panathenaic Stadium, the following two Games, at Paris and St Louis left few urban legacies. In Paris (1900) the Games were exclusively held in natural settings (Lucas, 1904).

The dominance of the Olympic Stadium (1908–28)

Although tethered to the Franco-British Exhibition of the same year, the London Games of 1908 produced a milestone for Olympic design, when the first piece of Olympic architecture, the White City Stadium, was built on former agricultural land at Shepherd's Bush in west London. Aiming to showcase the technical achievements of the new century, the stadium was gigantic in size and was characterised by avant-garde industrial aesthetics. In operation however, it was flawed due to attempts in the design to reconcile too many, often conflicting, functions for different sports through one architectural solution.

In a rethinking of London's approach, Stockholm 1912 developed a range of venues for separate sports in the northern suburbs of the city. The centrepiece was the neo-Gothic athletic stadium, meticulously built in reddish stone to be in harmony with the context of Scandinavian cities. The Olympic Stadium was the backbone of the Games where most contests and ceremonies were concentrated, and it consumed most (87 per cent) of the budget. Commended by De Coubertin himself, Stockholm's practice soon became a prototype for later cities to follow. Until the late 1920s, the pattern of Olympic development can be summarised as: purpose-built Olympic Stadium (covering most of the competitions) + small rented halls (for a small number of essential indoor events) + improvised adapted watercourse (for aquatic sports).

From a town planning perspective, Olympic development and urban design in the 1910s to 1920s did not impinge greatly on host cities; yet purposefully created athletic stadiums effectively defined an Olympic 'node' (if not a 'quarter') in urban fabric terms; creating a location with new landmarks and identities. Further, there was a manifestation of the cultural diversity of the host society, or the era, through different architectural dialects; for instance, industrial craftsmanship in London (1908) and Paris (1924), Gothic revival in Stockholm (1912), Beaux-Arts in Antwerp (1920) and Modernism in Amsterdam (1928). Aesthetic and symbolic expression subsequently became an important theme of later Olympic urban development.

The rise of the Olympic quarter (1932–56)

The Los Angeles Games of 1932 was a breakthrough for Olympic urban development as it created the first genuine Olympic Village (comprising 550 wooden cottages set up in a 101ha compound at Baldwin Hills on the edge of the city). This allowed the last indispensable component of De Coubertin's 'Modern Olympia' to be incorporated, and extended the content of Olympic urban design from sports premises to housing. William Garland, the Games' chief organiser, was perhaps the first to perceive the potential benefits that could be brought to host cities by Olympic intervention. Under his leadership, Los Angeles prepared an inventory of new facilities, including the epic Memorial Coliseum, a swimming arena and a fencing pavilion. These were located in a 65ha site that had once been Exposition Park, and which would later become the city's late-night entertainment district. The Coliseum remained the largest Olympic arena built until the Sydney Games of 2000.

The Berlin Games of 1936 consolidated the trend for the development of substantial facilities in forming an 'Olympic quarter' (the Reichssportfeld), and resulted in a 130ha site at Grunewald in western Berlin being developed as a sporting and cultural area. The site included a new stadium with 100,000 seats, a swimming centre, an open-air amphitheatre, large assembly fields and service buildings, all built in rigid neoclassical forms and linked by monumental axes. A 16km-long ceremonial boulevard, the 'Via Triumphalis', was specially routed to articulate the Olympic site and the city centre through the Brandenburg Gate.

A self-contained village encompassing 194 bungalows was created in a verdant 55ha site 14.5km west of the Olympic complex, with full training and leisure facilities. The Berlin Games has been seen as a turning point for the Olympics, moving from modest sports celebrations to sumptuous, multi-dimensional spectacles. Although controversially coloured by the politics of the Nazi regime, the urban settings of these Games were superb and were not surpassed for many years.

Post-war economics meant the London Games of 1948 had to rely on existing facilities for most venues and left little impact on the city's built environment. The following Games in Helsinki (1952) and Melbourne (1956), however, continued the tendency to produce more facilities for the expanding Games and to integrate the planning procedure into the local urban agenda. Helsinki made two significant contributions: the creation of the first pastoral Olympic Park in which 'buildings and landscape were perfectly harmonized in an expression of dignity and loftiness' (Gordon, 1983: 3); and the combination of the Olympic Village development with municipal housing schemes, a feature commonplace in later Games.

Up to the 1950s, the breadth and depth of Olympic urbanisation remained moderate by modern standards. This was partly due to the lack of enthusiasm for urban expansion in host cities and the amateur status promoted by the Olympic Movement, which limited commercialisation and political interference. Since 1960, however, Olympic urban planning has become more ambitious with wider impacts.

Figure 3.1
The Berlin Stadium for the 1936 Games (now used as a football/sports stadium)

The age of urban transformation (1960–2012)

Along with rapid progress in the world economy, social mobility and communication techniques, the 1960s witnessed a wave of radical urban growth. Increasing land speculation and the persistence of the suburbanisation process helped drive urban expansion at an unprecedented rate. Meanwhile, Western planning ideology became heavily influenced by architectural modernism, leading to calls for urban transformation towards more rational and functional settlements. Inevitably, Olympic urban development of the 1960s and 1970s was impacted upon by these zeitgeists.

The Rome Games of 1960 provided the first paradigm of the Olympics as a catalyst for major urban change, where the delivery of Olympic venues as key elements in urban intervention gave way to a wider urban design programme. The main sporting facilities for the Rome Games were clustered in three separate sites in the northern and southern outskirts of the city, stretching the urban plan in two directions. The main sites were connected by a new thoroughfare and, besides Games-related facilities, the city also developed a new water supply system, new hotels, a new jetport, and improved public transport, street lighting and urban landscaping. The largest project involved the road network connecting Olympic venues to the rest of the city, occupying 75 per cent of the land used for the event (Munoz, 1997).

The role of the Olympics in triggering urban transformation developed further in Tokyo for the 1964 Games. The Games provided a timely opportunity to remedy the city's poor civic infrastructure and to fast-track the already proposed ten-year development plan. Tokyo spent nearly US$2.7 billion (or 3.2 per cent of Japan's GNP in 1965) on an ambitious urban renovation scheme, which included extensive developments of urban amenities, housing, tourist accommodation, and waste and sewage disposal systems (TOCOG, 1964). At the plan's core was a carefully contrived, multi-hierarchy transport network crisscrossing the whole city, embracing eight new expressways, 22 motor links of various kinds, 90km of underground routes and monorail, and a 500km Shinkansen (bullet train) route connecting Tokyo, Kyoto and Osaka (Gordon, 1983). Interestingly, of Tokyo's vast Olympic expenditure, the largest portion (more than 95 per cent) was channelled into urban improvements rather than into sport. This sparked some IOC concerns though what had been planned (and was achieved) in Tokyo did help transform the city into a modern, prosperous metropolis.

Financial strictures and impacts of civic opposition meant that the Mexico City Games of 1968 could not afford developments on the scale of Tokyo; rather, many existing facilities were refurbished for Olympic use. Described as a 'Games of long walks', Mexico City followed the decentralised approach to its limit, and placed new urban developments strategically in areas where future growth was expected. With new and refurbished venues scattered widely over its sprawling urban area, the city's public transport system came under great stress. The Olympics stimulated the construction of the city's metro but did not benefit from it – the first 12km line was inaugurated in 1969, one year after the Games. The most successful urban work that distinguished Mexico City from previous hosts was its 'Olympic Identity Program', which introduced strong decorative elements and signposts to the whole city, particularly the Olympic routes, and created a carnival atmosphere. This strategy has been widely adopted by later Games organisers.

By comparison with the distributed Mexican scheme, the Munich Games of 1972 adopted a very centralised approach and located most Olympic venues and the Athletes' Village on one concentrated 280ha site of derelict land at Oberwiesenfeld, just 4km north of the city centre. Munich's Olympic plan was characterised by land-use modification and urban renewal. Oberwiesenfeld had once been a pre-war airstrip and then a dumping ground for building wastes. The 1963 City masterplan had earmarked the site for the development of a sports and entertainment centre over a 15- to 20-year period, yet, under the Olympic banner, development speed increased.

In order to efface the arrogant impression of the 1936 Berlin Games, Munich Olympic Park was designed to embrace an enchanting style and humanistic taste, and to avoid any metaphor of monumentality. The site was enriched by a green landscape of hills, hollows, water and woods, in the midst of which lay a set of venues unified by a wave-form and net-structured roof, giving a sense of freedom and flux. The Olympic Village was constructed in the vicinity of the site with diverse building types and vivid spatial layers to echo the theme. Yet, the hostage-taking of Israeli athletes by terrorists in the Olympic Village ultimately produced criticism for its open character and convoluted layout, and highlighted security as a crucial point in Olympic design.

The pattern of centralised Olympic urban development continued with Montreal for the 1976 Games, where the local authority was keen to use grand projects to reshape the city, as had been the case with its 1967 Exposition. Due to the lack of federal financial support, the initial idea was to promote a 'modest, self-financing' Games. Existing facilities were widely used and Olympic construction was focused on the Olympic Stadium, swimming arena, velodrome and the Athletes' Village; together forming the Maisonneuve Olympic Park close to Montreal's downtown area. As with Munich, the site had been earmarked for sports and recreational use by earlier urban plans and already contained some athletic facilities. The Olympic development package also included some improvements of urban infrastructure such as the creation of a new international airport at Mirabel.

Although Montreal's planning was as meaningful as that of previous Games, the implementation was plagued with problems. Designed by Robert Tailibert, Montreal's Olympic facilities have been noted as 'among the most complex concrete structures ever attempted' (Malouf, 1980: 58) – the most striking features of which were colossal, self-stabilising roof shells and an 18-floor leaning tower designed to house a retractable fabric canopy overhanging the main stadium. The ambitious structure, new techniques and materials, interwoven with lax project management, global inflation and local labour strikes resulted in a debt of Can$1.5 billion; the Games were nearly postponed. The development of the Olympic Village was also problematic. The original proposal was to build five residential compounds spreading over a radius of several kilometres from the Olympic Park to be in line with the city's housing scheme. It was, however, rejected by the IOC, who by then preferred a concentrated approach in the wake of the Munich tragedy. The result was to locate the village in the vicinity of the sports facilities and compress 980 suites into two giant pyramidal towers; the consequent use of 34ha of urban green land caused a wave of local protests.

Ironically, despite all the efforts made, the Games seem to have produced little benefit to local communities. Thirty years after the Montreal Games, the sports complex has had difficulties in sustaining its original functions, and the stadium has even been suggested for demolition. The remote and expensive Mirabel airport also became an example of unnecessary infrastructural improvements; it was closed in 2004. Montreal's Olympic urban development package shows the risk of creating 'white elephant' legacies and resulting long-term debts.

The lessons from Montreal inevitably affected the planning of subsequent Games. Both Moscow (1980) and Los Angeles (1984) attempted to avoid the construction of over-extravagant projects. Nonetheless, Moscow's Olympic inventory still embraced more than 90 construction sites across the conurbation (Gordon, 1983). The Soviet planning philosophy had long been influenced by rationalism and the satellite-city theory stemming from the early Modern Movement. Moscow's masterplan of 1971–90 zoned the city into eight planning agglomerations, with each centred on an economic, recreational and social-cultural core. Moscow's Olympic scheme was largely devised in line with this vision. Olympic venues were established in six different zones as part of the city's sub-centre development plan. The 107ha Olympic Village (now home to 15,000 Muscovites) was built in an urban extension south-west of the city that had earlier been earmarked as a residential quarter. The Olympics also boosted the city's underdeveloped hotel sector and broadcasting and communication facilities.

The Los Angeles Games of 1984 represented a more heterogeneous approach, deviating from the mainstream of Olympic urban practice dating back to the 1960s. The whole concept was to create an 'ephemeral Olympic scene' rather than to support any substantial urban change. Due to opposition from local taxpayers, the 1984 Games became an entirely privately sponsored event and in order to minimise expenditure on installation, the organisers mobilised existing facilities as far as possible and used a number of makeshift structures. In the whole plan, no meaningful Olympic precinct was defined and venues were dispersed throughout the city's vast area. Being the only candidate city and a city already possessing 24 of 31 venues needed to stage the Games, Los Angeles had unique advantages to realise this strategy.

The old Memorial Coliseum was once again refurbished as the main venue and the student dormitories at three local universities were temporarily converted to Athletes' Villages. The whole city was ablaze with colourful streamers, banners, balloons, signposts, light towers and all kinds of graphic-design works. Yet behind these sparkling 'urban confetti' the Olympics brought little change to the urban fabric. Nonetheless, with a profit of US$225 million, the 1984 Games were a clear commercial success.

The theme of utilising the Olympics for implementing local urbanisation plans was revived with the Seoul Games of 1988 and the Barcelona Games of 1992. From the late 1980s there were increasing needs for inner-city regeneration in post-industrial cities to regenerate their run-down central areas. The Olympics provide opportunities for such operations. In Seoul, 120ha of flood-vulnerable land occupied by urban slums at Chamsil, south-east of the Han River, was transformed into Seoul Sports Complex and Athletes' Village. In the case of Barcelona, the decaying industrial and port area of Poblenou, a waterfront district that had separated the city from its beach and fragmented the neighbourhood, was rehabilitated with stylish

Figure 3.2
The Barcelona Stadium for the 1992 Games

apartments, new sewage system, new coastal ring-road, new marina (Olympic Harbour) and other amenities along the 5.2km of barrier-free costal strip. Both in Seoul and Barcelona, extensive urban regeneration projects were carried out throughout the city in preparing for the Games: metro networks extended, airports redesigned and expanded, telecommunications systems modernised, new hotel and new cultural facilities established, and street scenes aesthetically enhanced. These are good examples of what might be achieved by way of Olympic urban intervention.

At the Centennial Games of Atlanta in 1996, most venues were located within a 3km circle of the 'Olympic Ring' in the heart of the city; many others were constructed on a temporary basis at Stone Mountain Park, 25km east of downtown Atlanta. The Olympic Stadium was designed as a combination of an athletic ground and a baseball diamond so that it could be converted into a ballpark after the Games. Many new and reused facilities were developed in cooperation with local colleges, including the Olympic Village (students' dormitories at Georgia Institute of Technology). To provide the Olympic concourse and a commemorative legacy, the organisers set up an 8.5ha Centennial Olympic Park in the city centre with a rich collection of horticultural works.

Atlanta's general urban infrastructure, however, was less impacted by the Olympics. The organisers, in following the Los Angeles model, did not appear to appreciate the lack of existing facilities comparable to those of Los Angeles, and neither was the Olympic Movement in the same situation as in the late 1970s. The lack of substantial investment in the city's infrastructure resulted in some criticism. Also, the intention to revive Atlanta downtown through the development of centrally located venues does not appear to have been successful: several post-Games studies suggest that the decline of many of the poorest communities in central Atlanta continued (Stone, 2001).

The Sydney 2000 Games were widely labelled as 'green' with development guidelines to govern the design, construction and maintenance of Olympic facilities. The main site for the Games was at Homebush Bay, an area of heavily contaminated land approximately 15km inland from Sydney Harbour that had been earmarked for environmental rehabilitation. Homebush was also the demographic centre of the greater Sydney region, strategically linking two major Central Business Districts: Darwin Harbour in the east and Parramatta in the west. The Olympic development thus attempted to agglomerate Sydney's amorphous urban tissue and consolidate the connections between regional centres.

Consisting of 14 grand venues, the Homebush Bay site formed the largest venue cluster in history. This included the 115,000-seat Stadium Australia: the largest-capacity Olympic Stadium created, featuring retractable seating areas to support versatility, and demountable overlays to enable venue resizing after the Games. Renewable energy sources, particularly solar panels, were demonstrated throughout the Olympic site and the Athletes' Village. In order to restore the ecosystem of the region, a 420ha site surrounding the Olympic venues was converted into the Millennium Parklands with diverse landscaped topography. As with other host cities, the Olympics also brought forward improvements to Sydney's general built environment, particularly in the area of hotel stock, motorways, rail links and public areas in the central city.

There were also potential problems: although Sydney was cited as a benchmark for eco-sensitive design for future Games, its green credentials in completing land decontamination and other sustainability goals have been questioned in view of such a hasty Olympic timetable. In addition, many venues at Homebush Bay have experienced low usage since the event.

The Games returned to their birthplace, Athens, in 2004. Given the special meaning of the Olympics to Greece, local communities held high aspirations to showcase successful organisation and to reinvent Athens as a thriving post-modern metropolis. Olympic projects were carried out in almost every corner of the city, but principally accumulated in four precincts. The main site was Athens Olympic Sports Complex located in a north-eastern suburb 9km from the Acropolis. The site already contained some quality venues and in preparing for the 2004 Games it was reshaped by Santiago Calatrava incorporating his futuristic, but also expensive, roof structures. Other major developments took place at the Faliron coastal zone, Hellinikon, Goudi and Marathonas. The 2,300-unit Olympic Village was built at the foot of Mountain Parnitha, 25km north-west of the city, aiming to attract more migrants to this sparsely populated area after the Games.

Athens also built new metro- and tram-lines to link main Olympic sites with other urban zones, strengthening the city's articulation along its north-east to south-west axis perpendicular to the sea. There were also new air terminals, new plazas and new hotels. Many archaeological remains were restored and supported with museum facilities. However, Athens' Olympic urban development was also overshadowed by worrisome delays in construction and cost overruns. The environmentally sensitive design concept, given such a promising focus in Sydney, was less meaningfully incorporated in Athens. Most Olympic venues have since been heavily underused and are generally inaccessible to the general public except when occasional large events have been held. There has been a good deal of negative press criticism, much of it valid, and all emphasising the need for well-planned post-Games usage of facilities.

Olympic urban development impacts have continued with the Beijing Games of 2008 and are planned for the London Games to be held in 2012. Beijing effectively used the Games to raise its international profile and remedy some severe environmental problems. Most of the venues were constructed in a 405ha Olympic Park on the northern edge of the city's central mass and adjacent to the old Asian Games Park. The idea was to make full use of the existing sports premises left from the 1990 Asian Games and to reinforce, in a symbolic sense, the city's north–south axis, with a series of key Olympic buildings placed on the northern end of a ritualistic axis lined up with the Tiananmen Gate at Beijing's geographic centre.

In supporting the Games bid, Beijing's Olympic urbanisation plan did not follow the 'south-eastward strategy' identified in the city's earlier masterplan (Beijing Municipality, 1991). Criticisms therefore emerged that this would further aggravate the current development imbalance and social inequity. Nevertheless, this deficiency may be made up to some extent by ambitious ongoing plans to expand metro and light-rail networks to encompass the whole urban area, particularly towards the south. Extensive infrastructure improvements and urban beautification activities were also created beyond the Olympic precincts.

Comparatively, London's Olympic plan for 2012 is more consistent with the city's long-term efforts to regenerate its degraded eastern boroughs, which started with the redevelopment of the Docklands in the 1980s and continued in the Mayor of London's Plan 2004 (GLA, 2004). Most of the new venues and the Olympic Village are being constructed in a 200ha site at Lower Lea Valley, 13km east of the city centre, and will be served by new transport facilities including the high-speed 'Olympic Javelin' shuttle train. The development for the London 2012 Olympics will be discussed in more detail in Chapter 10.

The content and scales of Olympic development

Taking a historical view of Olympic urban design and development, one finds that although it has been performed with the aim of achieving generally similar objectives within a limited timescale, each city exhibits different outcomes in terms of scale, intensity and level of detail. Consequently, very different and distinct footprints in the local urban environment have been produced. Given such heterogeneous outcomes, the question arises as to what makes a successful Olympic scheme in terms of urban design and development. Several features are relevant for investigation: the content and scales of intervention; the urban entity defined; the vision of urban integration represented; and their relationship with host cities' long-term development demands.

Table 3.1 summarises the possible elements of Olympic urban intervention. In addition to the requisite Olympic facilities, new developments normally focus on the infrastructure associated with transport, communication, tourism and civic services. These are each essential for host cities to cope with the substantial increase in visitors during the event. Lower imperatives are improvements to

Table 3.1 The content of Olympic urban development

	In staging a Games a host city needs . . .	This may lead to the development of . . .	. . . and may contribute to the host city by providing . . .
Direct-related	Competition venues and training grounds Olympic Villages Official and media villages Administrative buildings IBC and MPC	Sports facilities Multi-purpose halls Residential facilities Office buildings	More entertainment facilities Fair/convention support Additional housing estates More business opportunities and inward investments
Primary indirect-related	Capable transportation system Capable communication systems Appropriate tourist services	Airport expansion Road network expansion Mass transit system Telecommunication infrastructure Hotel accommodation Commercial establishments Hospitality premises	More transport capacity, efficiency and convenience, and various environmental effects (positive and negative) Higher quality of living through better communication A boost to the tourism and convention industry
Secondary indirect-related	Satisfactory and pleasant environments for daily activities Better public domain Elements showing identity of the event Cultural promotion premises	Water and sewage systems Waste disposal stations Power plants and grids Environmental beautification schemes Open spaces, parklands and street elements Monumental structures Museums, galleries and exhibition spaces	Higher quality of living through better civic infrastructure and services Higher quality of living and extra ecological value New urban landmarks Cultural legacies

cultural amenities, street greening and works in the public domain that help improve the image of host cities under the international spotlight. Although the primary objective of all these developments is to meet the logistic needs of running the Games, they are often planned and designed with the aim of catering for the city's long-term growth, and often involve large-scale and high-risk investment over a lengthy period.

The content and scale of Olympic urban development can be examined by looking at the capital investment in Olympic construction at each Games. The variations are shown in Figure 3.3 where all values have been converted into US dollars with year base 1995 for comparison. It shows that the highest investment, made by Beijing for the 2008 Games, was approximately 32 times higher than that of Los Angeles in 1984. There are also striking differences in the development of supportive infrastructure: in Barcelona (1992) and Athens (2004), about two-thirds of the total expenditure was spent on this component, and in the case of Tokyo and Beijing, the ratio is even higher. By contrast, in Montreal (1976) only 13 per cent of the investment was in indirect Olympic projects. In general, Games with modest infrastructural investment, or those concentrating on the development of

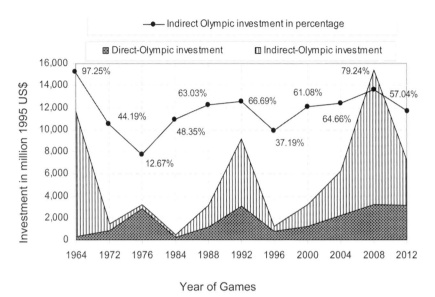

Figure 3.3
Financial investment in Olympic construction, Tokyo 1964 to London 2012

competition-related facilities, are unlikely to have promoted mass urban transformation and may also have fewer subsequent longer-lasting benefits.

Of course, this is not a simple story of 'spend more, get more', as shown by Helsinki and Munich – host cities in which limited resources were used to leverage improved urban amenities and to create stylish spaces. In contrast, Montreal and Athens seem to indicate that lavish investment does not guarantee wider urban improvement and sustainable legacies. Decisions on what should be included in the Olympic development package require wisdom in decision-making, and come from a thorough understanding of the city's traditions, attributes, problems and needs. Also required are: a sharp insight into, and ability to predict, future local development trends; a holistic planning strategy with scientific analysis of positive and negative features; a democratic consultation process to ensure public interest and support; and sufficient economic capacity to enable the development to take place.

Urban integration of major Olympic sites

The integration of major Olympic facilities into a host city's urban fabric is fundamental to the success of planning interventions; it is also a factor influencing other ventures (private and joint public–private) that might exploit land development before and after the Games. The history of Olympic site integration indicates six main city models, each with its own advantages and limitations, which could be used or adapted based on local factors as a guide for future host cities. Figures 3.4 to 3.9 illustrate schematic drawings of the six theoretical models and city examples.

The decentralised model presents an urban adjustment form in which venues are scattered over a wide area with little or modest clustering (in this text, a venue cluster is defined as more than four major venues and their auxiliary facilities being built in proximity). No apparent main Olympic site is defined and because new developments are separated from each other, they have low impacts on the

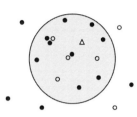

Decentralised:
London (1948)
Mexico City (1968)
Los Angeles (1984)

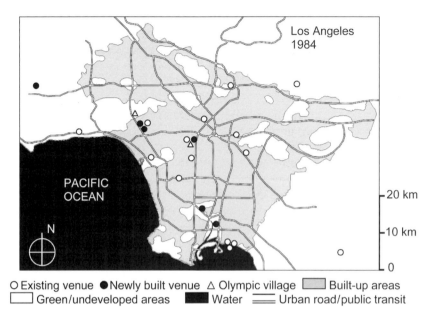

Figure 3.4
*Decentralised model of Games
development (example Los
Angeles 1984)*

O Existing venue ●Newly built venue △ Olympic village ▢ Built-up areas
▢ Green/undeveloped areas ■ Water ═ Urban road/public transit

Olympic site precincts and moderate impacts on the overall urban fabric and
transport infrastructure. Nevertheless it provides the flexibility to deploy new
venues within existing neighbourhoods, which allows the largest number of local
people to access the facilities by walking or cycling from their home or work. Also,
because large-scale land procurement is not normally required, this model is easier
to implement, less sensitive to criticism, and generally incurs a lower cost.

Inner-city mono-clustering:
Helsinki (1952)
Munich (1972)
Montreal (1976)
London (2012)

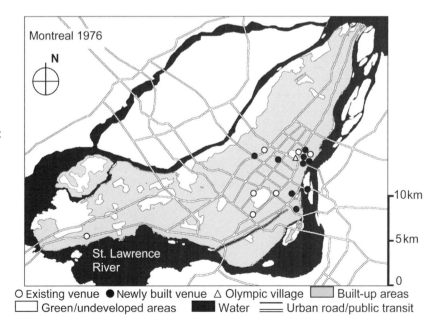

Figure 3.5
*Inner-city mono-clustering
model of Games development
(example Montreal 1976)*

O Existing venue ●Newly built venue △ Olympic village ▢ Built-up areas
▢ Green/undeveloped areas ■ Water ═ Urban road/public transit

The inner-city mono-clustering model presents an urban contraction form with most venues concentrated on one large site within the city's central mass and others dispersed across the metropolitan area. The main Olympic precinct may involve large-scale construction work and need extensive development land. This may lead to profound inner-city regeneration as well as risks of high costs and disruption to local communities (e.g. population displacement). A centrally located concentrated site enables easy access for both athletes and spectators, although transport infrastructure that links the main site with other parts of the city may need to be enhanced prior to the Games.

The inner-city poly-clustering model presents another urban contraction form, but with most venues clustered on several medium-sized sites within the city's central mass, and with others dispersed. Ideally, Olympic precincts are distributed with a sense of balance, with each of them involving substantial construction work and requiring relevant development land. As with the inner-city mono-clustering model, it may trigger inner-city regeneration and create new urban sub-centres. The scaling down of the level of venue concentration may reduce difficulties in land procurement, site management and population relocation, with a lower risk of arousing local objections to the development. This model also tends to reinforce the city's transport infrastructure network through linking the different Olympic sites with other parts of the city.

The periphery-clustering model presents an urban expansion form, with most venues clustered on one or more site(s) on the urban periphery and with others dispersed. Because there are more low-density brownfield areas in a city's outskirts, this model provides potential for large-scale Olympic construction schemes to take place with fewer negative socio-economic consequences. Through this model, a new urban quarter centred on Olympic facilities can be shaped in pursuing a

Figure 3.6
Inner-city poly-clustering model of Games development (example Barcelona 1992)

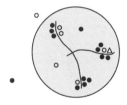

Inner-city poly-clustering:
Tokyo (1964)
Moscow (1980)
Barcelona (1992)

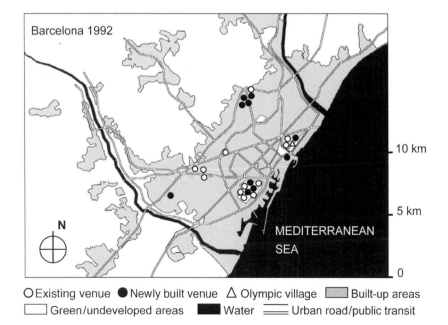

○ Existing venue ● Newly built venue △ Olympic village ▢ Built-up areas
▢ Green/undeveloped areas ■ Water ═ Urban road/public transit

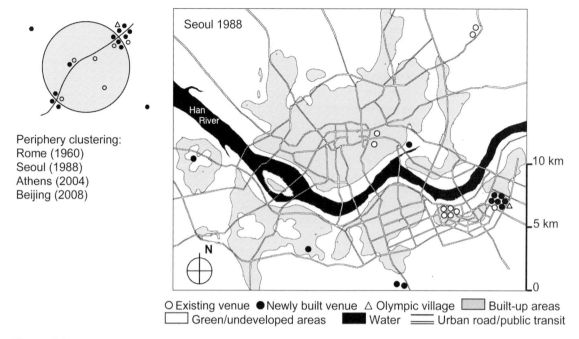

Periphery clustering:
Rome (1960)
Seoul (1988)
Athens (2004)
Beijing (2008)

O Existing venue ● Newly built venue △ Olympic village ▢ Built-up areas
▢ Green/undeveloped areas ■ Water ═ Urban road/public transit

Figure 3.7
Periphery-clustering model of Games development (example Seoul 1988)

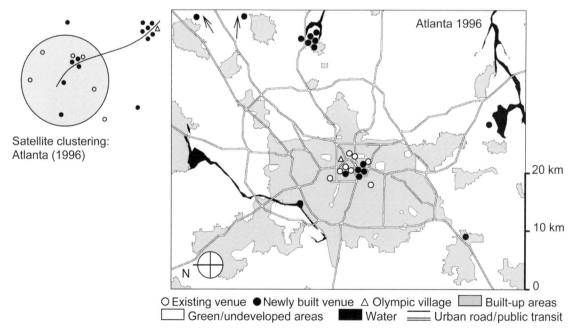

Satellite clustering:
Atlanta (1996)

O Existing venue ● Newly built venue △ Olympic village ▢ Built-up areas
▢ Green/undeveloped areas ■ Water ═ Urban road/public transit

Figure 3.8
Satellite-clustering model of Games development (example Atlanta 1996)

polycentric urban form. In order to handle a large number of Olympic visitors, enhanced transport infrastructures linking the remote venue cluster(s) and the original city core are likely to be required. Often this leads to the extension of the city's underground or light-rail networks to the newly developed areas and hence may help a previously sprawling urban form to adapt towards a more organised transit-orientated urban form. Potential drawbacks are limitations on inner-city renewal, risks of greenfield encroachment and urban sprawl. It is the most frequently found form for Olympic host-city development.

The satellite-clustering model has been identified only once; and then not completely adopted, by Atlanta for the 1996 Games. It presents a regional adjustment form, with a large number of venues clustered on an Olympic site far from the main urban mass and others dispersed or partially clustered across the metropolitan region. This model has modest impacts on the inner city but more significant regional impacts. It favours development of new satellite towns with new or reinforced transport infrastructures linking them to the old city. The remote location of the venue cluster may, however, bring travel inconvenience to athletes and spectators attending competition; further, to enable the new satellite development to function, significant expenditure may be required on basic infrastructure and service networks.

Finally, the joint-clustering model presents a regional combination form, in which many venues are clustered around the main Olympic precinct, tactically located between two urban masses. Others are dispersed or partially clustered across the metropolitan region. This model has modest impacts on both city masses but favours regional integration and may promote a polycentric urban form on a wider scale. Transportation infrastructure linking each regional centre and the Olympic site is likely to be strengthened, yet this model also increases the risk of

Figure 3.9
Joint-clustering model of Games development (example Sydney 2000)

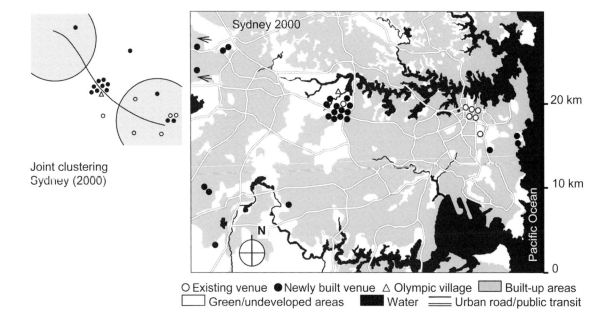

Joint clustering
Sydney (2000)

O Existing venue ● Newly built venue △ Olympic village ☐ Built-up areas
☐ Green/undeveloped areas ■ Water ═ Urban road/public transit

urban sprawl by creating widespread building across a region. One way to avoid this happening might be to develop the Olympic-orientated urban nucleus as a compact and self-sufficient settlement with mixed development features.

The consideration of urban integration methods, either explicitly as part of planning or implicitly associated with other strategies, should respect the distinct character of host cities in terms of urbanisation, demographic change, socio-economic reality and environmental deficiencies. Interestingly, the scale of inner-city population change might be used as one of the indicators to shed light on host cities' general development conditions and needs. Figure 3.10 classifies several Olympic cities into three categories based on the inner-city demographic change centred on the Olympic year. In the cities of Group A, there are dramatic population increases before and during the Olympic preparation, suggesting strong development pressures and expansion needs for these cities' urban fabric. In the cities of Group B, urban population is slightly increased or remains stable before and during the Olympic host, implying that in these cities socio-economic conditions are mature and urban growth is in a benign stage with moderate needs for expansion. The cities of Group C are generally in a state of decline characterised by an urban population decrease before and during the Olympic intervention, suggesting the needs of inner-city regeneration in physical and economic terms to attract both inhabitants and business to return. From this it might be inferred that different integration models should be applied dependent on the city type in this respect.

In general, the decentralised model is appropriate for cities having good civic infrastructures, with no obvious environmental deficiencies to be redressed by planning processes, yet needing a partial adjustment of its urban fabric to balance development. Inner-city clustering models are suitable for cities suffering from inner-city decline, suburbanisation and sprawl. The model can help to re-nucleate an evenly dispersed urban form and introduce large green and public spaces to the city's central mass. The periphery-clustering model is suitable for cities experiencing considerable population growth with outward development pressure and expansion needs. It can help to define the development orientation and convert a rather spread form to a more linear-shaped transit-orientated type. The satellite-clustering model is suitable for large conurbations where internal development pressures need to be organically dispersed and multi-hierarchy settlements need to be reinforced in the whole region. The joint-clustering model is suitable for the coordination of two closely located developing urban areas for a strategic development.

Summary

The Olympic Games in travelling around the world have left a rich spectrum of urban heritage legacies that, taken together, are a unique and indispensable contribution to the success of the modern Olympic Movement. The idea of a 'Modern Olympia' is not a truly geographic concept and the 'Olympic City' is not a distinct urban genre; rather, they are flexible phenomena constantly enriched by the practice of host cities and reinterpreted through the preparation for each new Games. Large-scale Olympic urban development provides solutions and problems for both the Games and local communities. On one hand it may bring desirable

Group A:

Growing cities with
dramatic increase
of inner-city
population during
the Olympic period

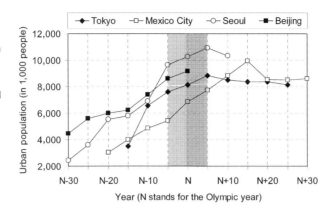

Group B:

Stable cities with
slightly increased or
unchanged inner-
city population
during the Olympic
period

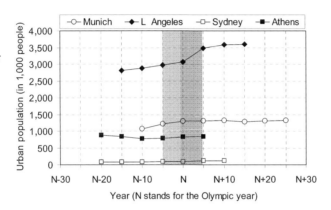

Group C:

Cities with
regeneration needs
with declining inner-
city population
during the Olympic
period

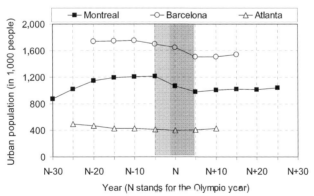

Figure 3.10
*Inner-city population change of
host cities shown centred on
the Olympic year*

social change and an enhanced global reputation; on the other, financial difficulties
and a range of criticism. Each Olympic urban scheme therefore has to find a balance
between sports, ritual, social, economic, environmental and symbolic considerations,
and take account of longer-term realities. Nevertheless, Olympic urban design and
development has emerged as an essential part of the modern Olympic Movement,
extending the Olympic footprint well beyond the Games period, but at the same
time indicating needs for better analysis, understanding and assessment.

CHAPTER 4

Sports venue design and development

Introduction

This chapter is concerned with the development and impact of Olympic sports venues taking a historical perspective up to the present day. It deals with the development of Olympic architecture from basic surroundings of simple sport fields, to high-specification and energy-intensive complexes. Certain sustainability issues are investigated with a focus on the function, structure and environmental impacts.

The IOC currently deals with at least 31 different types of venues in accommodating the 28 main types of sport (35 including sub-categories) and 300 events composing a Summer Olympic Games (IOC, 2004). Initially, Olympic host cities provided sports premises to satisfy the basic requirements of competitions with temporary accommodation for the delegations. The venues were simple, small in number, and often without formal settings. Over time, the quantity and quality of sports and other supporting facilities increased, then after the Second World War two trends emerged affecting the development of competition venues in terms of scale and structure. One was the shift of many sports from natural, outdoor settings into artificial, indoor environments; encouraging development of more expensively constructed, energy-intensive and operationally complicated sports halls. Another was the separation of sports facility types so that more and more special arenas were added to the Olympic architectural family (for instance the velodrome, shooting range, tennis court, equestrian ground, sailing course and hockey field). Overall it is possible to identify four main driving factors behind the evolution of venues:

- the development of the sports;
- improvement in venues' required service level;
- marketing and economic interests; and
- environmental imperatives.

Olympic sports development

The Olympic Games are seen as an assemblage of many individual sport championships attracting many competitors and fans. The range of sports included depends on several factors and there is always pressure for wider coverage. The content of the Olympic programme has in fact changed many times since 1896, only reaching a stable point in recent years. Figure 4.1 lays out the main 28 summer Olympic sports and the Games at which they were included as men's and/or women's events. A number of other sports were staged only at early Summer Olympic Games (pre 1936), such as cricket, croquet, golf and lacrosse.

These Olympic sports can be classified into three groups:

- Basic physical exertions (such as running, swimming, throwing, jumping, weightlifting, canoeing, rowing and sailing), which belong to the oldest sport disciplines tracing back to the early ages of human civilisation.
- Physical exercise related to military or fighting activities (including archery, shooting, fencing, equestrianism, boxing, wrestling, judo and tae kwon do). As

Figure 4.1
Change over time in occurrence of summer Olympic sports

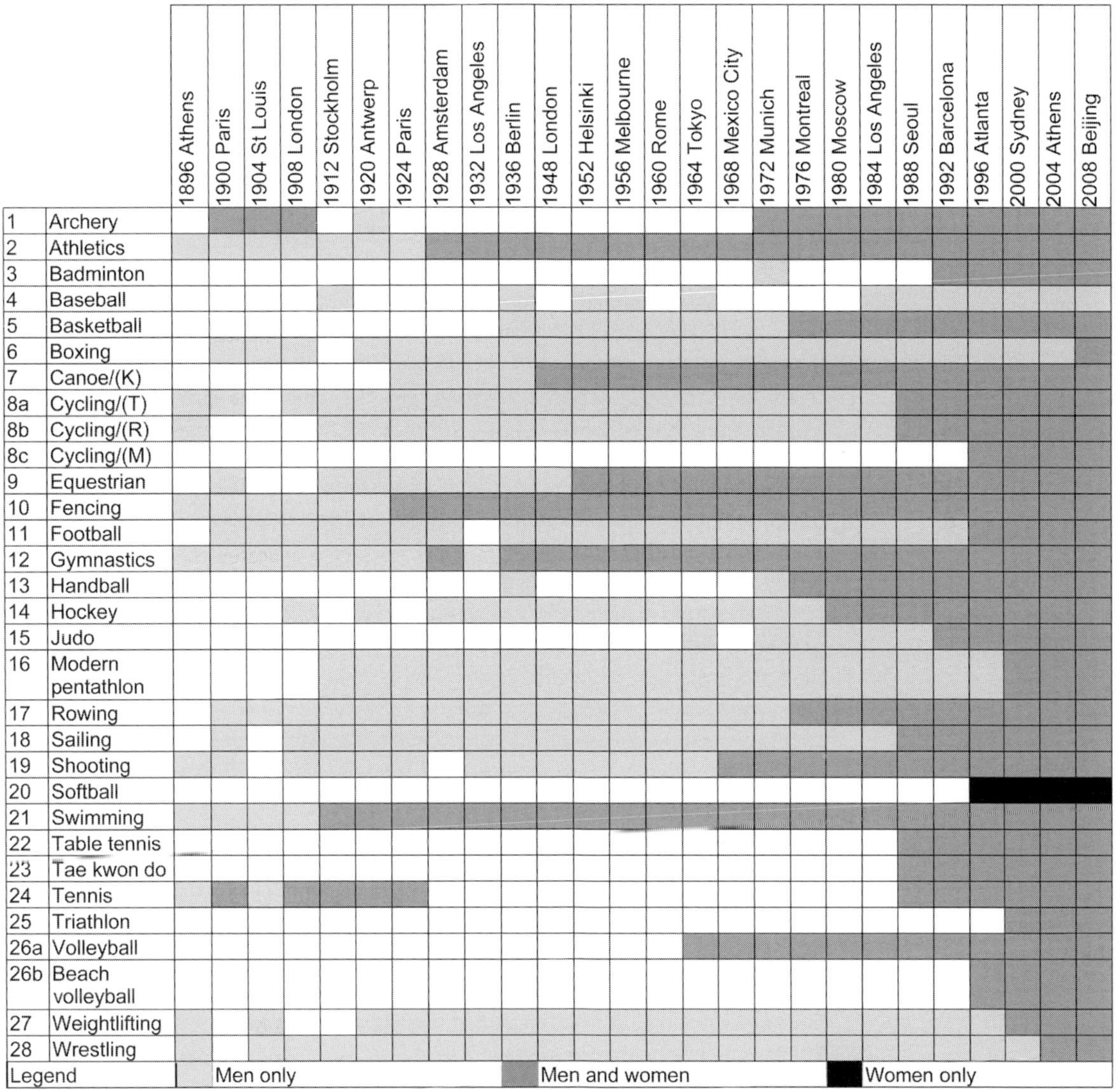
1896 Athens
1900 Paris
1904 St Louis
1908 London
1912 Stockholm
1920 Antwerp
1924 Paris
1928 Amsterdam
1932 Los Angeles
1936 Berlin
1948 London
1952 Helsinki
1956 Melbourne
1960 Rome
1964 Tokyo
1968 Mexico City
1972 Munich
1976 Montreal
1980 Moscow
1984 Los Angeles
1988 Seoul
1992 Barcelona
1996 Atlanta
2000 Sydney
2004 Athens
2008 Beijing
1 Archery
2 Athletics
3 Badminton
4 Baseball
5 Basketball
6 Boxing
7 Canoe/(K)
8a Cycling/(T)
8b Cycling/(R)
8c Cycling/(M)
9 Equestrian
10 Fencing
11 Football
12 Gymnastics
13 Handball
14 Hockey
15 Judo
16 Modern pentathlon
17 Rowing
18 Sailing
19 Shooting
20 Softball
21 Swimming
22 Table tennis
23 Tae kwon do
24 Tennis
25 Triathlon
26a Volleyball
26b Beach volleyball
27 Weightlifting
28 Wrestling
Legend
Men only
Men and women
Women only

with the first group, most of these sports have ancient origins but adapted to new competitive rules.

• Modern sports related to public amusement and sport spectacle. They are mainly ball games: football, basketball, baseball, softball, handball, volleyball, hockey, badminton, lawn tennis and table tennis. Most of these games are played by teams rather than individual players.

Clearly the development of venues is inextricably linked to the sports they serve; in the following sections a review of the development of such venues is provided.

The early 'mono-stadium' model

In its early years the modern Games was dominated by the sports of the first two categories; these could just about fit into one athletic stadium, which was the centre-piece of early Olympic development. The infield was used in various ways: as turf for the football tournament; with fences for equestrian routines; with demountable podiums for boxing, gymnastics, wrestling and weightlifting; and, as in London (1908) and Amsterdam (1928), even excavated for a swimming pool and ringed by a cycling track. At the 1912 Games in Stockholm the expenditure for the Olympic Stadium was 87 per cent of the cost for the entire venue construction (SOCOG, 1912). In addition to the stadium, smaller rented halls were utilised for essential indoor events, and an improvised/adapted watercourse used for aquatic sports.

This 'mono-stadium' development model did not match increasing Olympic needs; it became more and more difficult to reconcile the emerging, and often conflicting, requirements of different sports in one architectural solution. The White City Stadium for the London Games in 1908 showed the functional interference of the over-inclusive design. Developed by James Fulton, the stadium had a single-tier stand capable of holding 80,000 spectators; the running track was surrounded by a 604m concrete cycling track with banked turns, and the infield had a 17m x 100m swimming pool. A collapsible tower was also erected beside the pool for high-diving competition.

The inappropriateness of these settings was illustrated by the experience of Italian marathon runner Dorando Pietri. The official film clips showed that Pietri was too exhausted to balance on the inclined ramp at the edge of the cycling track, falling several times before reaching the finish (Gordon, 1983). The complexity of the stadium format inevitably impaired spectator view and proximity to the events. In addition, concentrating sport events in one venue meant the competition was spread over a longer period with Summer Games before 1932 no shorter than 79 days. With the competition time being shortened to 16 days at the Los Angeles Games and thereafter, many competitions ran concurrently at separate sites. These factors triggered innovations in creating new types of sports premises.

Natatorium (aquatic arena)

The first derivative sports facility that was separated from the conventional athletic stadium was the natatorium. As one of the four sports contested in every modern Games, swimming events were held in natural waters in the early Olympiads.

Stadium, Franco-British Exhibition, London, 1908

Athens 1896 luckily had the picturesque Bay of Piraeus as the competition venue, but in 1900 (Paris) swimmers had to negotiate the muddied and hazardous Seine at Asnières.

At St Louis and London, crude unfiltered and unheated artificial pools were provided but with no wind protection. Stockholm used a natural waterway with a beautifully decorated grandstand built at the water's edge with seating for 7,500. The designers also used pontoon bridges to mark the three other sides and coated the bottom of the 'pool' with sand to keep the water clear.

By 1924, Paris had a much-improved setting with the first real swimming stadium, the Stade Nautique des Tourelles, designed by Leopold Bevière and engineered by Bureau Hennebique. It had an 18m x 50m pool basin with filtering and heating facilities. The pool was ringed by a narrow deck and surmounted on all four sides by concrete seating galleries with total capacity of 10,000 spectators. The novel setting caused a sensation and led to several Olympic records. It also used pool lane markers for the first time, and reduced the length from 100m to 50m allowing swimmers more turns and powerful leg thrusts.

A further modernised natatorium appeared in Berlin; it was a graceful 16,000-seat stadium in crude limestone with a pair of opposing grandstands with two pools, one for swimming and one for diving. A sculptural tower with cantilevered springboards was laid out along the venue's longitudinal axis and this layout became the design standard for international swimming pools. Twenty years later, the first indoor swimming arena was constructed in Melbourne for the Games of 1956.

Figure 4.2
An illustration of the White City Olympic Stadium, London 1908 (source: IOC, Lausanne, © IOC)

Figure 4.3
Swimming and diving pool for the Berlin Games in 1936, undergoing renovation in 2007

The natatorium became the focus of Olympic venue development at the Tokyo Games of 1964, where a lyrical, imaginative, tensile structured swimming arena was created. Since the 1970s, the natatorium has been normally regarded as the most important Olympic architecture apart from the Olympic Stadium. The expression of design importance was reinforced at the Beijing Games with the inclusion of the 'Water Cube'; a building in appearance reminiscent of bubbles from the outside.

Velodrome

Cycling emerged as a sport in the nineteenth century; the early Olympic velodrome was no more than a simple and inclined concrete circuit without seating facilities. London (1906) and Amsterdam integrated a cycling track to the athletic stadium, resulting in criticism but also bringing the cycling events more attention; however, until the Second World War, the velodrome was a minor Olympic venue.

Hilding Ekelund designed the more modern Helsinki velodrome including a 6,200-seat grandstand covered by a delicate steel–concrete-framed roof. The first all-seat Olympic velodrome was built for the Rome Games with cyclists entering through an underground passage beneath the stand (CONI, 1960). In Munich, the velodrome specification called for an open-air construction, but 'one which should be unaffected by weather conditions as far as possible' (OCOM, 1972). The result was a semi-enclosed solution where spectators and the track were roofed-over by a cantilevered canopy.

Figure 4.4
Tokyo National Swimming Arena designed by Kenzo Tange and URTEC for the Games of 1964, Tokyo (source: IOC, Lausanne, © IOC)

The first indoor velodrome was at Montreal; designed by Robert Taillibert, the 6,000-seat arena had a shield-shaped roof spanning over 170m and supported only by four massive abutments. The roof's concrete arches and transverse ribs were

Figure 4.5
The Water Cube Aquatic Centre of the Beijing Games 2008

organically interlinked by acrylic blister skylights, which 'drench the whole space in beautifully diffuse light' (Gordon, 1983). Montreal's velodrome cost US$$_{1976}$ 86.5 million, and boosted the design impact of this building type. Moscow, Sydney, Athens and Beijing consolidated the status of the velodrome as one of the Olympic architectural backbones.

Equestrian arena and other venues

Equestrian events held originally in the Olympic Stadium gradually moved outside, being held on natural plots at Antwerp and Amsterdam, and at the Riviera Country Club in Los Angeles (1932). In Berlin, a vast grassy plateau (the Maifield) was laid out adjacent to the main stadium and ringed on three sides by low bleachers for 50,000 spectators and used for polo matches. Martti Valikangas designed the first real Olympic equestrian centre for Helsinki; since then, a separate structure has normally been provided at each Games. Tokyo had an equestrian park including an open-air dressage/polo ground, a jumping course, stables, a dispensary, a blacksmith centre, a quarantine stall and also (in case of rain) a purpose-built riding hall. After the Tokyo Games, the Olympic equestrian complex usually comprised both open-air and indoor arenas.

Archery and shooting events were also provided with their own premises, because the advances in modern bow and shotgun craft called for a longer projectile range than the stadium infield could possibly provide. Gymnastics, wrestling, weightlifting, boxing and fencing became indoor events and hastened the development of large sports halls. And the Olympic Stadium, after these sports were removed, has been simplified only to accommodate athletic competition and ritual ceremonies.

The main Olympic Stadium and athletics

The iconic role of the Olympic Stadium has a cultural and symbolic meaning and has taken aesthetic forms ranging between traditionalism and modernism, externalism and functionalism, localism and internationalism.

Olympic athletic events underwent a considerable change during the twentieth century, which impacted on the track design and consequently the layout of the whole stadium. Having found the U-shaped Panathenaic hippodrome problematic at Athens in 1896 (see Figure 2.1), designers experimented searching for a better plan. The length of the running track, for instance: this was 333m at Athens (1896), 500m at Paris (1900), 536m at St Louis (1904) and London (1908), 382m at Stockholm (1912), 400m at Antwerp (1920), back to 500m at Paris (1924) and finally the 400m standard at Amsterdam (1928).

After the Second World War, the predominance of athletics in the Games declined; the focus of the Olympic urban development shifted to the holistic planning of all competition facilities. Professionalism and innovation has also played a part in venue development.

Service level for venues

The IOC has used the term 'service level' to describe the general level of logistics provided to Olympic stakeholders in each Games, and there is pressure to continuously improve upon services to showcase 'the best Games ever'. In this text, the 'service level of venues' has a much narrower meaning; it refers to the supporting apparatus, spatial arrangement and environmental conditions that are provided to enable the athletes to compete to the best of their abilities, and to ensure the spectators a certain standard of comfort.

Whereas normal daily sports have an intimacy with the natural environment, the highest standard competitions are somewhat different. Athletes are inevitably affected by the environmental conditions: wind, water turbulence, glare, noise, etc., which may affect performance. Environments should enable fair play and performance levels approaching physical thresholds; this clearly affects venue design.

The need for change

Some early Olympic venues, such as the River Seine, were neither pleasant for athletes nor comfortable for spectators. The official report from the first Athens Games (OCOA, 1896) described the first-day cycling competition at Athens with: 'The weather on that afternoon was anything but mild, a bitterly cold wind blew across the plain and whirled up the dust Inside and outside the enclosure, whose low walls afforded hardly any shelter from the severe blasts.' Lucas (1904) reviews the athletics events of Paris in his report as: 'part of the course lying in a clump of trees; the course of the sprints was wet and soggy, and hammer-throwing was impeded by trees.' Gordon (1983) comments on the water-filled trench used as a swimming pool for Antwerp with: 'the water in the trench never rose above 60 degrees Fahrenheit, a level at which limbs numbed and teeth chattered.'

In London (1948), running competitions were interrupted several times because the track at Wembley was flooded (Bale, 1994). Similar conditions occurred in

Melbourne, where wind and rain often made it difficult; the strong wind more than once blew away the crossbar for the pole vault (Abitare, 1983). At Mexico City, the high altitude (over 2,100m) caused discomfort and brought some chaos to the endurance events.

These dissatisfactions each prompted change, with measures pursued to improve competition conditions. The swimming pool has undergone successive technical refinements in keeping the water clean, temperature mild and minimum subsurface turbulence. Advances in synthetic materials brought resilience to the running track and less frictional force to the cycling circuit. Warm-water irrigation systems aided stadium turf vitality, and 'smart seating' technology delivered more comfort to the spectators – the seating in Mexico City was claimed by one local journalist to be 'a grudge against humanity' (Real Talk, 1967).

Trend towards enclosure

Although it may be better to stage competitions in a controlled environment to minimise external effects; it would be impossible, as well as undesirable, for the Olympics to become a purely indoor event. At early Olympics, however, technology, resources and costs limited construction of large, column-free spaces. Several stages of development are evident: initially those sports requiring neither large performance area nor high spectator capacity became the first to move indoors (for instance wrestling, fencing, weightlifting, badminton and table tennis). With the development of construction techniques, the 1960s saw a boom of so-called 'super sports arenas' for larger scale events. The Palazzetto and Palazzo dello Sport at Rome were based on pre-stressed and post-tensioned concrete techniques; the National Gymnasium complex at Tokyo was a catenary cable and tensegrity system; the Sports Palace at Mexico City used lightweight materials and mesh dome structure; and the sports arena at Munich utilised a tensile net and membrane canopy. These were some of the most epic spaces created for the Olympic Games and allowed sports requiring a large pitch or seating area to be played under roofs. Gymnastics, basketball, volleyball, handball, hockey, cycling and aquatic events also moved indoors; in recent Games, almost 50 per cent of total events were indoors.

The advent of long-span structures allowed development of overhanging grandstand canopies in the stadium. Light steel cantilever trestles had been tested at Paris (1924) and Amsterdam but, until Melbourne, stand roofs were still normally supported by a row of columns erected in the middle of the seating tier; no matter how delicate and slim, they were annoying elements for unobstructed lines of sight. The Flaminio Stadium built for the Olympic soccer events at Rome explored some new thoughts, on which the thin roof was cantilevered forward from an array of heavy in situ concrete supports behind the stand. The system was further developed in the Aztec stadium of Mexico City and the lavish Olympic Stadium of Montreal.

The airy tent roof that crowns the Munich Olympic Stadium presented a heterogeneous approach. The pre-fabricated, cable-suspended, net structure provided more freedom in creating space with less structural weight, and also led to the establishment of computer-aided mathematical programmes for cable network analysis. The stadium at Sydney designed by HOK+LOBB (Figure 4.7) and

the roof addition of the Athens Olympic Stadium by Santiago Calatrava (Figure 4.8) can be seen as extensions to the development with supporting spans as much as 300m.

Panstadia (1999) and SAS (2001) identified the 'first generation' of modern stadiums as those from the first half of the twentieth century with no roof or only modest shelter for spectators. The 'second generation' emerged in the 1960s as a response to the impact of television and had large covered areas 'placing greater emphasis on comfort and ensuring a safe environment to watch sport – the same levels of comfort and security as the living room' (Panstadia, 1999). The 'third generation' included the cable-drawn fabric canopy of the Montreal Olympic Stadium (schemed in 1973, finished in 1987) and the sliding roof segments of the Toronto Skydome (completed 1989), potentially merging all the advantages of an open-air stadium and indoor arena. But these were very expensive and the cost and type of roof coverings for Athens in 2004 and Beijing in 2008 have been a focus of concern.

For completely enclosed arenas, lighting, heating, cooling and ventilation systems create significant energy demands to achieve desired comfort levels. In Helsinki and Melbourne, only limited heating was used; whereas in later arenas (Palazzo dello

Figure 4.6
Impact of columns at Wembley stadium Olympic opening ceremony, London 1948 (source: IOC, Lausanne, © IOC/Lothar Rübelt)

Figure 4.7
The Olympic Stadium, Sydney, for the 2000 Games, showing retractable seating and the trussed arches and cantilevered canopy of the roof

Sport at Rome and aquatic centre at Mexico City), spaces were both ventilated and air-conditioned to reduce the interior temperature.

In the natatorium of Munich, a complicated micro-climate control system was created. Fresh air was ventilated into the arena through a series of ducts suspended beneath the roof while stale air was collected under the seats and forced out at outlets in the façade. Space temperature was 24°C to 26°C with an airflow rate of 600,000m^3 per hour. Halogen lamps produced 4,800 lux horizontal and 1,900 lux vertical light intensity in the competition area and 400 lux for spectator zones (the level of illumination in Olympic venues is mainly driven by needs of television broadcasting). An electrical supply system of capacity 2,200 kW was required to meet demands. Despite the systems, it was reported that the fabric canopy for the pool had minor problems of condensation (Gordon, 1983).

Marketing and economic interests

The Olympics are large global businesses with the Summer Games delivering about US$$_{1995}$ 2 billion to the Organising Committee and the IOC, excluding government

Figure 4.8
The Olympic Stadium, Athens, for the 2004 Games, showing the roof construction

subsidies. Olympic fundraising began with the first Games at Athens in 1896, where private donations and various forms of financing aids contributed to its success. The structure of the Olympic revenue has substantially changed since the 1970s, as shown by Table 4.1; television rights (approximately 40 per cent) and marketing sponsorship (approximately 25 per cent) are now the most prominent with competition tickets sales (approximately 20 per cent) also significant along with merchandising and memorabilia (approximately 5 per cent). These economic interests determine the existence and vitality of the Olympic Movement, and have been reflected subsequently in the venues' architectonic features. For Olympic sponsors, their advertising and signage are prohibited from display at competition venues (Rule 51 of the Olympic Charter, IOC, 2007); thus the economic benefit

Table 4.1 Revenues of the Summer Olympic Games from Munich to Sydney (US$₁₉₉₅ million)

Source	Munich 1972	Montreal 1976	Moscow 1980	LA 1984	Seoul 1988	Barcelona 1992	Atlanta 1996	Sydney 2000
TV	60	84	180	419	523	706	872	1124
Donations	0	0	0	0	170	119	0	n.a.
Stamps	3	20	14	0	7	7	0	0
Coins	735	219	149	53	187	56	15	0
Lottery	204	482	835	0	184	195	0	0
Merchandising	4	6	58	22	20	15	72	48
Ticketing	59	70	46	228	49	92	417	316
Sponsorship	0	40	18	219	215	564	497	459
Other	40	45	38	262	137	314	170	0
TOTAL	1105	966	1338	1203	1492	2068	2043	1947

Sources: Preuss, 2000 and OCOG-80, 1980

comes from the media, the ticket marketing and the memorabilia service. That is to say, Olympic venues are first a temporary 'studio' for broadcasting to be seen by billions of spectators from their living room; second, they act as 'urban theatres' for sports events and have seating capacity in support of ticket sales; and third, they are 'service centres' with commercial space for the merchandise retail sector.

The media and Olympic venues

The Olympic Games is a mass-media event; Sydney attracted 10,000 athletes, but also 20,000 journalists, threefold that of Los Angeles in 1984. The Sydney Games was watched by 3.7 billion television viewers (IOC, 2002) and television has become an engine driving Olympic prosperity: as Samaranch (IOC President 1980–2002) said before Atlanta, 'The media more than anyone else measures the success of the Games' (Gratton, 1999). In supporting media coverage, several elements of Olympic architecture are produced: the media village, and the two largest non-competition venues, the Main Press Centre (MPC) and International Broadcasting Centre (IBC).

The involvement of the media began in the early twentieth century: at Stockholm, press representatives were allocated special areas in the stands to watch the Games undisturbed by other spectators. Two small pavilions were built close to the main stadium for telegraph and post services; forerunners of the later MPC and IBC and radio broadcasts commenced at Paris in 1924. At Amsterdam and Los Angeles (1932), writing rooms, telegraph and telephone booths for the printed press, darkrooms and display spaces for photographers, and boxes for teletypists and radio correspondents were set up within the Olympic Stadium. Separate entrances were designed for contestants, spectators and the media representatives. Television broadcasting arrived at Berlin, but only expanded after satellite transmission technology was developed in the 1960s, leading to further additions to sports arenas such as commentators' cabins, camera platforms, interview studios and signal control centres.

Mexico City had the first full colour-television coverage with satellite relay around the world, and levels of illumination in most indoor arenas had to be substantially increased. Whereas black and white television transmission required intensities of 150–300 lux, at least 1,500 lux was needed for high-definition colour broadcasting. This increased the energy requirements for lighting as well as for the mechanical services needed to remove the heat generated. Lighting energy use was further increased due to more night-time events in the competition schedule, although in recent Olympic arenas, more advanced lighting management systems have been used that differentiate between televised competition and non-televised practice periods. Traditional opaque stand canopies, which may cast strong shadows, as at the Aztec stadium at Mexico City, may cause some problems for television. If canopies are replaced by transparent materials new problems occur, such as the chequerboard shadows, produced by lattices, affecting the athlete's attention, and also the consequent loss of shade for spectators.

A compromise was adopted for the main stadium at Sydney, where a translucent roof with various transparencies in different parts was designed. The front rim of the roof had panels with 30 per cent transparency, which reduced to 20 per cent

at the mid-third and 15 per cent at the rear. John and Sheard (2001) predicted that seating in future stadiums would have more sophisticated sockets for plugging in personal headsets with interactive controls allowing a choice of information.

Figure 4.9
The press stand in the Memorial Coliseum, Los Angeles 1932 (source: IOC, Lausanne, © IOC)

Ticketing and spectator capacity

The number of Olympic television viewers is steadily increasing, but on-site attendance has fluctuated (Table 4.2). Although at Atlanta and Sydney ticketed spectator numbers increased, at Athens (2004) the figure returned to the three-million level of the 1970s. Olympic site visits are affected by many issues: price, accessibility, event interest and time of day; all affect the ticket sales. Geographic location and international profile of a host city may impact on foreign visitors, while local population and sporting traditions influence local attendance; however, for high-demand events, the number of spectators is limited by the seating capacity of a competition venue.

The most important decision in planning a new Olympic venue, or converting an existing one, is the number of spectators to be accommodated. There is a dilemma: on one hand, larger audiences contribute to an impression of a spectacular

Figure 4.10
Umbrella used to shade a television camera, Wembley Stadium, London 1948 (source: IOC, Lausanne, © IOC/Lothar Rübelt)

and successful Games; higher ticket revenues can also be generated. But on the other hand, the larger scale increases the capital and running costs, and leaves difficulties for post-Games usage. Often, figures for Games' attendances seem to be over-estimated by the aspiring organiser; even if the enlarged venues were filled with enthusiastic spectators, the extra economic benefit might be small because many amenities, services and staffing costs have to be increased accordingly for additional spectators. Once the additional circulation, escape and safety-barrier space are taken into account the cost per person may actually be greater than benefits derived.

It is therefore important not to extend venue capacity beyond that which is known to be 'necessary'. One of the clues that help to identify this 'necessary' value is the recommended standard from the International Federation for each sport, approved by the IOC. Another source of information comes from previous Games, where past ticketing data may shed light on finding an appropriate referential range. Figure 4.12 illustrates the capacity of the main Olympic Stadium in each Games.

In general the capacity of Olympic venues has increased over the 40-year period considered and Figure 4.13 shows the distribution of seating capacity at major

Table 4.2 Olympic ticketing data from Rome to Athens

Venue	Total tickets sold	Total tickets available	Average seats' occupation (%)	Average price in US$$_{1995}$	Ticketing revenue in million US$$_{1995}$
1960 Rome	1,408,075	3,669,966	38.4	–	–
1964 Tokyo	2,061,183	2,143,635	96.2	11.02	22.7
1972 Munich	3,311,105	5,003,204	66.2	17.67	58.49
1976 Montreal	3,195,170	4,913,800	65.0	21.77	69.56
1980 Moscow	5,466,321	6,070,717	90.0	8.47	46.32
1984 Los Angeles	5,720,000	7,284,000	78.5	36.5	227.56
1988 Seoul	3,305,944	3,592,589	92.0	14.7	48.61
1992 Barcelona	3,811,916	4,161,518	91.6	24.09	91.81
1996 Atlanta	8,384,290	9,762,347	85.9	38.93	416.64
2000 Sydney	6,679,792	7,539,269	88.6	47.37	316.42
2004 Athens	3,598,444	5,300,000	67.9	51.88	186.70

Data from multiple reports of Olympic Host City Organising Committees

Games venues (excluding the main stadium and football grounds). It can be seen that from Rome to Sydney the number of small-scale venues (capacity <5,000) diminished, while large-scale venues (capacity >20,000) slightly increased.

Some sports traditionally use higher capacity venues (mean value >12,000), including athletics, football, baseball, equestrian, rowing, gymnastics, aquatics and basketball; whereas some others such as archery, weightlifting, shooting, fencing, badminton and table tennis use facilities with mean value of capacity ≤5,000. The range of capacities for certain sports has also varied, perhaps reflecting popularity variations in regions with different cultures.

Figure 4.11

The beach volleyball court and stands for the Athens Games 2004

Figure 4.12

The spectator capacities of the main Olympic Stadiums, Athens 1896 to London 2012

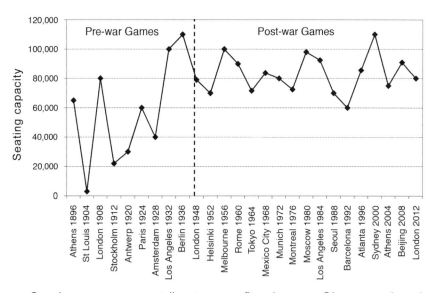

Over-large venues potentially trigger conflicts between Olympic needs and after-use adaptation. Meinel (2001) argued that taking an overview of the 40 or so competition facilities and adding up the required spectator capacity, one arrives at a figure of 800,000. This might be reduced by 20 per cent by skilful scheduling and combining several events at one site, but the remaining 640,000 still represents a daunting challenge for finding post-Games uses for any host city; events that can draw crowds of that size do not come along with great frequency. As a result, many Olympic sites have suffered with long-term under-utilisation and have failed to be economically sustained. The point is reinforced in relation to the Sydney Games by Moore (2000) who reported that promoters preferred to put on their shows in the 10,000-seat Sydney Entertainment Centre rather than in a half-empty Olympic Super Dome even though the rental was similar (the Dome's operating

Figure 4.13

Olympic venue seating capacity, Rome 1960 to Sydney 2000

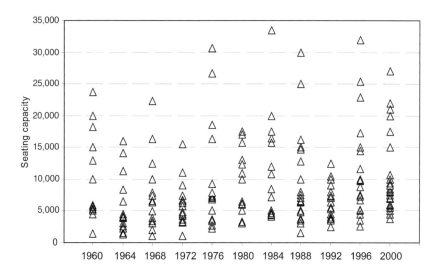

losses were estimated to be running at AU$5 million per year). There is an appeal to some of the IFs to revise the demand for accommodation. As Meinel (2001) pointed out in the Second IOC/UIA joint conference on sports architecture, 'a 10 to 20 per cent reduction in capacity would considerably ease the strain in the host cities or regions'.

Temporary facilities

The utilisation of temporary facilities can either eliminate or reduce the long-term burden of maintenance, and can also reduce environmental impacts. Temporary stands were used at a number of pre-war Games although such stands were generally of low capacity reflecting engineering constraints at the time. If temporary facilities are to be effective they also need to be standardised and be modular to allow for reuse.

Boosted by German industrial craftsmanship and computer modelling techniques, Munich saw an increasing application of modular-based installations. In some of its main venues, such as the Olympic Stadium and the swimming hall, a considerable number of seats were therefore moveable to other sites after the Games. At Barcelona, facilities were rented from a gradually maturing market, leading to extensive use of temporary stands at each venue – a total of 89,557 seats (a third of the entire venue capacity) were provided in this way (COOB'92, 1992). The example of Barcelona showed the importance of temporary facilities in aiding a smaller city to host a big event without leaving too many 'white elephant' legacies. Completely temporary venues have been used in recent Games, such as Stone Mountain Park Velodrome (Atlanta) and Bondi Beach Volleyball Court (Sydney).

Good design can allow the shift of venues to new sports uses such as the Atlanta Olympic Stadium, which was converted to a baseball park. This was successful with modular pre-cast concrete seating tiers removed after the closing ceremony; however, many believed it compromised the athletic venue where original plan was a combination of oval and triangle, with some seats far from the track (ACOG, 1996). The Sydney Olympic Stadium was more successful in adapting between athletics, soccer pitch and Australian Rules Rugby ground. The lower sections of the seating bowl were mounted on steel tracks and could be moved to change the shape of playing field within eight hours (OCA, 1999). Retractable seats are not temporary utilities but they provide flexibility for after-Games use.

Of course temporary facilities are not confined to seating devices, but include a wide range of products that are essential to the running of an Olympic event. Tents, marquees, canopies, trailers, kiosks, booths and portable cabins were widely used in recent Games as well as more complicated units such as toilets, portable telecommunication centres, mobile electricity generators and mobile air conditioners to meet Olympic standards.

Commercial space

Retail space is important at the Games events for selling souvenirs but there is also potential for commercial space that could be introduced in and around sports venues to enhance the long-term economic viability. Some owners and managers have been very energetic in exploiting these opportunities: leisure facilities, exhibitions, conferences, catering, shopping, etc. have been integrated into sports complexes. Unfortunately the rigid structure of a seating bowl, its structure and its access points, restrict the flexibility to insert large facilities. One alternative is to add these facilities on to the stadium separately but attached. Sheard (2001) envisioned a conceptual scheme 'Arena 2020', which was a mixed-use complex where leisure and commercial facilities were no longer auxiliary elements of a stadium; rather, the stadium became an essential part of a multi-functional entity of city fabric. However, even if 'Arena 2020' represents the future for large-scale, international-class sports facilities, its applicability to an Olympic venue is limited at present, because the high initial expenditure would be unlikely to be favoured by the IOC and any organising Committee. Nevertheless, with strategic master-planning, potential development space could be left in appropriate locations to convert basic sports arenas and their surrounding precincts into more useful venues; this was a guiding design principle for two of the main venues for Beijing, the 'Bird's Nest' and 'Water Cube'.

The environmental imperative

The final driver comes from the imperative of environmentally sustainable develop-ment, which is of particular relevance to the theme of this text. Environmental considerations for the venue design are not new issues for the Olympic Movement; since the end of the Second World War, with the growth of the Games both in scale and specification, public concerns about the impact or potential impact of Olympic urban development have posted challenges on a number of occasions. At the same time, there were also several notable instances where Olympic designers in pursuit of a positive environmental footprint have demonstrated good stewardship.

The third pillar of Olympism

Environmental issues were rarely addressed by Olympic decision makers in any organised and pressing manner prior to the 1990s; however, there are some good earlier examples. In Rome, the rowing course used a new floating-cable lane marking system to replace the traditional overhead suspended system, which enabled use of the natural Albano Lake rather than excavating a man-made water course. The design was a great success and the 'Albano system', as it came to be called, was quickly adopted as the International Rowing Federation (FISA)'s standard (Gordon, 1983). At the Sapporo Winter Games, the men's downhill course was specially paved so that it could be restored to its original state afterwards in order to conserve nature (IOC, 1999a). In Munich and Seoul, run-down urban areas were deliberately selected as main Olympic sites and were therefore rehabilitated as pleasant urban neighbourhoods. One can also see a series of confrontations occurring over this period between Olympic development and local people, often centred on environmental issues.

The first environmental impact study on the Olympic Games dated from those of Lake Placid in 1980, and by the 1990s increased awareness of the importance of energy and environmental protection issues caused a change in opinions. In the belief that the Olympic Movement and the 'environmental movement' shared the common ideal of building a 'peaceful and better world' for humanity (as expressed in the principles enshrined in the Olympic Charter), the IOC felt its duty to act as a catalyst in fostering environmentally sound actions within the Olympic Movement and beyond.

In 1992, the IOC, together with many IFs and NOCs, signed the 'Earth Pledge', formally confirming their commitments to environmental protection and enhancement. In 1994, the IOC signed a cooperation agreement with the United Nations Environmental Programme (UNEP) to develop joint initiatives. In the same year, 'environment' was approved as the third pillar of Olympism after 'sport' and 'culture'. In 1996, the Olympic Charter was modified to refer to the environment, and it now states that one of the IOC's roles is 'to encourage and support a responsible concern for environmental issues, to promote sustainable development in sport and to require that the Olympic Games are held accordingly' (IOC, 2007: 14).

In 1999, the Olympic Movement's Agenda 21 was adopted at the Third World Conference on Sport and the Environment, but the most tangible and influential action was that since 1994 candidate cities for both Summer and Winter Olympic Games have been evaluated on their environment plans. The IOC's bidding procedure includes issues of environmental protection, environmental impact measurement, sustainability of Olympic legacies and compulsory ecological studies. These now occupy a significant fraction of the candidature file and are of importance in the process of choosing the host city. In particular, emphasis has been given to Olympic infrastructure, the largest share of the preparation stewardship. Environmental parameters and long-term sustainability should be taken into account from the outset, and be geared towards the minimisation of any negative environmental impact.

Although the formal expectations for environmental sensitivity and sustainability are expressed in quite general terms, the driving forces are now expressed forcefully through public and political expectations.

Environmental initiatives in venue development

In 1994, the Winter Games in Lillehammer became the first Olympics to address environmental issues and publicise their efforts. Thereafter, each of the Olympic organising authorities has launched, and implemented at different levels, their own environmental sustainable development (ESD) guidelines. Contemporary host cities, Vancouver and London, have also released their own plans to ensure that environmentally sound design features will be included in the development brief. The design of Olympic venues is also affected, to a greater or lesser extent, by environmental considerations in terms of land usage, material selection, structure deployment, energy management, water and resources conservation, waste disposal and function optimisation.

The main environmental requirements of recent Olympic venue development can be summarised as follows:

- Establish an Environment Management System (EMS), including the creation of planning tools or environmental guidelines for large building projects; the development of new green building standards, purchasing guidance and products lists; and the conduction of environmental audits at various stages of design and construction. These requirements have been more effective in some host cities than others.
- Apply environmental protection and enhancement measures, including the creation of Olympic parkland by remediation of contaminated and degraded land; the protection of natural habitats and threatened native species; and the carrying out of regular environmental impact assessments. These efforts help to enhance the surrounding landscape and ecological vitality of a whole site, which has been recognised as an important parameter of a venue's development.
- Establish a resources management system, including the promotion of the application of energy-efficient facilities; maximisation of use of green power and renewable energy; acting as a showcase of natural lighting, cooling and ventilation strategies; and the use of water conservation, treatment and recycling techniques. These are tangible measures geared towards 'green' infrastructure, some of which rely on innovative technologies whereas others use low technology but with intelligent design and planning.
- Instigate a waste management system, including promotion of reduction, reuse and recycling of waste, reuse of existing facilities and recycling of building materials. The Super Dome for Sydney claimed to be the first Olympic venue having a direct 'site to recycler' waste management system. During the construction, 26,000m^3 of concrete found on and around the construction precinct was crushed and reduced on site, which contributed 18 per cent to the total of amount of concrete used for the whole project. At another site, the Sydney Showground, 1,200 tonnes of building materials including bricks, metal and timber from demolishing were skilfully reused on site. The construction waste recycling rate of these two sites reached 92 per cent and 60 per cent respectively (OCA, 2000). Later Games figures are even higher.
- Improve other features, including the construction of environmentally friendly transportation systems (promoting public transport to reduce the use of private cars); the use of light-weight structure to reduce the material usage; the wide application of sustainable building materials such as timber (e.g. Radiata Pine for Sydney's Dome and Pavilions) and materials with low embodied energy such as high strength, light-weight steel components; the preconceiving of the venue's long-term use scenarios in the initial design stage; and the promotion of public environmental education programmes, encouraging the involvement of local stakeholders.

Implementation of environmental strategies

The use of renewable energy to power venues has been a common feature of recent Games. In Atlanta, a photovoltaic energy system consisting of 2,856 amorphous silicon solar cells was installed on the roof of Atlanta Aquatic Centre, which generated up to 40 per cent of electricity demand at this facility. A similar system was applied at the Super Dome in Sydney, which also had 19 Towers of Power stretching along the main Games' boulevard. Sydney's Olympic Village has a total photovoltaic electricity production capacity of over 1 million kWh each year. Likewise, Beijing included installation of geothermal pumps, solar power and wind turbines in its Olympic Park planning. Renewable energy generation devices at competition venues have often been more for demonstration than practical supply so far. However, the purchase of 'green' power from the electricity market can also help the development of local renewable energy businesses by creating a demand. The electricity supplier for Sydney, Energy Australia, utilised a variety of sources including solar power, wind power, hydropower and landfill gas.

In compliance with environmental requirements, high-efficiency equipment (lights, air-conditioning and water fittings) with certain levels of control has been widely adopted in venues of Atlanta, Sydney, Athens and Beijing. At the same time, natural lighting and passive thermal-comfort strategies have been incorporated with the help of state-of-the-art research. For example, in designing the main stadium for Sydney, computer simulation techniques were used to examine the temperatures, air movement and daylight distribution throughout its enclosed area as well as estimating solar heat gains (Lomas et al., 1997). The analysis led innovations to be included in the design of the building's layout, profile and envelope.

At Sydney, to reduce the heat gain in the summer, glazing areas in the façade were assessed and shading strategies applied; also natural displacement ventilation was used to minimise the use of air-conditioning. The hollow core of the spiral ramps at the four corners of the stadium and several vertical air shafts made up a solar chimney system, allowing hot air in the space beneath stands to be extracted at high level by stack effect. Fresh air was allowed to circulate from the louvres below the windows on the pitch side of the stadium and the entrances to the concourse. Since, in the hottest season, ventilation alone was unlikely to maintain thermal comfort, several natural cooling strategies were also explored, including using the night venting to cool the exposed concrete ceiling and walls. If all possible measures had been implemented, it was estimated that approximately 30 per cent of overall energy would have been saved compared to conventional benchmarks.

Other environmental design features shown by recent games included rainwater collection and storage systems; minimising the use of construction materials with negative environmental impact; and conducting life-cycle assessment (LCA) for prime venues as a part of decision support systems.

Summary of Olympic venue development

Building and construction requirements for Olympic Games events have grown in parallel with competitor and spectator numbers. Several driving factors have been described that have fuelled the evolution of Olympic venues from simply-equipped, mono-functional, open-air sports-grounds to an array of highly specialised, multi-functional, environmentally controlled arenas. Some factors, such as the Olympic sports and service level, have been stable for recent Games, yet others, such as the media and environmental protection, are still active in steering change. Four principal aims influence the procurement of each Games venue: to ensure optimum competition conditions; to provide spectators with comfortable environments; to allow the event to maximise its media impact; and to minimise negative

Figure 4.14

The spectacular 'Bird's Nest' Stadium for the Beijing Games 2008

environmental impacts. These issues constitute the basic framework from which to evaluate competition facilities.

The criteria for examination of these issues are based on a number of resources. Both the IOC and the International Federations have established technical standards in terms of competition settings and media services for different sports events. For amenities and comfort level of spectators, the decision rests with the organising committee of each Games. The IOC has also undertaken two projects that may impact on future venue development. The first was the work developed by the IOC Games Study Commission, which, in assessing ways to control cost, size and complexity of the Games, made several recommendations related to service level in general. The second project developed venue standards for all Olympic facilities, defining aspects of venues related to spectators, including seating type and quality, concourse widths, and provision of services. Research in related fields, such as on outdoor thermal comfort (Bosselmann et al., 1988; Noguchi and Givoni, 1997; Nikolopoulou, 2000) and the optimum viewing distances in stadium (John and Sheard, 2001; BIADR, 2002), also provided important information that may be taken into account.

The basic contents of design manuals for particular sports architecture are clearly important and worthy of study. Certain parameters such as seating capacity, spatial versatility and energy and water consumption are important elements in the overall evaluation framework, and will be used later as indicators to examine the environment performance of Olympic venues. In general, except for venues such as indoor swimming arenas, sports stadiums are not a building type that is thought of as polluting and energy intensive. Some, however, are water-intensive in terms of pitch irrigation and hygiene needs for large numbers of spectators. To establish the environmental benchmarks for different types of Olympic sports facilities in energy and water usage is a daunting but significant task required for the future.

Another essential aspect of the evaluation is adaptability of Olympic venues to changing demands, which is crucial to post-Games use. Most Olympic venues are still standing, and though some, such as the 1896 Athens stadium, no longer satisfy modern needs, many, such as the Gothic stadium of Stockholm and the Los Angeles' Memorial Coliseum, still enjoy a range of sporting uses. Others, including the Berlin, Colombes (Paris, 1924) and Rome stadiums, have been technically upgraded to serve new requirements. And some, such as the 1956 Melbourne swimming arena and the 1976 Montreal velodrome, have been redesigned. Recent Olympic Stadiums are in regular use although a number are reported to struggle in finding sufficient spectators/customers. Many questions should be posed in relation to the adaptability of Olympic facilities and their future value. Competition venues are only part of the whole picture, however, and in the next chapter another important component is examined: the Olympic Village.

CHAPTER 5 Olympic Village design and development

Overview of Olympic Villages

The previous chapter discussed Olympic competition venues; in this chapter the Olympic, or Athletes' Village, is investigated. Compared to competition venues, the Olympic Village can more easily be integrated into a host city's masterplan as a new residential quarter, and it therefore has more intimacy with the city's urban fabric in terms of strategic development and expansion. This intimacy has been recognised by many researchers, as Munoz (1997) pointed out: 'The study of the Olympic Village throughout this century is the study of the history of ideas about how to develop the city, how to plan it, and how to manage it.' It is clear therefore that any discussion about villages will also be closely linked to that of urban design, planning and development. A sustainable village is important not just for its impact during the Games but also for the long-term post-Games use and also the influence it might have on the wider housing market.

The commitment of an organising committee to prepare an Olympic Village is laid down in the Olympic Charter, the host city contract, and the technical manual on the Olympic Village and NOC services. According to the IOC, the Olympic Village is an 'accommodation complex reserved exclusively for competitors and accompanying personnel' (IOC, 1994). It does not accommodate the IOC and IF officials, referees, IOC guests, Olympic sponsors or media representatives; these personnel normally occupy quality hotel rooms close to the main competition sites or, in some cases, a separate officials' village. This chapter concentrates only on issues of the Olympic Village itself and excludes other accommodation.

Compared to the sports venue's competitive atmosphere, the Olympic Village demonstrates more a spirit of brotherhood, mutual inspiration, solidarity and humanity. It has consequently become a mainstay of Olympism. In a publication from 1994 the Olympic Village was described as 'the central point where athletes from all over the world live together before and during the Games, thereby helping to further the noble ideals of understanding and friendship among athletes from all countries and all Olympic sports' (IOC, 1994). The village should provide a safe, well-protected and comfortable residential environment, essential for the athletes' mental and physical preparation, away from the distractions of the outside world. A poor competition venue may detract from a particular sports event, but a poor Olympic Village may compromise the quality of the whole Games.

At a time when the Games seem to be dominated by economics, urban design and spectator concerns, the Olympic Village has emerged as perhaps the last stronghold of traditional Olympic values. Yet as with competition venues, the Olympic Village has also undergone many changes in respect of building scale, architectonic specification and relationship to a host city. From the barrack-like camps that characterised early Games, to large-scale housing schemes now integrated into the urban residential fabric; from simple shelters with the sole function of board and lodging, to stylish compounds providing a whole set of amenities and services; the development of the Olympic Village has reflected the trend of other Olympic facilities towards gigantism, and consequently a higher level of consumption of resources.

The most direct impact comes from the increase in the number of Olympic participants, creating soaring space and resource demands. Figure 5.1 shows the change in the number of participants in the Summer Olympics; note the number of athletes taking part in the Games of Athens in 2004 was double that in Moscow in 1980.

The second impact arises from the cultural, social and leisure dimensions of the village. These have been important since the 1960s, when the village was recognised as a hub of socialisation and multi-cultural exchange, as well as for physiological and psychological recovery of contestants. Since the 1970s, most Olympic Villages have provided three zones: a residential zone where athletes and NOC officials are accommodated; an international zone where they are entertained; and a sports centre where they train.

The third impact arises from the development needs of the host city; in particular its residential infrastructure and backdrop of different historic periods, which can determine the form of the Olympic Village and its insertion into the city's built environment.

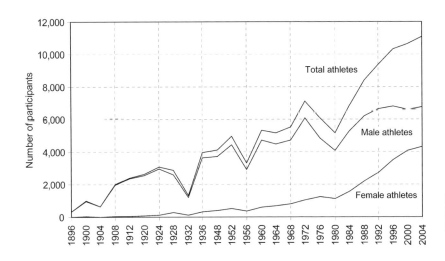

Figure 5.1
Number of participants in the Summer Olympics, Athens 1896 to Athens 2004

Historic evolution of the Olympic Village

The origin of the Olympic Village concept arises from De Coubertin's ideas of creating a 'Modern Olympia'. In a pamphlet published in the *Olympic Review* describing his vision of the Olympic city, the Olympic Movement's founder suggested the need for 'an expandable sort of hotel' to accommodate delegates or participants in the Olympic celebration. He had considered the requirements in some detail:

> They [Olympic participants] need comfort but would be willing to put up with a certain degree of simplicity and uniformity in food and lodging. The architecture and layout of this institution, of course, would take their cue from these special conditions. Around it, space would have to be provided for setting up a camp, and also some sort of barrack buildings to house the athletes during the Games.
>
> (De Coubertin, 1909c)

However, these ideas took some time to realise; even in the 1920s most host cities had an accommodation committee to investigate local hotels and negotiate appropriate tariffs and reservations for Olympic delegates. On some occasions when there was not enough hotel capacity to house the number of visitors, alternative accommodation resources were secured. The Games of Amsterdam was a typical example, where the athletes' lodgings were scattered up to 60km distant including hotels, guest houses, schools and 18 ships hired in the Amsterdam port area (TNOC, 1928). These discrete accommodation locations prevented athletes from having a communal life, and also increased transportation problems.

Pre-war villages to Berlin

In Stockholm, the Swedish committee accommodated its own athletes in houses situated next to the Olympic Stadium. These houses, though without any Olympic design involvement and being primitive in the level of service conditions provided, could be seen as a prototype of later Athletes' Villages.

A more significant impact was Paris in 1924, however, where wooden barracks were established in an area near the Colombes Stadium for some of the athletes. From photographic records, the Paris village looked more like an urban slum than athlete domiciles with coarsely built, low-eaves huts alongside narrow, muddy lanes. Nevertheless it was a purpose-built facility and included almost all the features of later Olympic Villages. There were two drawbacks: first it was on a relatively small scale and was only used by a portion of Olympic delegates; second it was only a temporary construction and was demolished soon after the Games. As a result, many Olympic scholars believe the first real Olympic Village made its debut in Los Angeles in 1932.

Several researchers (e.g. Wimmer, 1976; Munoz, 1997; Thomas, 1999) considered economics as the catalyst for the common village plan in Los Angeles. At the pre-Games IOC congress in Berlin, two accommodation proposals were put forward for discussion: the purpose-built Olympic Village and the use of the city's hotels. The second scenario appeared to be more costly for delegates. Considering the remote location of America for European athletes, a reduction in costs was a good strategy to encourage participation. Also the project could stimulate employment at the time of the Great Depression as well as profits for local developers. The Los Angeles event was also supported by a group of businessmen including real estate developer William Garland, who was both contracted for the Olympic Village project and chaired the organising committee. As a result, 550 prefabricated white and rose coloured wooden cottages were built in a 101-hectare compound on Baldwin Hills at the edge of the city; each accommodated four athletes in an area of 89m^2. Female athletes were lodged in the Chapman Park Hotel near the city centre, consistent with the convention at the time of separating the sexes in Olympic residences.

Compared to Paris, the Los Angeles Village was innovative in planning and design with industrialised modular elements (for quick on-site assembly and quality control); toilet and washing facilities in each unit; communal open space; an emergency hospital; an open-air theatre; a library; a gymnasium; and other training fields. According to the post-Games' official report, even the selection of the site had been made with care for the temperature in Southern California, which had been as high as 40°C in the year before the Games. Baldwin Hills was chosen because the average summer temperature was lower than the city centre (OCLA, 1933).

The success of the Los Angeles Village also inspired both the IOC and the German organisers for the Berlin Games. Although the city did in fact have enough hotel capacity to hold all the Olympic visitors, at the IOC congress in Vienna in 1933, most participants were keen to build a concentrated village (OKOB, 1936). The decision was to use the military land at Döberitz, about 14.5km from the Olympic Stadium. As with Los Angeles four years earlier, the site for Berlin's Village was also carefully selected from the environmental point of view. The 55-hectare plot was beautifully landscaped with birch groves and small lakes; and the predominant westerly winds in summer would provide unpolluted fresh air to the site. Designed by Werner and Walter March, 194 whitewashed, tile-roofed bungalows were organically clustered around a contoured plateau; each consisting of ten to twelve simply furnished rooms; two people to a room. Service facilities in the Village were more comprehensive than previously including an indoor swimming hall and various entertainment rooms, making the Olympic Village more self-contained. Unlike the design of previous villages, nothing in the Berlin Village was temporary. It had been designed to be a billet for German army officers after the Games. Berlin's advanced Olympic Village had a military style, but from technical and functional points of view it was not surpassed for many years.

Post-war villages from London to Melbourne

The first post-war Games was held in London in 1948, the only city perhaps capable of hosting the Games in Europe at that time, despite struggling with reconstruction and economic stringency. In the post-war circumstances the organisers were unable to build large new facilities: 'No building program could possibly have been entertained in a country with the immediate post-war housing and building problem of Great Britain in 1946 and 1947' (LOCOG, 1948).

This meant a wide range of residential infrastructures in the greater London region had to be requisitioned and converted into athlete accommodation, including two Royal Air Force camps at Uxbridge and West Drayton, one military infirmary at Richmond Park, a series of schools in Middlesex, and three colleges in the outskirts of the city for female competitors. A total of 27 makeshift lodgings were arranged within 50km, making the transportation issue a considerable challenge. Food was scarce and living conditions inevitably poor, as Monique Berlioux (IOC director 1969–85) wrote in her memoirs: athletes were 'squashed up five to a room and with only one toilet for every thirty people' (Berlioux, 1991). Despite the difficulties, the main blocks were equipped with services such as laundries, banks, mini-cinemas and small shops; the installation of amenities accounted for 22 per cent of the whole Olympic construction budget (Baker, 1989).

The first post-war Olympic Village was therefore built in Helsinki; in fact, the city had prepared a village in Käpylä for the cancelled Games of 1940. The most important innovation was that it had been designed from the outset to be a permanent self-sustaining community as part of a long-term municipal social housing plan (commonplace in later Games). The village comprised dozens of simply shaped apartment blocks, three or four storeys high, and coherent in colour and design details. Each dwelling included two to three rooms plus a kitchen, a bathroom and a small balcony (typical for a Finnish family at that time). Pre-existing landscape features of the site were preserved wherever possible. The first 545 units had already been built for the cancelled 1940 Games and had been used by refugees in the interim period. When the Games were re-awarded to Finland for 1952, a new Olympic Village therefore had to be built on a site adjacent to the earlier developments. Designed by Pauli Salomaa, the second village inherited many architectonic features of the previous, though simpler in form and smaller in spatial dimensions, due to the post-war economy. In fact it only had the capacity to house some of the athletes; those taking part in rowing, shooting, equestrian and wrestling events were accommodated in local colleges and war-affected housing. Women were placed in the city's nursing school, 1km away from the Olympic Stadium. At the IOC congress in Rome in 1949, the Helsinki committee explained its scaled-down approach:

> It is not in our opinion today possible to carry through the idea of Baron De Coubertin that all athletes should be brought together in an Olympic Village. With all extra buildings, stores, dining rooms, kitchens, etc. the organisers would have to build not a village, but a city.
>
> (Frenckell, 1949)

Following the request of the Soviet Union, who entered the Games for the first time, a third village had to be built especially for their athletes and those from the Eastern Bloc countries to separate them from Western delegations. This was located at Otäniemi, 10km from Käpylä Village, and later became student housing.

In Melbourne the trend to combine the development of the Olympic Village with the municipal housing programme was consolidated. A large village with 841 semi-detached houses was set up on a 60ha site in the city's suburb of Heidelberg, 13km north of the Olympic Park. Interest-free funding was provided by the local council from the Commonwealth State Housing Scheme. These houses were one- or two-storey villas with small gardens, typical of colonial style and to be used by immigrants once the Olympics were over (Bailey, 1993). For those athletes taking part in the separate equestrian events in Stockholm, makeshift accommodation was offered in the Karlberg Military Academy and in Nasby Castle, formerly the Swedish Naval School.

Villages from Rome to Moscow

By the 1960s, economies had recovered from the war and rapid development could be seen everywhere. Accompanying the new wave of modernisation and commercialisation, and also owing much to the popularisation of private transport, major cities underwent dramatic expansion. Within this scenario Olympic building became an agent for regional development rather than a solution to a temporary need; Olympic Villages could fulfil urgent housing needs after the Games and hence became a more desirable construction element, less sensitive to criticism. Their dual function – as athlete dormitories in the short-term and residential dwellings in the long-term – sometimes brought conflicts in spatial layout and division. If the after-use (for family living) was given priority, Olympic usage (based on collectivism on one hand and individual flexibility in training and competition on the other) was inevitably compromised and this is an issue that remains to the present day. From the 1960s onwards, the form of the Olympic Village has often been of a multi-storey apartment block rather than De Coubertin's 'barrack village' concept, being largely driven by the prioritisation of post-Olympic adaptation. As a counter to the deficiencies, cultural and entertainment elements were reinforced wherever possible to create a carnival atmosphere within the Village.

Wimmer (1976) described the Olympic Village for Rome, located at Campo Paroli inside the northernmost curl of the River Tiber, as 'the first modern residential quarter'. The village, designed by Cafiero, Libera, Luccichenti and Moretti, consisted of 33 apartment buildings ranging from three to five storeys, totalling 1,348 units. Influenced by the functionalism of Le Corbusier, buildings in the Campo Paroli village reflected a succinct style from exterior identity to interior elements. Interestingly, Le Corbusier himself commented on Rome's village design and his 'Ville Radieuse' proposal, finding many common features (Brandizzi, 1989). The enclosed spaces between the apartment blocks acted as lively piazzas for athletes, where facilities ranging from restaurants and shops to billiard rooms, and open-air cinemas were established. It was the first time that leisure activities in the Olympic Village were included to support the social and recreational needs of athletes (CONI, 1960).

The Tokyo Games of 1964 combined Olympic urban development with an ambitious city regeneration plan; with a total investment of 11.6 billion US$_{1995}, it was the most costly Olympic installation package so far. Because the Olympic venues for competition and training were scattered over Tokyo's numerous wards and prefectures, the main Olympic Village was placed in a central location to allow equal convenience in reaching Olympic sites by normal means of transport. A former camp for US military personnel known as 'Washington Heights' in the Yoyogi area was chosen as the location. The precinct already had a large number of modern houses and needed relatively modest adaptation to match Olympic requirements. Approximately 250 two-storey wooden cottages and 14 four-storey reinforced-concrete buildings (3,125 rooms in total) were provided for the 7,000 participating athletes and officials. Other spaces available in the site were converted to service facilities for communal use. One deficiency of the compound was its limited area at only 66 hectares and it was difficult to accommodate adequate training grounds. As a result of the distance between Yoyogi village and several competition sites with potential transportation problems, four additional 'villages' were set up based in local hotels.

The trend of decentralisation of Olympic venues was continued in Mexico City with development in areas where growth was expected. Although Mexico City had a less ambitious overall Olympic plan than Tokyo, the Olympic Village itself was considered superb. In fact two Olympic Villages were built on the south periphery of the city: the Miguel Hidalgo village for athletes and journalists, and the Villa Coapa for judges and entertainers taking part in a wide programme of cultural events – an indispensable component of the 1968 Games and dream of De Coubertin's Olympic vision: to unite arts and sports.

Designed by a large team of local architects, both complexes were made up of large apartment blocks, a building type that had been used as Olympic accommodation in Rome. The Miguel Hidalgo village consisted of 29 white/red-coloured brick buildings, 13 of which were ten storeys high and the rest six storeys, making a total of 904 condominium units (5,044 rooms); whereas the Villa Coapa was a mixture of houses and low-rise flats with 686 units (3,474 rooms). These buildings were surrounded by modestly scaled, richly verdant areas, generous in amenities and coherent in design features. Their planning also reflected the influence of 'neighbourhood unit' theory prevailing in the 1960s. Ironically, the Miguel Hidalgo village only had 30ha of land, far less than that of Tokyo, but sufficient training grounds were available within the compound due to the high-rise accommodation units. Two ancient Maya pyramids discovered during the constructional process gave the community an unexpected historic identity.

Munich adopted a centralised approach to locate most of their Olympic venues and Athletes' Village on one concentrated site: the 280ha of derelict land at Oberwiesenfeld 4km north of the city centre. Within the precinct, the Olympic Village was organically formed by a series of heterogeneous buildings differing in size and layout, housing up to 12,000 residents. In order to echo the delightful style and humanistic taste of Munich Olympic Park, the design of the village also manifested a sense of freedom with regard to form, structure and position on the site. The skyline of the complex was dominated by three snaking tiers of terraced apartment blocks (7 to 14 storeys in height), each linked at their east end to a 20-storey slab-tower administrative building. Among these high-rise prefabricated concrete blocks, three- to five-storey maisonettes and bungalows were positioned almost casually, making the spaces between buildings vivid and rich of layer both in horizontal and vertical dimensions. Two features distinguished Munich's village from earlier ones: the introduction of a pneumatic waste collection system as a part of environmental initiatives; and the separation of pedestrian paths from vehicular traffic route at different levels within the site.

The Munich village marked a peak in terms of complication of building design and site masterplanning. The village was criticised in this manner: 'as rich and powerful as the architectural forms are, there is a sense of crowding and a loss of clarity in certain of the routes of circulation that even Hans Hollein's overhead system of Path-finders could not entirely restore' (Gordon 1983). And worse: the kidnap of Israeli athletes by terrorists within the Olympic Village and their subsequent massacre brought into question the open character and tortuous space linkages of the Village that perhaps increased problems of security. These deficiencies found immediate response in the design of the next Village for the Games of Montreal.

Shortly before the events at the Munich Games, Montreal had submitted its proposal to build a Village consisting of five different buildings spread over several kilometres. The concept was to integrate the new developments into the city's long-term public housing scheme, but it was rejected by the IOC in June 1973 who by then were more in favour of a concentrated village approach for reasons of convenience and security. The lessons of Munich called for a simpler and more compact building solution to be employed for ease of surveillance, rather than a tangle of housing clusters. As a result, designers of Montreal's village, Roger D'Astous and Luc Durand, compressed almost everything into four giant stepped towers grouped two by two, with elevator cores.

These sculptured, visually spectacular structures, extending up to nearly 600m in length and rising in continuous setbacks to a height of 19 storeys, provided a total of 980 flats, each with terrace, cross ventilation and a view. The usual public and amenity resources were positioned in the lower levels of these buildings with more noisy facilities (such as cinemas, restaurants and discotheques) placed in the International Centre across the street to prevent congestion of the Village itself and ensure a quiet environment for residents.

The compact nature of the building meant the living space per head was less than some earlier villages. Each apartment, with one to three bedrooms, was shared between 5 to 14 occupants: a space-standard close to that of London in 1948, but with living conditions better than its post-war predecessors. The accommodation had purpose-made furniture and appliances especially designed for each studio type with several functions being ingeniously combined together. As with previous Games, the organisers encouraged an intimate atmosphere by defining an 'international zone', but more than before, security was prioritised. For the first time, the entire Village was surrounded by a high wire fence with any access subject to a strict check and heavily armed guards wandering around walkways; a scene perhaps not very harmonious with the advocacy of Olympism.

Montreal's village project had also been controversial from the very beginning; the use of 34ha of urban green land for the development had caused a wave of local opposition (Radwanski, 1973; Harrison, 1973; Le Devoir, 1973), and its massing profile was accused of being unnecessarily over-scaled to the low-rise surroundings (Gordon, 1983). The features that most concerned critics were the exposed exterior corridors for access to apartments: devices crucial to the whole design concept but obviously ill-suited to the climate. Games' officials, however, claimed that they provided for easy surveillance of horizontal movement throughout the building complex. Though the criticisms cannot be ignored, Montreal's Village remains as an enduring architectural symbol of the Games. Those who predicted problems after the Games found themselves disappointed with the apartments offered as housing soon fully occupied with a long waiting list (Essex and Chalkey, 1999).

The last Olympic Village in this grouping was that built for Moscow, which marked the extreme of the 'urban residential quarter' scenario. Moscow's regulated Master Plan 1971–90 zoned the city into eight planning agglomerations, each one equipped with an economic, recreational and social core. To a large extent, Olympic urban development for the 1980 Games was implemented in line with this planning strategy. By the end of 1979, sports infrastructures had been established in six different zones and the Olympic Village was built in an urban extension area in the south-west of Moscow that also had been earmarked as a residential quadrant much earlier.

Although the Olympic Village has been often combined with social housing programmes, this has generally been a secondary objective because its development site, size and form largely depended on the location of the main competition venues as preferred by the IOC. Moscow exhibited a different approach with the Olympic Village as a specific urban element. The 107ha of village were divided into three zones: the residential zone comprised of 18 homogeneous pre-fabricated slabs, 16 storeys each, being arranged in rigid order along a broad pedestrian concourse. All parking was at the perimeter. These buildings were typically 'international style' and contained two- or three-bedroom dwelling units with kitchenettes, bathrooms and small balconies; although of good size, they appeared a little austere and monotonous, and short of Olympic identity. A further zone included logistic facilities and a large sports complex for training, while the cultural centre was equipped with the typical leisure resources provided in previous villages. Because of the boycott of the Games by a number of Western nations, the village was used by only 8,310 athletes but later lived in by 15,000 Muscovites.

Villages from Los Angeles to Beijing

In recent decades, the development of the Olympic Village has employed a more diverse approach, which might be grouped into three categories. The villages of Seoul and Barcelona produced urban apartment compounds but also showed features of land modification; the two North American cases of Los Angeles and Atlanta ventured to opposite extremes to create ephemeral Olympic Villages with leased properties; while Sydney and Athens redefined the values of the suburban village in a more environmentally sustainable way. Beijing stands on its own due to methods of planning and delivery; it reflects some aspects of Moscow central control and decision-making, yet overlaid with private-sector final use.

The Seoul and Barcelona Games continued and extended the role of the Olympics as a vehicle for urban change and followed the trend (which began in Helsinki) of inserting the Olympic Village into the urban residential network. The Olympic housing programmes in Seoul and Barcelona were different however in that they did not exploit new urban territories (Rome and Mexico City), nor did they bridge a gap in the city's existing fabric (Munich and Montreal). They instead formed part of urban land-use renovation and rehabilitation plans. In the case of Seoul, Chamsil on the south bank of the Han River was a slum and floodplain area that had been occupied since the 1960s by low-quality housing suffering from environmental problems (McKay and Plumb, 2001). Seoul Olympic planners took over this site in 1973, designated 60ha for the development of a Seoul Sports Complex and the remaining 63ha for a future village. In Barcelona's case, the run-down seafront area of Poblenou, consisting of derelict warehouses and railway sidings was chosen. Barcelona's Olympic Village was a key part of the municipal policy of creating a thriving neighbourhood connecting the sea to the town centre.

The two Olympic Villages were made up of various apartment blocks, zoned by function of residence, training or leisure. In Seoul, because of lack of housing arising from rapid city expansion in the 1970s and 1980s, the organising committee deliberately created a large village containing 86 blocks ranging from 4 to 26 storeys. Interestingly, a successful marketing programme had been launched in Seoul and all the apartments were sold (for a total of US$$_{1995}$ 203.6 million) even before the Games were held (SLOOC, 1988). In Barcelona, the 72ha main village area consisted of very diverse buildings, mostly six-storey blocks, stone-yellow in colour, with large windows and shaded balconies to the living rooms. In view of the lack of hotel rooms and the experiences of Seoul, Barcelona also set up further 'villages': for media representatives at Vall d'Hebron and Montigalà; and for juries and referees at Parc de Mar. Although all four villages were nearly fully occupied during the Olympics, they were too large (and perhaps expensive) to be absorbed by the local population afterwards. It was reported that even a year after the Games, 33 per cent of the apartments were still not sold, highlighting the risk of small cities undertaking such projects (Reth, 1993).

Los Angeles and Atlanta deviated from the mainstream of the 1960s and 1970s by using temporary accommodation. The priorities of private sponsorship in the 1984 Games favoured maximum use of existing facilities to reduce expenditure on new installations. The Los Angeles organising committee decided not to build any new Olympic Villages but to use student residences at three local universities

Figure 5.2
A view of the waterfront in Barcelona at Poblenou with the Olympic Village in the mid-distance

temporarily converted with necessary technical, service and logistic facilities, and perimeter fencing (the University of Southern California: 7,000 beds; the University of California at Los Angeles: 6,000 beds; and the University of California at Santa Barbara: 1,000 beds). One innovation, which distinguished the sites from previous examples, was the introduction of strong decorative elements with Olympic identity. These succeeded in turning the separate villages (as well as competition venues) into 'a common and easily recognisable celebratory presence during the Olympic Games' (LAOOC, 1985).

In a similar way, Atlanta used the campus of the Georgia Institute of Technology as the Olympic Village because of its proximity to the city centre. Since 10 out of 26 competition venues were also scattered around the greater Atlanta region, eight satellite villages were also established to reduce transportation loads. In addition to some 200 existing facilities in the Georgia Tech, a small range of new constructions were also undertaken in the south-east corner of the campus, including a new Olympic Plaza, a large multi-functional shopping mall and two high blocks (accommodating up to 9,400 athletes in total). Few long-term legacies accrued, but of note was that in Atlanta's Village, for the first time, all rooms were air-conditioned, significantly increasing electricity requirements.

The Olympic Villages for Sydney and Athens represented a change from 'urban quadrant village' characterised by high/mid-rise apartment blocks to a 'suburban estate village' model. Each had features of manor housing: low density, semi-natural landscapes, and impressions of countryside life, thus linking back to Baldwin Hills (Los Angeles) and Heidelberg (Melbourne). The Olympic Village for Sydney was part of a 90ha residential development at Newington adjacent to Homebush Bay, the main competition site. It was designed for 15,000 Olympic visitors with

Figure 5.3
Housing in the Olympic Village at Sydney 2000, showing roof-mounted solar collectors

approximately 520 two-storey courtyard villas, 350 low-rise apartment units and 350 specially made modular dwellings. When the Games were over, the demountable modular houses were relocated for mining camps and Aboriginal residences, clearing the land for a further development of permanent houses. The facilities in the 'international zone' were subsequently converted to a community centre incorporating retail, recreational, educational and hi-tech industrial sectors.

Two features made the Sydney Village unique. First, a diverse aesthetic style and design concept was secured by entrusting the project to an architect consortium rather than an individual designer, which avoided a stereotyped clone of one standard template for the whole site. Second, a range of environmentally benign initiatives had been applied in the development of Newington Village in line with Sydney's pledge of delivering a 'green Games'. Each house featured passive thermal strategies for heating, cooling and ventilation including the careful calculation of glazing size, awning angle and insulation thickness matched to local climatic requirements. The village also used photovoltaic cells to produce electricity: houses had 12 roof-mounted inverter type panels (grid connected) with output capacity 1,400–1,600 kWh/yr. A dual water-supply system reduced the consumption of potable water, and nearby wetlands were used by the village as a natural recycling water plant. In addition, the site demonstrated a more compact urban form with a density of 28 homes per hectare, compared with the usual eight, of Sydney's suburban sprawl (Towndrow, 1998). These factors contributed to making the village a successful, self-sustaining residential community after the Games. As a commercial development funded by semi-private resources, it also contradicted the myth that environmentally friendly technologies for housing were prohibitively expensive to implement on a large scale.

Figure 5.4
Housing in the Olympic Village at Athens 2004

Athens developed a village in a low-population suburban area (similarly to Sydney) some 25km north-west of the city centre at the foot of Mount Parnitha. The aim was to 'upgrade the neglected area of the north-west section of the greater Athens area' (ATHENS 2004, 2004). Within the 124ha there were 2,300 apartments in 366 small flat-roofed buildings, two to four storeys in height, light coloured, of minimalist style, and decorated with delicate metal balconies. As with the Sydney Games, the Athens organising authority had also committed to integrate environmental principles into the project. However, the promise was not fully incorporated in the final product due to economics and lack of time, highlighting the risks that environmentally sustainable development may be compromised without a thorough planning and management mechanism.

The Olympic Village for Beijing was designed to house over 17,000 occupants in an area of the main Olympic Park to the north of the city centre. The flats, located in multi-storey apartment buildings, housed either four or eight athletes in unusually luxurious accommodation for China. Solar energy was used for some of the site and water could be drunk from the tap (not typical in China). It is expected that all will be sold into the private sector after post-Games refitting and at exceptional prices, even for Beijing, of up to £500,000. The arrangement conforms to the city's plan with its predominant centralised control.

Analysis of Olympic Villages

Table 5.1 summarises Olympic Village physical characteristics. Martin Wimmer (1976) has suggested a classification of Olympic Villages on the basis of building typology and development scale, while Munoz (1997) proposed several ways of categorisation in terms of architectural language, ekistics knowledge and spatial relationship to the city. In this study, the historical period (reflecting different stages of urbanisation in Western society) is used as a guide to the evolution of Olympic Villages, which may also correlate with some other village characteristics. Figure 5.5 illustrates the common factors.

It appears that Olympic Villages that developed in the same historical period have certain homogenous features in terms of building type, site location, neighbourhood density and potential after-use, suggesting links that may affect other design parameters. It is also observed that most village developments have been located within 6km to 15km from the host city's centre, suggesting Olympic Villages have been used for, or created, urban expansion.

Six periods of Olympic Village development can be seen, commencing with the first real villages of Los Angeles and Berlin in the 1930s. These were typically low-rise cottages or bungalows at remote suburban locations, suggesting new settlements rather than urban fabric enhancement. The second period, from Helsinki to Mexico City, was at a time of fast urban growth in western cities and urban population increasing at a rate of 2 per cent per annum. General housing shortages prompted Olympic Villages to be integrated into social housing schemes with a trend towards mid- and high-rise apartment blocks. The Olympic Villages built during this period were located in the peripheral areas of host cities often linked by new roads and expanded public transport networks.

Table 5.1 Summary of Olympic Village building, Los Angeles 1932 to Athens 2004

Olympic Games	Area (ha)	No of buildings	No of living units	Designed capacity	Largest occupation	Designed density (persons/ha)	Distance to Olympic stadium (km)	Distance to city centre (km)	Building type	Post-Games use
LA 1932	101	550	550	2,200	1,868	22	8	21	Prefabricated wooden 'cottages'	Demolished
Berlin 1936	55	194	2,300	4,550	4,300	83	15	30	Pitch-roofed brick bungalows	Army officer billet
Helsinki 1952										
Käpylä	–	13	1,630	4,800	4,655	–	4.5	6	3–4-storey brick apartment blocks	Social housing
Otäniemi		6	200	600	580		8	10		Student dormitories
Melbourne 1956	60	841	2,680	6,260	4,818	104	14	14	2-storey brick semi-detached houses	Social housing
Rome 1960	35	33	1,348	6,500	6,305	186	5	9	3–5-storey pre-fab apartment blocks	Social housing
Tokyo 1964	66	263	3,125	7,000	6,678	106	4.4	7	2-storey wooden cottages and 4-storey concrete apartment blocks	Hostel/ demolished
Mexico City 1968	30	29	5,044	10,088	8,206	336	3.5	15	6–10-storey brick apartment blocks	Social housing
Munich 1972	40	95	4,722	13,487	10,562	337	On-site	4	High- and mid-rise pre-fab apartment blocks, bungalows	Social housing
Montreal 1976	34	4	980	11,000	9,027	324	On-site	4	19-storey concrete apartment blocks	Social housing
Moscow 1980	107	18	8,640	15,280	8,310	143	10	14	16-storey pre-fab apartment blocks	Social housing
LA 1984										
USC Village	18	–	–	7,000	6,829	389	On-site	5	Mid-rise brick apartment blocks	Student dormitories (as before the Games)
UCLA Village	26	–	–	6,000	4,400	231	13	18		
UCSB Village	8	–	–	1,000	850	125	48	distant		
Seoul 1988	63	86	9,180	15,780	13,945	250	On-site	15	4–26-storey concrete apartment blocks	Commercial housing
Barcelona 1992	53	12	1,814	14,200	13,994	268	5	3	Mid-rise apartment blocks	Commercial housing
Atlanta 1996	109	122	7,239	15,078	14,985	138	3	4	Mid- and high-rise apartment blocks	Student dormitories
Sydney 2000	90	1,220	6,250	15,300	15,108	170	On-site	15.5	2-storey cottages, temporary module houses and low-rise apartment blocks	Commercial housing
Athens 2004	124	366	6,990	16,000	–	129	14.5	25	2–4-storey brick apartment buildings	Commercial housing

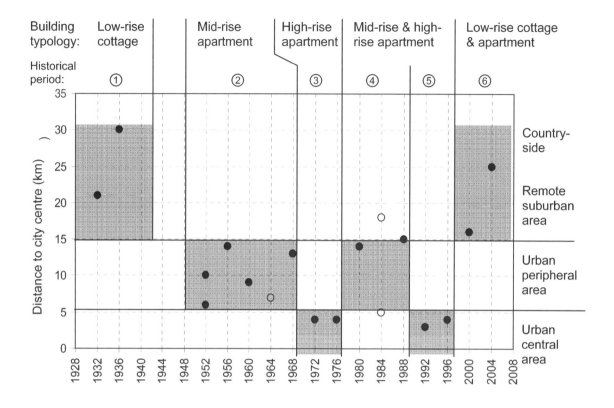

Figure 5.5

Correlation of building type, site location and historical period for Olympic Villages from Los Angeles 1932 to Athens 2004

During the third period (Munich and Montreal), Olympic Villages were centrally located and used high-rise buildings in line with central urban density. In the developed world, rapid urban expansion had come to an end and there were opportunities for redevelopment of the centre, marking an era of urban fabric consolidation and adjustment. The fourth period of the 1980s showed very different approaches in three Olympic cities. Moscow and Seoul were experiencing rapid urbanisation processes as Western cities had during the 1960s. Olympic Villages in these cities appeared to have similar characters to those in the second period. In Los Angeles, however, with some urban decline, the ephemeral village implementation reflected local housing needs. The fifth period includes the two Games of the 1990s in which the need for environmental and economic sustainability stimulated the movement towards urban regeneration. The villages built for Barcelona and Atlanta reflected these issues and their sites moved towards the urban centre and formed part of host cities' revival plans.

Sydney represents the start of a sixth period: the development of Olympic Villages reverting to the suburban estate model and showed that the idea of a 'garden city' was still meaningful in the twenty-first century. The villages now aimed to establish an organic, multi-hierarchical settlement within a greater urban region, with the help of the latest technologies in transportation, communication and environmental protection.

Olympic Village development is clearly linked to the urbanisation of the host city, eventually becoming part of the local housing stock, and responding to the demographic change of the city. This theme will impact upon current and future Games, evident in Beijing with its urban peripheral model (in accordance with the rapid urban growth of the Chinese capital), and also in the plans for London 2012 with a relatively centrally located village in the Lower Lea Valley to regenerate its East End. This theme provides a useful indicator for evaluation of Olympic Villages within urban development.

Post-Games use of Olympic Villages

As with the competition venues, the post-Games use issue is also important for the Olympic Village. Early schemes in Paris and Los Angeles were temporary facilities without consideration for post-Games use, though the pre-fabricated wooden module cottages in Los Angeles were later reassembled elsewhere. The Döberitz Village for Berlin, designed to be a permanent military billet afterwards, was the first Olympic Village to have a meaningful post-Olympic function from the outset. Since Helsinki, however, the dominant design trend for Olympic Villages has generally been to combine with urban housing schemes for use by local residents when the Games were over.

Up to the 1980s, Olympic projects were funded principally by public resources, resulting in most units being taken into the social housing system after the Games, and allocated to low-income groups. The villages for Helsinki, Melbourne, Rome, Mexico City, Moscow and some of the apartments for Munich and Montreal fit this model. From the 1980s, investment from the private sector has gradually taken the leading role and, driven by profitability issues, Olympic Villages have become more commercial with high-quality or even luxury features, aiming post-Games for middle-class occupants. The villages developed for Seoul, Barcelona, Sydney, Athens and Beijing have to some extent followed this model.

The commercialisation of the village projects has brought some benefits: efficiency in cost-quality control, better use of construction material and apparatus, flexibility in design of housing unit types, and even motivation to shorten the construction period and promote innovative technologies. They have also developed some negative features, such as paying less attention to the athlete's needs and promoting gentrification at the expense of previous occupants/use of the area.

Villages have also been used for student accommodation subsequent to the Games, examples being the Otäniemi village at Helsinki, the Olympic towers for Atlanta, and some of the apartments for Munich and Montreal. Some villages have also disappeared: the demountable module dwellings (550 units) in Los Angeles 1932, and in Sydney 350 units were rebuilt in other places. The Yoyogi Village in Tokyo was first transformed into a youth hostel and later demolished.

In general, most of the existing Olympic Villages have been successfully incorporated into urban life. As Millet (1996) pointed out, 'there has been no historical failure of any Olympic Village model'; at worst there have been lessons to be learnt to optimise the service and design of the future Villages. The first such lesson perhaps came from the case of Rome, where its Village suffered with environmental deterioration; the reason being the poor quality of the materials used and lack of subsequent external maintenance. Even during the Games, there were complaints from athletes about faulty equipment and cracks on the walls and ceilings; the problems worsened after the Games resulting in a public enquiry in 1963. A total of 16 building contractors were taken to court in 1968 and some sentenced to prison for fraudulent use of building materials (Schmidt, 1971). The poor quality of the Rome village highlighted the importance of quality standards in pursuit of long-term value and sustainability.

A second lesson arises from Mexico City, where the village was left half-empty for several years after the Games; and in Barcelona post-Games occupancy was less than 100 per cent. For Barcelona, the cause was a relatively small city gaining too much expensive housing stock too quickly. In Mexico City, with a huge population of 19 million and reasonable Olympic housing prices, the problem was in the remote location (15km distant from Mexico City) and the lack of easy transportation. Moreover, until 1972 there were no shops and supermarkets nearby and a private car was still a costly asset in Mexico. Even when private car ownership gradually increased, new problems arose, as parking space was insufficient. A well-designed Olympic Village became an overcrowded neighbour-hood (Cardinali, 1983). Obviously, public transportation and parking spaces were not concerns of Olympic athletes but were of significance to long-term tenants.

Evaluation issues and sustainability

The Olympic Village is central to a host city's overall Olympic urban plan and its importance is recognised in the IOC evaluation. The primary criterion is to conform to the spatial requirements and standards prescribed in the IOC manual, thus to provide the athletes with an appropriate environment to prepare for competition. At the same time it should leave a sustainable legacy for the local community, and the architecture should be of high quality and contribute qualitatively to the existing urban context.

Initially, the convenience of athletes is paramount: the Village should be within easy access of the competition sites and particularly the training grounds. In the first International Symposium on Olympic Villages in Lausanne (1996), one conclusion drawn was that 30 minutes' travel time by road should be a maximum for athletes (Thomas, 1999); above this value incurs negative points during the evaluation. In providing for cultural interaction and the promotion of the spirit of Olympism, the settings and spatial arrangement of the village play a vital role. A technically sound solution may not be enough to guarantee a successful design scheme, and architectural means should be employed to encourage social activities and communication, and provide suitable public spaces and communal amenities. Small rooms and high-rise structures are now less favoured as they afford poor opportunity for socialisation and impact negatively on the team spirit. It seems that a relatively compact but low-rise development better fits Olympic needs.

Other issues that need to be considered are the 'asymmetries of the competition cycle', with potential distractions from athletes in the village who have completed their events. Tactical means of separating functional zones and separating transport helps enable athletes to pursue choices (e.g. to prepare for the competition, to train, to be at leisure, to rest or sleep, or to enjoy social activities) without jeopardising others' well-being; important considerations, as are safety and security. It is worth incorporating the following, too: distinctive signage systems, which also give identity and character to a village; redevelopment potential for post-Games use; and a barrier-free environment to aid use by disabled athletes for the Paralympic Games.

Finally, and of most significance in this text, Olympic Villages should be built as a demonstration of environmentally sustainable development both for the local community and for the worldwide audience of the Games. Organisers should plan for a suitably landscaped neighbourhood providing protection to existing site ecology and conserving resources such as energy and water. As an example of residential building, Olympic Villages can be appraised for their environmental performance by using a number of techniques developed for dwellings. In the UK this could include the Code for Sustainable Homes. These assessment method-ologies have evolved over several years and versions of them are employed in a number of other countries. In this book, no new environmental accounting pro-cedure will be created for the dwellings of the Olympic Village; rather, existing housing assessment techniques should be integrated into the Olympic evaluation framework. Typical factors considered are: energy use; carbon dioxide production; materials; water use; pollution; ecology; wastes; health issues; and transport/locational arrangements, though this last category might be considered through an overarching assessment for all Games sectors (including urban design and Games venues).

CHAPTER 6

The Olympic impact on host cities

Introduction

Previous chapters have established that Olympic events frequently involve large-scale infrastructural provision and substantial urban development, and hence are increasingly used explicitly as a tool for urban transformation purposes. The associated initiatives will inevitably have both short- and long-term impacts on the host cities and their communities, ranging through economic, social, physical, political and cultural realms, which can have both positive and detrimental outcomes. This chapter aims to explore the nature and implications of these impacts, and to provide a holistic perspective of what Olympic urban development might bequeath, including whether and how these impacts can be managed through specific development strategies. The impacts of Olympic urban development can be differentiated from the impacts of the Olympic Games themselves; the latter are different in scope and may be linked with more intangible political, economic and socio-cultural effects.

There are perhaps five ways in which cities can be impacted upon by Olympic urban development. The first category relates to physical and environmental impacts, involving efforts to change the urban landscape and affect, either deliberately or otherwise, the built and natural environment. The second category is essentially socio-economic and focuses on how Olympic development can assist with economic development, promote tourism and service industries, and provide a more attractive image for inward investment. The third category falls within the socio-cultural field and concerns how Olympic planning and design can strengthen local traditions and values, and increase civic pride and community spirit. The fourth category might be labelled socio-political, concentrating on what effects Olympic urban development might have on the society's legislation and governance, and whether internal or external conflicts such as social segregation will be mitigated or reinforced. The final category can be referred to as socio-psychological and is difficult to quantify but one that is often ignored even though it is important; this includes the memories and development legacies that the event leaves for local residents, and also concerns how Olympic urban development might transform a resident's perception or evaluation of their city. In the following sections, these five categories of impact are discussed in sequence, though there is much inter-linkage.

Physical and environmental impact

Olympic buildings have an impact on the environment as they are produced, occupied and used. For many host cities, improvement of the physical and built environment is one of the dominant objectives referred to when the benefits of hosting the events are cited. As previous chapters have established, the Olympics are distinct from other large-scale events by virtue of the sheer magnitude of facilities and infrastructural provision and by the penchant of organisers to capitalise ambitious urban schemes for city re-branding and place regeneration. Indeed, history shows that almost every genre of construction work could be undertaken under the banner of Olympic preparation, from underground rail expansion to the building of new commercial and leisure facilities for an expected tourism boom. Some initiatives, such as slum clearance and capital infrastructure alterations made to the public realm, aim to improve the physical appearance and attractiveness of the host city and its region, often irrespective of their impacts on the running of the Games.

The physical and environmental impact of Olympic urban development is reflected at various geographic levels. At global and regional scale, as with other development activities, they contribute to issues such as global warming and resource depletion. At urban level, Olympic development schemes can permanently affect the host city in the following areas: urban form related to the shape of the built-up area; the structure and capacity of the transport network; the spatial distribution of population and business; the overall urban density gradient; and directions towards which further physical growth can be stimulated. At sub-urban level, the development may alter the features of the cityscape in terms of grain, street grids, neighbourhood patterns, distribution of services and amenities, open spaces and the city skyline. At local level, the development may bring changes to building plots and their surroundings, the quality of public realm, accessibility to a place, biodiversity and street scenery. Certainly, all building projects have impacts on the environment, but its environmental impact is often seen in a more dramatic and intensive sense at the urban and sub-urban level.

One example that illustrates urban-scale impact is the urban expansion undertaken in Seoul for the 1988 Games, which transformed the Korean capital from pre-industrial city to a modern metropolis. The location of Seoul's old city had been selected, based on the ancient geomantic doctrine, to be on the north bank of the Han River. For centuries the river defined the southern boundary of the city's central mass and acted as a natural barrier restricting its southward expansion. The Chamsil district on the south bank of the Han River was deliberately chosen as the main Olympic precinct and extensive development of building complexes and urban infrastructure took place there in the years leading up to the Games. These activities quickly transformed the district into a booming new centre for the city. Korea's Olympic development not only substantially stretched the urban form of Seoul over the Han River and into the southern territory (in geographic and economic terms) but also converted the previously marginalised river into a dominant element of the city. A similar situation also pertained in other Olympic host cities to different extents, with great leaps of urban expansion in Rome, Tokyo, Mexico City and Beijing each driven by Olympic urban policies to a great extent.

As well as the broad strategic level, Olympic impact on the spatial dimension is often more clearly witnessed at smaller scales. For instance, in preparing for the 1992 Games, Barcelona adjusted its seafront elevation and skyline by rebuilding its declining coastal strip and in so doing re-established the links between the city and the sea. And as part of the 2004 Olympic development package, Athens transformed the 530ha brownfield site at the obsolete Hellinikon airport into Europe's largest park for sports and recreational use. These initiatives, though local, are still significant enough to change the immediate urban landscape in important ways, but the real key to success is to ensure long-term and continuing impacts.

For most Olympic host cities, environment improvements are made through various forms of urban beautification programmes aiming to enhance the aesthetics of the street scene, remove sources of physical pollution, and ensure health and hygiene standards throughout the city. Sculptures, decorative artwork and street greenery are often introduced together and major new parks and plazas created. In Tokyo, Moscow and Beijing, streets were widened and improved prior to the respective Games by the laying of new pavements, the installation of new street lamps, the realignment of advertising displays and rooftop neon lights. In Munich, Seoul and Sydney, more comprehensive programmes were implemented to decontaminate polluted dumping sites, noxious wastelands or damaged riverbeds. Remediation efforts are often followed by new methods and devices designed for waste and sewage control and disposal. In most circumstances, the local community is encouraged to participate in these projects through which environmental awareness can be positively reinforced leading to longer term awareness and benefits.

Although Olympic urban development has great potential to improve the physical environment of the host city or region, it may also pose additional environmental problems especially during the process of carrying out major construction projects. Hasty decision-making and implementation are always great concerns in Olympic development. The deadlines set for the construction of venues and the completion of support structures are often used as an excuse for major projects to bypass the usual procedures of development application review, including the environmental assessment and public consultation components. In Athens 2004, for example, the construction of the rowing centre at the Marathonas Lake was criticised for lacking adequate environmental analysis with potential to undermine the natural water resources and cause collateral damage in the area. Likewise, in Sydney, the cleaning of the contaminated Homebush Bay site has been criticised as not meeting international standards or 'best practice' in environmental issues because of the limited time assigned to the process.

Socio-economic impact

The motivation for hosting the Olympics clearly varies between cities, nevertheless one common goal can be identified: the desire to attract global capital flows and bring positive impacts to the local economy. Although jobs and revenue are created only in the short term, and usually used to offset the expenditure for organising the event itself, the long-term economic contribution of the Olympics is primarily thought of in terms of the possibilities they provide: increasing the awareness of the city or region as a tourism destination and a potential market for investment and commercial activities. As economic globalisation intensifies, the attractiveness of a city for tourism and business has been regarded as a key factor to maintain and strengthen its economic growth potential.

Previous studies suggest that the overall Olympic economic impact could be enormous: in Los Angeles (1984), Seoul, Atlanta and Sydney, the Games were estimated to have injected respectively $2.3, $1.6, $5.4 and $4.5 billion in then US dollars to the local economy. It is also estimated that the London Olympics in 2012 will add approximately £5.9 billion to the city's GDP and create as many as 40,000 full-time jobs over the 12-year period from 2005 to 2016 (in this, the largest GDP gain of £3.36 billion has been estimated to occur during the pre-Games construction period between 2005 and 2011).

Olympic urban development and its associated benefits in related sectors play a key role in shaping the overall cost–benefit equation for each Games. Olympic construction usually accounts for the largest spending attributed to the Games and this tends to exceed the direct income of the organising committee from ticket sales, television rights and sponsorship deals. Olympic projects notoriously suffer heavy cost overruns, often fail to deliver the supposed benefits and regularly provoke financial crises. The Munich and Montreal Games made losses of £178 million and £692 million largely due to their technologically complex and inherently expensive concepts for stadium design. And for those Games where considerable surpluses were made, such as Los Angeles in 1984 and Atlanta in 1996, Olympic urban development was comparatively moderate. The extent of any such surplus is, therefore, heavily dependent upon the level of new infrastructure required and how the expenditure is calculated within the financial appraisal.

Olympic urban development is not just consumption-based, it also creates added value from the investment. Not only do Olympic venues and improved civic infrastructure become permanent assets of host cities, but also many Olympic projects such as sports facilities and athlete housing are profitable after the Games on the basis of ongoing rental/lease or sale. In Seoul, it was possible to make a profit and sell the Olympic and media villages even before the Games had taken place (SLOOC, 1988). In recent Games the sale of housing for the Olympic Village 'off-plan' in advance of the Games with owners only taking up residency after the event has become a more popular financing route. Moreover, intensive construction of Olympic facilities and immutable deadlines for completion are likely to lead to more employment in the local building and associate sectors (e.g. component manufacture), as well as additional income and tax revenues. This has been the case in those host cities where major Olympic building activities took place: it was reported that among the 300,000 full-time jobs created by the Seoul Games, nearly one third were produced by the building industry.

Arguably the greatest economic impact of Olympic urban development is on the real estate market of the host city. Within this, the hotel and hospitality sector is the most affected due to the direct impact of Olympic-related visitors and the resulting demand for short-term accommodation. Most host cities experienced considerable growth in hotel room stock during the years of their Olympic period, with many rooms of high international standard. The residential market is also impacted upon by Olympic urban regeneration: a recent study carried out in the UK suggested that the housing market in the Olympic site area would experience a rise in rental values and prices well above the city's average (HBOS, 2007). However, the weight of this impact appears to depend upon the size and maturity of the property market in the host city. Studies indicate that in large and more advanced host cities, such as Atlanta and Sydney, the house price boom may have owed less to the Olympics than to other factors such as swings in the local economy and population increase (McKay and Plumb, 2001; Abelson et al., 2005). Past experience also shows that the overall Olympic impact on office, retail and industrial property markets is likely to be moderate, unpredictable and short-term. The unpredictability has been further highlighted by the severe worldwide impacts on the property sector of the financial markets; problems initiated by inflated real estate values. It is not yet clear how this will affect the Games in the long run but there are concerns for future financing of the Olympic Village for London 2012.

Rising property prices in certain localities, changes in the price and supply of building materials, and the creation of new jobs in the construction industry are all short-term economic impacts of Olympic urban development. There is also the so-called 'crowding-out effect' (Preuss, 2000) where local expenditure streams and manpower are diverted from essential public services to the budget for Olympic infrastructure. The local population may also experience increased taxes levied in order to balance the city's accounts. However, the real benefits of Olympic urban development to the local economy are measured in the long term through the reform of an urban area's natural and built environment, and the restructuring of the demographic make-up, which can result in enhanced lifestyles and better working conditions. This goal is essential for post-industrial cities helping to foster wealth-creation and encouraging entrepreneurs and commercial leadership. As Amis (2005: 15) points out, 'there is a need to ensure that land and housing are used to their maximum potential in a city that is marketing itself as a major global competitor'. Several cities considered to be less advanced before the Games, such as Tokyo, Munich and Barcelona, were successfully transformed and developed more service-based economies featuring high consumption and high income following changes associated with Olympic intervention. This phenomenon has been addressed by several studies undertaken by Essex and Chalkey (1999) and Preuss (2000) with the conclusion that the Olympics tend to bring more positive economic impact to poorer cities in greater need of large-scale investment and infrastructure improvement, and less to cities with a developed infrastructure and low unemployment.

Socio-political impact

Although the Olympic Charter forbids capitalising on the Games for political benefit, the modern Olympic Movement has had to contend on many occasions with wars, protests, boycotts, walkouts, terrorism and many kinds of political and diplomatic turmoil. Indeed, in a world where countries actively compete for recognition and status, the prestige of the Games and the substantial attention that they attract offers unparalleled opportunities to make a statement on the world stage. Historically, the 're-imaging' of a city or country is a resonant motivation for hosting an Olympic event. The Games of Tokyo and Munich symbolised the return of Japan and Germany to positions of robust economic standing and a place of high esteem in the international community; the Games of Seoul and Barcelona celebrated the peaceful transition of South Korea and Spain to greater democracy and liberalism. In fact, almost every host nation consciously or unconsciously seems to utilise the Olympics to showcase its power and success, or to reassert its ideology, potentially rendering the Olympic maxim 'politics should be kept out of sport' of little worth.

Given the size and complexity of Olympic building projects and scale of resources they require, Olympic development is often difficult to implement without economic and policy support from local, regional or even central governments. Frequently, the cost of significant supportive infrastructure is covered by governments through special grants, allocation of national lottery funds and other measures. In many host countries special legislation (e.g. the Olympic Act) is enacted to give local authorities the statutory power for land assembly where there is a compelling case in the public interest. For instance, to secure land in Lower Lea Valley for the 2012 Olympic Park the London Development Agency (LDA) has been granted Compulsory Purchase Orders to acquire land under the Regional Development Agencies Act 1998. This is to safeguard the delivery of the Olympic facilities on time in case private agreements cannot be reached with landowners and site occupants due to unwarranted objections. Sometimes the intervention of high-level governments in Olympic development is essential to save the Games from disaster. For instance, had the Quebec government not intervened at the last minute in the construction of the Montreal Olympic Park, the 1976 Games could well have been delayed.

As the Olympic Games cannot be well organised without the support of political resources and strength, in turn, it inevitably impacts on the normal planning process and decision-making, for better or for worse. For better, it may force the city to embrace international legal norms in dealing with issues such as land acquisition and urban displacement, and help to refocus public governance from bureaucratic politics to a style of dynamic business leadership; for worse, it may precipitate development programmes agreed within a very condensed time framework, and which overrides public participation, changes the nature of eviction procedure, and intensifies social segregation. The displacement of low-income households and squatter communities arising from Olympic-inspired urban renewal has emerged as a motivating factor for anti-Olympic protests. Before such discussion, more explanation can be given relating to the Olympic political impacts identified above.

The first identified positive impact occurs through the promotion of civic housing rights in host cities where the legal framework is less well established. One particular case is Seoul where a new model of slum redevelopment ('joint development' or 'partnership renewal') was introduced by the metropolitan authority on the eve of the 1988 Games. This helped to engage with squatter communities and avoid the strong opposition to development schemes that had been experienced in previous slum-clearance initiatives. Greene (2003) argued that to some extent the hosting of the Olympics helped consolidate the housing rights movement in the 1980s in South Korea and added legitimacy to the newly formed Asian Coalition for Housing Rights. A similar situation was found in Beijing where, arguably, the pressure generated during the preparation of the 2008 Games contributed to the amendment of the Demolition and Eviction Act in 2003 and the release of the Property Rights Act by the Chinese People's Congress in March 2007.

The second political impact of Olympic development is in help to promote a new form of urban politics that may be based less on bureaucracy and more on competitive and more efficient practices. Hall (1987) suggested that the decisions affecting the hosting of a large-scale event grow out of a political process that not only involves the interests of political authorities, but also those of private, profit-orientated organisations. This is particularly the case in host cities where the market economy is more advanced. In Atlanta, Sydney and now London, the Olympic delivery bodies seem to have embraced more entrepreneurial-driven forms of governance, with a broad range of non-governmental, often private, organisations incorporated into the decision-making and policy-formulation process. With new urban political imperatives, a decision to bid for the Olympics, and how to prepare for it, is not made solely by local or regional governments, but often involves business corporations. For example, the first cost–benefit analysis to inform the decision on whether London would bid for the 2012 Games seems to have been made by the global engineering company Arups, rather than the Greater London Authority. In that sense, large-scale sporting events can be seen to mobilise corporate elites and local politicians to form profitable alliances that not only boost local construction, retail and tourism industries, but also attract substantial development funding from both public and private resources.

A negative impact of Olympic development is that it is often treated as a special urban issue separated from the normal planning and delivery process. However the Games have their own timelines of preparation and dates for bidding are set by the International Olympic Committee (IOC), as are the requirements for the content of the bid. The requirements for venues and infrastructure may not be appropriate to be dealt with in normal methods of city functioning. In that sense, the Olympics often fast-track planning and development at the local level which inevitably leads some to feelings of a lack of consultation and discussion. In addition, due to the great uncertainty of the Olympic bidding process, it is common for candidate cities to make somewhat unrealistic statements on the grounds that it is only a preliminary document and winning the bid is the primary objective. Due to this uncertainty, the developments promised in the bidding file are often not closely scrutinised by local interest groups until the bid has been successful and the IOC and International Sports Federations begin to take action. This is where a conflict occurs and the organising authority may find itself in a dilemma in choosing between breaking bidding promises and ignoring the voice of the local public.

Almost all Olympic development involves campaigns to persuade the citizens of the host city that the plan is justified and can bring national and international prestige to their hometown. Nevertheless, Olympic passion does not guarantee public approval and overriding reasoned opposition may lead to serious consequences. At the Games of Mexico City many ordinary Mexicans questioned the Olympic development as an unnecessary extravagance when there were severe social problems with many people living in conditions of poverty and poor housing. The opposition climaxed in violent clashes between student activists and the armed police with many people killed and injured in the so-called Tlatelolco massacre, just 10 days before the 1968 Games. Preparation for the Seoul Games was also accompanied by fierce protests and harsh suppression in the 1980s; and when crises break out, compromises and makeshift solutions have to be found to ensure the

Olympics proceed. The history of Olympic development, as Hiller (2003: 103) points out, is 'strewn with untold instances of design, location, and financing issues that pushed ahead based on a sense of urgency about the imminent event that required quick action.'

Olympic development may also increase social segregation due to its emphasis on beautification and removal of eyesores rather than addressing fundamental social problems. For example in Seoul walls were built to hide slums and poor-quality housing from television coverage during the marathon race; many street stalls were also ordered to move into back alleys out of public sight during the Games. Ironically, this kind of 'beautification' initiative not only occurs in less-developed host cities; in Atlanta, for instance, city ordinances were introduced to beautify areas surrounding Olympic venues. This involved the removal of poorer residents, closure of hostels and the 'designing-out' of the homeless by methods such as use of sleep-proof benches and intermittent sprinklers. Atlanta Olympic development has been criticised as 'the ruling regime taking advantage of the Olympics to mount an attack on the city's underclass' (Gold and Gold, 2008: 308). These cases illustrate how the Olympics can project a positive global image by disguising rather than solving social problems.

Olympic urban displacement

Displacement can be defined as when a household is forced to move by conditions impacting on the dwelling and its immediate surroundings. Past experience shows that the conditions forcing people to move can manifest themselves in various ways: socio-economic displacement occurs when residents are priced out of, or are marginalised in their neighbourhood; this is often linked to the process of gentrification. In a physical sense, residents may be removed by legal or illegal enforcement, or through unfair negotiation dominated by developers, often culminating in processes of eviction, forced or otherwise. In environmental terms, residents may also be forced to leave due to degraded living conditions caused by natural factors or human impacts (e.g. increased traffic noise). Large-scale events, particularly the Olympics, often exacerbate involuntary resettlement arising from each of the causes above. In Seoul, for example, 48,000 buildings, housing approximately 720,000 residents, were demolished for redevelopment during the years preceding the Games. Most of the evictees did not receive replacement housing within the redevelopment site (Kim, 1998). In Barcelona, the market prices of old and new housing were reported to have risen by 240 per cent and 287 per cent respectively between 1986 and 1992. Meanwhile it was estimated that 59,000 people left the city to live elsewhere (Brunet, 1993). In Sydney, soaring house sale and rental prices occurred in the lead-up to the Olympic event; the number of homeless also increased (Jewell and Kilgour, 2000). In Athens in 2004, it was reported that 79 forced evictions and 323 lawsuits were lodged by the Greek government to remove Gypsy communities during the Olympic period (COHRE, 2006). And in preparing for the 2008 Games, it was cited that some 580,000 inhabitants of Beijing were re-housed two years before the Games to make space for Olympic construction (Slavin, 2006).

It should be noted that many of these figures and statistics lack official endorsement. It seems that organising authorities are reluctant to make serious enquiries about displacement associated with their events; the most influential studies in the field therefore are normally undertaken independently and by dissident critics of the Olympics. This, however, poses questions of accuracy for these data, and, in fact, accuracy is a fundamental problem with any displacement survey, as Atkinson (2002: 9) has acknowledged: 'the fact that displacement has been inferred more often than directly measured is directly linked to the difficulties of developing methodologies capable of tracking those who are displaced.' Without effective and widely accepted means of evaluation it would be hard to reveal the true level of displacement associated with the Games. There may be an overestimation of the number of displaced households by critics and perhaps an underestimate by the organising authority.

Sometimes the information conveyed by the statistics is fragmented and biased, leading to fallacious arguments. For example, in Sydney the house price boom between 1993 and 2001 had less to do with the 2000 Olympics than many commentators had thought, as similar rises occurred in other large Australian cities over the same period (Abelson et al., 2005). Also, according to Maennig (1997) the rent price increases in Barcelona in the late 1980s could not be fully attributed to the Olympics. These studies highlight the importance of building a comprehensive view backed up by clear data to understand the Olympics' impact on host cities.

It is also necessary to separate displacement from desirable changes in the social and built environment brought about by Olympic development, for instance improvements in living conditions, voluntary migration and necessary slum clearance. For many people, resettlement can have mixed outcomes: displaced residents may suffer capital loss and dislocation from workplaces and social networks, but they may also benefit from moving in other respects, such as gaining a larger dwelling or an improved living environment. In Seoul's case, the Olympic site Chamsil was occupied in the 1960s by housing affected by major environmental problems (Stratton, 1986: 219). In Beijing's case, the squatter villages destroyed did not have sewage and drainage systems or individual toilets, with many families sharing a common water supply. For such communities, regeneration may be welcomed by the people it benefits, and in Seoul a survey of displaced residents affected by the Olympic project in Sang Kye Dong suggested that most interviewees believed their living conditions had been improved (Kim, 1998). A recent investigation by the Beijing Bureau of Statistics indicated that 70 per cent of the respondents supported the Old and Dilapidated Housing Redevelopment programme in the city with 37 per cent of the respondents asking to be moved from their substandard settlements (NBSC, 2003).

For Seoul and Beijing, slum clearance and inner-city regeneration were each part of long-established urban agenda extant before the winning of their Olympic bids and continuing beyond the event. In these cities, the Olympics should not be seen as the main cause of mass displacement, although it cannot be denied that even with justified slum redevelopment schemes, conflicts between the displaced residents and the developers exist. These normally focus on the level of compensation, the place allocated for relocation, the means of eviction and the legal rights of tenants. A failure to address these issues can lead to strong long-term resistance and ensuing difficulties.

Although property or landowners are usually offered 'fair' payments based on the appraised value of their existing estates, and perhaps the priority to purchase low-cost social housing on or close to the redevelopment site, given the 'escalating land costs and rampant exploitation by real estate speculators' in Olympic districts, they have no guarantee of return (Greene, 2003: 172). This has been highlighted by the situation in Beijing where average redress for displacement was around US$30,000 per household in 2005 whereas an ordinary apartment in a suitably desirable inner-city neighbourhood cost nearly twice as much (Huang and Xu, 2005). In Seoul and Beijing, compensation was actually paid at a higher per square metre rate for a demolished property than the average market price for a newly built equivalent in the same area. However, because many informal settlers lived in very cramped shack-like buildings before being displaced, the total compensation amount was relatively low and unlikely to empower them to afford suitable commercially available housing in the locality. In most Olympic cities, illegal and unauthorised properties are included in the negotiation process but with much lower levels of compensation. The homeless and informal settlers living in makeshift shelters or caravans are normally denied any legal recognition and evicted from the site with minimal relocation payments. From the analysis above it can be seen that the negative impact of the Olympics in terms of urban displacement may have been a little exaggerated. However this cannot be used to ignore the fact that on many occasions Olympic development does lead to gentrification and pressures for relocation or eviction.

A further category of displacement arises from environmental disturbance caused by Olympic development. Although Olympic projects normally aim to improve the built environment, large urban schemes can have negative impacts on their surroundings and inhabitants. For example, large stadiums and other Olympic buildings may block views and shade buildings or gardens. In Olympic history there are many cases of local resistance to development arising from environmental disputes. In a case in 2006, a group of Beijing residents campaigned to stop the construction of an Olympic power substation close to their community, for the fear of exposure to high-voltage radiation (Yi, 2006). Despite the fact that for the construction of major Olympic venues there is an expectation to undertake full environmental impact assessments, smaller components and supportive infrastructure may be given less attention during decision-making processes. As a result, resettlement may become a more attractive proposition for some local residents if their opposition fails to prevent the development.

Socio-cultural and socio-psychological impacts

The Olympics are seen as the greatest sporting and cultural event and they can raise national pride and provide opportunities to show the host country at its best. Indeed, as culture itself is one of the three pillars of Olympism, cultural manifestation has always found a place in Olympic development, through the use of architectural language, spatial context and aesthetic elements in planning and design. Symbolism and metaphors are expressively used in almost every Olympic urban package to make each occasion distinguished (and perhaps more photogenic and more spectacular) than the last. Large Olympic buildings offer the opportunity for important scientific and cultural exchange and at the same time they provide a unique platform upon which a host city can place aspects of its history, its culture and the collective dreams of its citizens before a world audience.

Each fresh celebration of the Games has a very different cultural theme and manifesto, which are also reflected in the forms of major Olympic venues. Some, such as Torben Grut's Stockholm Olympic Stadium for the 1912 Games and Kenzo Tange's National Gymnasium for the Tokyo Games, were inspired by vernacular architecture and craftsmanship, and designed to showcase the essence of regional traditions and values. Some others, such as Gunter Behnisch's tensile tent roof that crowns the Munich Olympic Stadiums, Robert Taillibert's giant concrete 'flying saucer' for the Montreal Games, and the epic 'Bird's Nest' and 'Water Cube' of the Beijing Games, embraced avant-garde ideas and the innovative technologies available in their times. The messages conveyed by these buildings are clear-cut: to present the host nation as a modern, advanced, creative and capable society.

Olympic development can also increase local pride and community spirit by improving the built environment of the city and by providing more sports and cultural amenities. Increased sports participation provides a sense of well-being through fun and enjoyment, leading to self-fulfilment and achievement, and encourages social interaction and cohesion for those who may otherwise feel socially excluded. Truno (1995) reported a notable increase in participation in sports activities in Barcelona following the hosting of the 1992 Games; there was an increase of 46,000 users for the city's sports centres by 1995, with a significant increase in female participants. Similarly, surveys undertaken in Atlanta after the 1996 Games and more recently in Beijing for the 2008 Games confirmed that the Olympics contribute to a strengthening in sports practice among the general public in the host region, with people feeling more open-minded, more confident in facing challenges and more aware of social norms and justice.

Finally, Olympic development can also contribute to transforming the image of the host city and people's perception of the city. This facilitates tourism and economic development, for instance the renown of Calgary increased significantly after the city held the 1988 Olympic Winter Games. Similar phenomena were also witnessed in other hosts, particularly smaller and perhaps then less well-known cities such as Munich, Montreal and Barcelona. These cities successfully repositioned themselves on the world map through their respective Games and consequent urban development endeavours.

Summary

The purpose of this chapter has been to identify the multi-faceted impact of Olympic urban development on host cities and their communities. Some of the impacts are more visible than others creating objectives and challenges for host cities, such as in physical and environmental impacts. This is significant for countries in economic transition or in rapid industrialisation, such as China, which in 2004 was home to nine of the world's ten most polluted cities, one of which was Beijing itself. On a broad scale, preparations for the event can provide a means of justifying new investment in civic infrastructure and efforts to enhance the city's landscape and physical appearance.

Socio-economic impacts of Olympic development are also tangible and can be quantified through comprehensive evaluation processes. Economic benefits are often the prime motivation for the hosting of the Games. The construction of Olympic facilities plays a key role in programmes of urban renewal and more generally in updating the built environment. This is helpful in attracting foreign trade, investment and highly qualified migrants to advance the economic development of the region.

Some impacts are less tangible and may extend beyond the local or even national population. These include socio-cultural, political and psychological impacts brought about by Olympic development. The essence of the power of the Olympics to promote a country – to herald its new ideologies and aspirations, to revive traditional values and concepts or to facilitate changes in systems and governance – is produced by the focus of world attention and the combination of exposure and pressure to perform that this brings. Olympic development, both as a social product and as a process, serves as a medium through which all kinds of symbolic and narrative characteristics can be exhibited, and conveyed to a world audience.

The discussion has highlighted positive as well as negative aspects and has considered urban regeneration, the creation of new business and revenue, increased civic pride and solidarity, economic development, housing, civil liberties, displacement and other issues. Understanding these impacts is a necessary precursor to the assessment of Olympic urban development for sustainability.

Evaluating Olympic urban development for sustainability

PART III

Infrastructural requirements to stage the modern Games

CHAPTER 7

Introduction

The International Olympic Committee is the supreme authority of the Games with responsibility for selecting a host city in line with the requirements of the Olympic Charter. Though every set of Games is different, each bidding host city must describe how it will provide the necessary infrastructure as part of the process to win the bid. The processes are complicated but the bid is expected to consider environmental concerns. In this chapter a range of features associated with the bid and infrastructure needs will be analysed with the aim of examining suitable integration within an overall sustainability evaluation framework that is developed later.

The International Federations (IFs) administer each individual sport and establish and enforce their own standards on competition venues; these standards are normally endorsed by the IOC and effectively become IOC standards. For each Olympic candidate city, it is necessary to win approval for competition and training facilities from the respective IF before the voting stage at the IOC Congress. Therefore, a city must convince the IOC and the IFs that it has, or will develop, sufficient and appropriate infrastructure on a number of levels.

The cycle of IOC involvement in Olympic development

As the franchise owner of the Olympic Movement, the IOC has a great impact on the decision-making and the management of Olympic projects; an impact surpassing that of a host city itself. Dubi (2003) pointed out that the IOC's direct and indirect involvement extends across 15 years, as shown in Figure 7.1.

During the first stage of the cycle, a potential applicant city needs to explore the viability of a bid before official submission. For any city, a good introduction to the process comes from the many published Olympic documents, including the Olympic Charter, the Host City Contract (HCC), and serials of technical guidelines and rules released by the IOC (such as Agenda 21 and technical manuals). It is these rules that ensure an Olympic Games has the infrastructure and logistical support required. Even when cities realise they cannot win an immediate bid, impacts of Olympic rules may still be felt on the city's urban development: for instance, by the earmarking of a plot of land for sport and recreational use in the future. One example was Sydney, where government-owned land at Homebush Bay was set aside as a future Olympic site by the city council two decades prior to the city's formal bid in 1993.

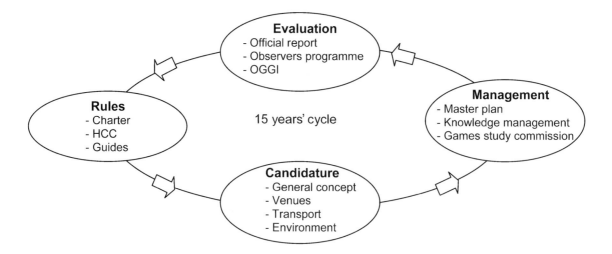

Figure 7.1
The cycle of the Olympic Games

Entering into the 'candidature' phase marks the start of the direct dialogue between a city and the IOC. Each candidate city is given a manual for the Olympiad, specifying a number of criteria; the core of the manual is a questionnaire consisting of requests for information divided into over 200 compulsory questions in approximately 17 themes (which the IOC has identified as being most important in the preparation and assessment of an Olympic bid). These include requirements for the general urban infrastructure, sport venues, transportation network, accommodation facilities, urban environment, etc. The standard Candidature File is a written response to these questions, which forms the key part of the documentation necessary for the city selection process.

Besides being fed with information from the candidature files, the IOC also conducts an independent evaluation in each city. Since 1993, the IOC has sent out one integrated expert team (the Evaluation Commission) to visit each city for an on-site inspection; a report is then produced to the IOC executive board for assistance in voting. The report is crucial for it not only examines the details in the bid documents and whether they are a true representation of the facts, but also comments on any insufficiencies and suggests a technical ranking of the candidates. The highest ranking indicates technical superiority but does not guarantee winning the bid as the IOC members have the final vote. The report also provides a chance for cities to remedy weaknesses in their Olympic strategies since there is a period of several months between the revelation of the report and the cities' final presentations to the IOC voting session.

During the candidature stage, the IFs of each summer Olympic sport also send their technical teams to each applicant city for on-site examination. A homologation would be issued if the competition and training facilities for the sport concerned, either existing or being planned, satisfy the technical requirements laid out by the related IF. Cities must get as many as possible of their venues homologated by the 28 IFs, as the results are reported to the IOC members and consequently may impact upon the vote (in addition, many IOC members are also IF members).

Upon selection of the host city and the consequent establishment of the Local Organising Committee, the Games enter into the 'management' stage. During this stage, the IOC oversees Olympic preparations mainly through cooperation with the organising committee. This includes the regular debriefing and inspection of the ongoing projects, and provision of expertise to the front-line organisers from IOC departments such as the OGKS (Olympic Games Knowledge Services) and the Games Study Commission. Normally an organising committee has considerable independence to implement its urban and other plans, but any great deviation from previous commitments in its bidding files is subject to the approval of the IOC administration.

The last link of the 15-year cycle is the 'evaluation' stage. During the Games, IOC Observers at each Olympic site collect any relevant experiences and lessons that could be learned for the future. A few months after the Games, there is an extensive debriefing by the IOC to examine all key aspects for strengths and weaknesses. More recently the 'Olympic Games Global Impact' (OGGI) programme has also been enacted to study the Games at a wider scale. These practices plus the post-Games official report impact on any amendments to Olympic rules, and consequently preparations for the next cycle.

Specified infrastructural requirements

The IOC uses a range of documents to normalise the Olympic Games and ensure their standard and quality. Because the nature of the Games is a multi-dimensional event, the documentation is wide ranging, from competition procedures to security operations. Among the themes, infrastructure and urban setting is central, being closely related to the overall Olympic concept and other important issues, such as event management, financial operation, environmental impact and cultural identity. The key elements from the following documents are worthy of further discussion:

*   The Olympic Charter
*   The Olympic Bidding Manual (Candidate Procedure and Questionnaire)
*   The Reports of the IOC Evaluation Commission/Working Group
*   Technical Manuals on Olympic Venues
*   The Report of the IOC Olympic Games Study Commission
*   The Olympic Agenda 21
*   The IOC Manual on Sports and the Environment
*   The IOC Olympic Village Guidelines and Media Service Guidelines.

The Olympic Charter

As the highest codification of the Olympic Movement, the Olympic Charter provides fundamental principles, rather than technical detail, to guide the operation of the Games. Although it does not deliver much guidance regarding Olympic urban and sustainability issues, it has two features deserving of note.

The 'one city' principle

The 'one city' principle is that Olympic sites should be concentrated within one city as far as possible. The Olympic Charter does not define the 'scope' of a city but clearly covers the metropolitan administrative area. Events commonly held outside the city are those reliant on special geographic and topographic conditions that may not exist within the city's boundary, such as for sailing, canoe/kayak events, cycling and cross-country races. Sometimes the list also includes beach volleyball and equestrian events. Soccer is a special case: due to its popularity and number of matches, at least the preliminary rounds will be held (probably simultaneously) in several other cities. Apart from these special events, the majority of the Games should rely on the infrastructure of the host city and this rule limits Olympic development on a wider, regional level. Of course there could be benefits in sharing the Olympics over a relatively large area, such as spreading of Olympic legacies, reduction of venue procurement and maintenance costs, and increase in the viability of the facilities in the post-Olympic period. These advantages, however, have to be balanced by potential risks, such as the increase of overall cost (when more cities involved), the dilution of the integrity and effect of an Olympic event, and the increase in complexity of transportation, coordination and security management.

The one city principle has been a specific requirement of the IOC, except in the cases of Melbourne and Beijing, with their quarantine regulations causing equestrian events to be held in Stockholm and Hong Kong respectively. When Mexico City requested approval for football matches to be dispersed throughout the country, the then IOC president Avery Brundage initially ruled against it (Brundage, 1968), though it was eventually permitted. Four years later, Munich further negotiated with the IOC (due to its being the smallest host city in terms of population), and was permitted 11 out of 32 venues outside the city. Since then, the arrangement of a number of venues outside the host city has become more usual; even so, at present, any such venues are still subject to the rigid control of the IOC.

Infrastructural obligations of a host city

The Olympic Charter clarifies the infrastructural obligation of a host city in staging the Games as a responsibility to provide an Olympic Village for the delegates and essential approved facilities for the sports included in the Olympic programme. In addition, as already stated, Olympic development should leave positive legacies to the host city and have concern for environmental issues and sustainable development, though the Olympic Charter does not define the details of these obligations.

In terms of infrastructure, Millet (1996) summarised the land requirements for the development of a full Games package, as detailed in Table 7.1. The figures derived are approximately the minimum necessary for the construction of each venue, not including surrounding areas or parks, which are also usually developed. The table also excludes facilities for the marathon, walking races, cycling mountain races, modern pentathlon and triathlon. More than 40 venues (approximately 31 competition and 8 non-competition) may be required with estimated eventual land demands of about 400ha. These are substantial figures and this is for only the 'direct-Olympic-related' development (a fraction of the total Olympic package).

Although the Olympic Charter formulates general rules of the Olympic obligations binding host cities, a specific edition of Games has more elaborate and specific requirements concerning infrastructure, defined in the Olympic Bidding Manual.

Table 7.1 Land requirements for Olympic facilities

Outdoor competition facilities			Indoor competition facilities		
Venue type	No. of units	Estimated area (ha)	Venue type	No. of units	Estimated area (ha)
Archery field	1	5	Badminton	1	3
Athletics	1	8	Basketball	1	4
Baseball	2 (1 main)	5+4	Boxing	1	1.5
Canoeing/rowing	1	75	Cycling velodrome	1	4
Canoeing slalom	1	15	Fencing	1	1.5
Equestrian complex	1	20	Gymnastics artistic/ trampoline	1	3
Football	4 (1 main)	8+4+4+4			
Hockey complex	1	10	Gymnastics rhythmic	1	3
Shooting range	1	30	Handball	2	6
Sailing port	1	15	Judo/wrestling	1	1.5
Softball	1	3	Swimming	1 or 2	5
Tennis complex	1	4	Table tennis	1	1.5
Volleyball beach	1	3	Tae kwon do	1	1.5
Total	17	217	Weightlifting	1	1.5
Training facilities			Volleyball	1	4
total	80	20	**Total**	15 or 16	41

Accommodation facilities			Service facilities		
Venue type	Architectural area (m²)	Estimated area (ha)	Venue type	Architectural area (m²)	Estimated area (ha)
Olympic Village	300,000	60 (min)	IBC	50,000	3
Other Village (officials, media, etc.)	200,000	25	MPC	40,000	2
			OCOG headquarters	40,000	2
Olympic 'family'	10,000	5	Other service centres (security, logistics, etc.)	50,000	2
Youth camp	10,000	7			
Total	700,000	97	**Total**	180,000	11
Total	**Units: 40–41, land: 386 ha minimum**				

Source: after Millet, 1996

The Olympic Bidding Manual (Candidate Procedure Questionnaire)

The manual for cities bidding for the Olympic Games grew out of a modest pamphlet published in the 1950s, together with the Olympic Rules Book published in the 1970s. The commercial success of the Los Angeles Games in 1984 brought a new wave of inter-city competition to Olympic bidding. Aiming to standardise the city selection process, the IOC launched the first version of the current Bidding Manual in 1992 (for the 2000 Games), which has retained its basic framework and content since, albeit with some updating. The most important part of the Bidding Manual is the Host City Application Questionnaire, which aims to collect the blueprint for each candidate city in planning the Olympic event. In the version of the 2012 Games' Bidding Manual, there were 17 themes:

Theme 1   Olympic Games concept and legacy
Theme 2   Political and economic climate and structure
Theme 3   Legal aspects
Theme 4   Customs and immigration formalities
Theme 5   Environment and meteorology
Theme 6   Finance
Theme 7   Marketing
Theme 8   Sport and venues
Theme 9   Paralympic Games
Theme 10 Olympic Village
Theme 11 Medical service
Theme 12 Security
Theme 13 Accommodation
Theme 14 Transport
Theme 15 Technology
Theme 16 Media operations
Theme 17 Olympism and culture

(IOC, 2003)

Each theme comprises an overview and a question section. The former provides a specification of the host city's obligation in the field concerned; the latter has a twofold function: to collect the information that most concerns the IOC for analysis and inter-city comparison; and to guide the Games' preparation by highlighting the emphases identified from previous experience. Among the themes above, four are directly associated with urban and sustainable development issues: theme 1 for the overall urban concept; theme 5 for the environmental approach; theme 8 for the competition venues; and theme 10 for the Olympic Village. In addition, themes 13, 14, 15 and 16 all indirectly link to the development of supportive infrastructures of the city (visitor's accommodation, transportation system, telecommunication and media broadcasting). The main points of impact can be summarised as follows.

Sustainable development and site concentration

With environmental and sustainability issues gaining greater prominence in the Olympic bidding process, questions related to this point have been expanding both in quantity and the level of detail. The principle of sustainable development is a key area in the four themes directly associated with Olympic urbanism. In Theme 1 the applicant city is requested to justify the choice of the location of key Olympic facilities; explain how Olympic projects fit into the city's long-term planning strategy; describe the impact and legacy for the city's built environment; and elaborate the plan for overall sustainable development.

Theme 5 further highlights environmental elements of sustainability issues, asking the applicant city to present its environmental action plans and initial environmental impact assessment for all projects. Themes 8 and 10 respectively require the applicant city to specify the details of competition venues and the Olympic Village in terms of location, capacity, layout, energy load, construction schedule and post-Olympic use. All these parameters should be examined by the IOC Evaluation Commission on the basis of state-of-the-art knowledge in environmental sustainability; however, there is a lack of specific guidance and benchmarking data.

Among all the information gathered by the IOC questionnaire, the spatial distribution of Olympic sites is a key element in the overall planning concept. It has been recognised as impacting on the running of the Games, the long-term viability of venues, and the future evolution of the city's urban fabric.

The current versions of Olympic rules and technical manuals do not specify any criteria for the evaluation of site location, though when interviewed, Gilbert Felli (Director of IOC Department of Sports, Olympic Coordination and Relations with the IFs) said:

> The choice by a candidate city to adopt a centralised or decentralised approach to venue location is usually driven by the overall city master plan, location of existing venues and by existing and planned infrastructures. The IOC does not consider one approach to be better than the other as a general rule but rather looks at the specific case for each candidate city and evaluates the benefits and challenges of each.
>
> (Felli, 2003)

It appears that the IOC, in its generic support for sustainable development, wishes to leave the host city flexibility in identifying its own strategy for Olympic urbanisation. However, it is noticeable that on many occasions, the IOC has shown favour to a more concentrated site approach, for the purposes of easing event management, aiding local transportation and providing a more secure environment. IOC documents have also stated: 'all these [Olympic] facilities and the village must be conveniently located, preferably together' (IOC, 1957); and 'The events must all take place in or as near possible to the city chosen and preferably at or near the main stadium' and the Olympic 'village shall be located as close as possible to the main stadium, practice fields and other facilities' (IOC, 1975). Further, the Bidding Manual for the 2000 Games made the point: 'The geographical area occupied by the sports installations required to cater for the Olympic programme should be as compact as possible . . . this can be a vital element for the awarding of the Games' (IOC, 1992). Similarly, the Bidding Manual for the 2008 Games offered: 'Proximity of sites to each other and to the nerve centres of the Games (Olympic Village, IBC, MPC, etc.) and to the city centre is highly recommended. Site concentration, if planned sensibly, will certainly ease the running of the Games' (IOC, 1999c).

In considering the six development scenarios from Chapter 3, the IOC in the past seems to have guided site planning towards a high concentration model, the Olympic Park at Homebush Bay for the 2000 Games being an example. Interestingly however, such encouragement was removed from the Bidding Manual for the 2012 Games and changed to the following: 'Venues must meet requirements and be realistic with respect to the master plan of the Host City, resource efficiencies and post-Games legacy' (IOC, 2004). Perhaps this change of emphasis indicates a willingness to allow host cities to develop individual solutions that can support sustainable development. It also may suggest that the considerations of environmental sustainability have overtaken those of the Games' operational convenience. Nevertheless, the Bidding Manual for the 2012 Games introduced the concept of 'Venue cluster(s)' and implied that design of such would gain a more positive response in the evaluation.

Environmental protection

The Bidding Manual for the 2012 Games declared: 'It is fundamental that from the beginning of the candidature to the post-Olympic period, all measures are taken to minimise or eliminate negative impact on the environment and contribute to the harmonious integration of the Olympic Games into the natural surroundings' (IOC, 2004).

Theme 5 in the manual consists of environment and meteorology components. The applicant city is asked to provide detailed environmental and meteorological conditions of its surroundings, including geographical features, potential natural hazards, ambient air and drinking-water quality and climatic data. In particular, cultural heritage and environmentally sensitive areas have to be identified on the urban blueprint. Thus the Bidding Manual delivers a clear message that Olympic projects should be based on respect for the local environmental. Cities are also asked to elaborate their key environmental action plans at a holistic level as well as for individual projects. An initial environmental impact assessment for all Olympic venues and facilities is called for, to be presented together with relevant studies during the site visit of the Evaluation Commission. In particular, the IOC asks the candidate city to pay attention to the following aspects (these will also be important considerations in formulating the evaluation framework presented later in this text):

*   architecture and transportation infrastructure and landscaping;
*   reuse of facilities wherever applicable;
*   restoration of derelict areas;
*   avoidance of destructive land use;
*   protection of habitats and biodiversity;
*   minimisation of consumption of non-renewable resources;
*   minimisation of release of pollutants to the air and water;
*   sewage treatment/solid-waste handling;
*   environmental awareness programmes/collaboration with environment agencies;
*   environmentally friendly technology application.

Venue development

The Bidding Manual also provides some principles within its Venue Development Guide concerning the following points:

*   Venue development should be realistic with respect to the city's long-term masterplan, resource efficiencies and post-Games legacy perspective.

- Venue development should support the concept of sustainable development at large, from the general planning concept to specific venues (considering use of permanent or temporary facilities, environmentally sensitive materials and systems).
- For venue selection, three options: to use existing venues as a first priority where feasible; to build new venues only when there is a legacy demand and identified post-Games use; and to seek temporary solutions for those venues required for the Games but without a post-Games use. The IOC asks for this information to be clarified in the candidature file, as well as the post-Games use of all permanent venues.
- The characteristics of each venue, in particular those elements which may affect the successful operation of the sport programme (e.g. orientation, indoor/ outdoor, surfaces, dimensions, etc.). These must comply with the relevant IF's technical rules.
- Venue versatility has potential benefits both for the Games and for future use; it should be an important consideration from the early stages.
- Olympic sites must be easily accessed and allowed communication between the different zones, and allow different groups of users to move around the site.
- Venues should be safely and efficiently operated, keeping the primary focus on athletes.

These principles are not only applicable to sports venues, but also to those non-competition venues such as the Main Press Centre, the International Broadcast Centre and the Olympic Village. The IOC has also attempted to introduce an aesthetic dimension to the design of the Olympic Village contrasting with its rather cautious manner on the development of sports venues. It suggested architectural competitions, promotion of local culture and the use of innovative construction techniques (IOC, 2004).

Another sensitive factor is the travel distance between competition venues, the Olympic Village and the media premises; this point echoes the 'site concentration' principle. For comparison purposes the Bidding Manual requests much information regarding the exact travel distances (in km) and journey times by bus (in minutes, both at average and peak times) between the Olympic Village, Media Village, Media premises, transport gateway and each competition site.

The questionnaire also requests applicant cities to provide basic information on accommodation, transport infrastructure, media premises and telecommunication facilities, categorised in different themes. For accommodation, a city's hotel room inventory and room rates should be provided as the number of out of city visitors to each Olympic Games is likely to be between 400,000 and 800,000 (Preuss, 2000). Olympic visitors are of two types: the accredited members of the greater Olympic family and normal Games tourists. The former group includes IOC members, IOC functionaries, programme partners, special agents, consultants and guests, officials of the International Federations for each Olympic sports, future organising committee delegates, Olympic sponsors, media representatives and NOC deputies, etc. – a total of approximately 30,000 to 40,000 people. The number of normal tourists is rather difficult to predict (a tourist boom is one among several effects that Olympic cities seek), but studies have shown that the tourism market of each host city tends to react differently to the Olympic Games stimulus (Leiper and Hall, 1993; Leiper, 1997). Some host cities suffered a decline in visitors in the years before, during and after the Games (Fu, 2002). Experience from some Games showed the international tourist industry boosted by the Games in the long run, and the improvement in accommodation infrastructure would help to secure the trend. In the Bidding Manual the candidate city must detail all the existing and planned hotels within 0–10 and 10–50km radius using the internationally accepted star rating system. The priority of the IOC is of course to ensure enough hotel rooms for the members of the Olympic family with appropriate conditions and rates, yet the IOC also reminds the candidate city that sufficient rooms ought to be available to the public at a reasonable price and within appropriate distance from the competition sites, because they will have an effect on ticket sales.

The candidate city's transport network and operational plans for the Games are also considered as a theme. A successful event relies on an efficient, safe and reliable transport system to move all personnel and cargoes in performing their roles. Olympic-generated traffic will be in addition to the daily traffic that services the host city and region; questions in the Bidding Manual for the 2012 Games were based on: supply, demand, strategic planning and operational concepts, and traffic command systems.

The theme of technology relates to the applicant city's infrastructure in supporting the information and telecommunications requirements of the Games, including special devices installed in competition venues. In particular, information about the International Broadcast Centre and Main Press Centre is sought in detail.

Unlike the Olympic Charter, the Bidding Manual is a practical tool for applicant cities to understand Olympic needs, and for the IOC to understand the interpretation by the cities. By placing the questions, the IOC defines the scope and key issues of Olympic preparation; by preparing the answers, applicant cities integrate their urban and other strategies into the Olympic framework.

Reports of the IOC Evaluation Commission and the Working Group

When Melbourne won its bid in 1949 to stage the 1956 Games, it simply relied on an attractive bidding book and a set of promises; the site of its main stadium had not even been selected (Cashman, 1999). The commercialisation since Los Angeles in the 1980s has stimulated an Olympic bidding frenzy, and also the expansion of the voting power of the IOC members. Allegations of corruption placed the whole Olympic selection process under suspicion and there was support for a more transparent process to 'publicly rank cities according to strict, unambiguous criteria' (Jennings and Simpson, 1992). Responding to this appeal, the mechanism of technical evaluation of each candidate city was introduced along with the Host City Application Questionnaire in 1993 as an important update to the bidding procedure.

Alleged bribery scandals in the late 1990s resulted in a further reform of the candidature process, dividing the evaluation into two phases. In the first phase, all the cities interested in hosting the Games are 'pre-evaluated' by a Working Group in terms of their potential organisational feasibility given the time and resources available. Only some of the applicant cities may then be confirmed as formal candidate cities; this helps ensure that those cities are both adequately prepared for the event and able to conform to the IOC's policies. Those cities that do not go forward avoid the expenditure of a candidature bid. The second phase retains the earlier evaluation framework from 1993 but at a smaller scale, because some issues have been tackled in the previous round.

The Evaluation Commission Report (hereinafter referred to as 'E-report') examines the identical themes of the Bidding Manual one by one, while the Working Group Report (hereinafter referred to as 'W-report') focuses more on the city's 'hardware': the supportive infrastructure and urban development plans. The methods of these two evaluations vary according to their different purposes. The W-report adopts a credit-based ranking system in order to rule out unqualified applicant cities, and the E-report produces a comment-based checklist for the IOC members as a voting aid; both evaluations have strong impacts on the host city selection. In the bidding for the 2008 Games, the E-report concluded three bids out of five candidate cities as excellent (Toronto, Paris and Beijing), and two others (Istanbul and Osaka) as less convincing (IOC, 2001). In the final voting session Istanbul and Osaka were voted off during the first two rounds.

From 1993 to the time of writing, the IOC has produced a number of E- and W-reports. The E-report for 2008 and the W-report for 2012 can be used to analyse the IOC's policy and judgement benchmarks. Several principles implied in the Bidding Manual can be confirmed through such evaluation as described below.

Confirmation of the 'site concentration' principle comes from the W-report for the 2012 Games, in which the IOC reasserts: 'The use of the fewest venues possible, the rational clustering if venues in close proximity to the Olympic Village, including an Olympic Park cluster, and the legacy value of the new values, were considered important' (IOC, 2004). The criterion has been applied when giving credits to the applicant cities. The W-report used 'fuzzy' interval grades to value each city's proposal. In the bidding for the 2012 Games, cities with a centralised venue approach (Paris and Madrid) achieved high credits (8–9) in the 'sports concept' theme, whereas those cities with rather dispersed plans (Istanbul and Havana) received lower credits (4–7). An interesting case was New York, which proposed the so-called 'X plan' where a series of competition sites were set up along intersecting transport routes rather than clustering. The linear arrangement of venues had the potential to be as convenient as the compact model for access; and given the shortage of land in Manhattan, it was a thoughtful option. Nevertheless, the New York plan was marked with a '5–8', suggesting the IOC believed it had risks.

The transport theme in the W-report 2012 also supported this rating: Paris and Madrid were given high credits for their 'shortest travel distance' (8.5–9.5), whereas Istanbul, Havana and London (which proposed the longest average travel distance) were given low credits (4–7). Leipzig and Rio de Janeiro achieved medium credits (6–8). New York was also cautiously awarded a medium-level credit; weaknesses were considered to be operational and security factors (IOC, 2004)

From the above, it seems that concentration of venues gains advantages in the bid. Echoes were found in the E-report 2008, where Osaka and Istanbul were criticised either for the dispersion of venues or for difficulty in access, and the compact plans of Paris, Toronto and Beijing were commented upon as 'good sports concepts' (IOC, 2001).

The 'three-step' principle of the venue selection has also been confirmed by the evaluation reports. In the W-report 2012, the good use of old facilities and the development of new sports legacies were balanced in evaluating the venues. The cities of Madrid, New York and Paris won high credits based on the combination of full exploitation of existing assets and clearly defined legacy plans. However, the proposals of London, Moscow and Rio de Janeiro were regarded as less attractive. One may perceive additional influences in this principle; first to reduce the number of venues and hence unnecessary costs, second to ensure older venues comply with the Olympic standards. Leipzig and Havana attained the lowest credits in the W-report, because the German proposal used too many venues that appeared excessive and costly, and in the Cuban plan, although substantially employing existing facilities (as high as 70 per cent of the whole infrastructure package), few of the venues met the IOC guidelines. In bidding for the 2008 Games, Osaka's 'Sports Paradise' (based on key venues and the Olympic Village being constructed on three man-made islands interlinked by underwater tunnels) led to concerns from the IOC due to its extravagance in development scale and cost.

The importance of environmental issues was also confirmed with the inclusion of an 'environmental impact' component in the evaluation task. Given the complexity of the matter, the IOC's assessment was based on a broad context – any relevant initiatives conceived to improve local environmental conditions and any strategies to mitigate potential negative consequence of Olympic projects would bring the city credits. As most applicants now claim to have sustainable principles in their bid, the IOC also pays more attention to tangible implementation than empty policies. In the W-report, cities that gained high credits on 'environmental impact' shared a common characteristic in that Olympic projects supported urban regeneration schemes centred on the reclamation of problematic urban land. The declining industrial quarter of Paris, the run-down neighbourhood of London's East End, and derelict areas of Madrid and Leipzig were each selected sites for the Olympic transformation. It would seem that an important factor in London winning the 2012 Games was the attractive urban regeneration plan.

The credit-based system adopted by the W-report helps to rank a large number of applicant cities on the basis of wide-ranging criteria; it also reveals the importance of each issue viewed by the IOC from the assigned weighting factors of between 1 and 5. Themes that are subdivided have sub-weightings; Table 7.2 lists them.

The Table shows that the whole set of sports venues (perhaps 15 to 30 projects) and the single Olympic Village are equally weighted in the evaluation. More interestingly, the supporting facilities (general infrastructure + accommodation) are more highly rated in total than the Olympic venues.

The data can be further interpreted: Figure 7.2 shows that all the themes related to Olympic infrastructure development can be roughly divided into four groups (only values associated with future development categories are included). The issues that raise most IOC concern (highest total) are those associated with the overall planning concept, which includes the determination of the overall development objectives and strategies. The second-highest category deals with the existing urban conditions of an applicant city, which may be quite external to Olympic

Table 7.2 Listing of evaluation weighting factors used by the IOC Working Group

IOC weighting	Main theme	Subdivided issues	%	Overall weighting	Code
2.0	Government support, legal issues and public opinion	Government support and commitment	70	1.4	A
		Legal aspects	15	0.3	B
		Public opinion	15	0.3	C
5.0*	General infrastructure	Existing transport infrastructure	51	2.55	D
		Planned transport infrastructure (Olympic)	34	1.7	E
		Airport	5	0.25	F
		IBC/MPC (location and legacy)	10	0.5	G1 G2
4.0*	Sports venues	Existing venues	35	1.4	H
		Planned and additional venues	35	1.4	I
		Sports concept/legacy	30	1.2	J1 J2
4.0*	Olympic Village	Location	50	2.0	K
		Design concept	30	1.2	L
		Legacy	20	0.8	M
2.0*	Environmental conditions and impact	Current environmental conditions	40	0.8	N
		Environmental impact	60	1.2	O
5.0*	Accommodation	Existing capacity	50	2.5	P
		Planned capacity	50	2.5	Q
3.0*	Transport concept	Distance and travel times	50	1.5	R
		Transport organisation and traffic management at Games time	50	1.5	S
3.0	Safety and security	–	100	3.0	T
2.0	Experience from past sports events	Number of international events organised	60	1.2	U
		Quality of the events	40	0.8	V
3.0	Finance	–	100	3.0	W
3.0*	Overall project and legacy	How Olympic needs fit into the city	50	1.5	X
		Post-Games legacy	25	0.75	Y
		Overall athlete experience	25	0.75	Z

Source: IOC, 2004.

Note: * Issues linked to Olympic urban development

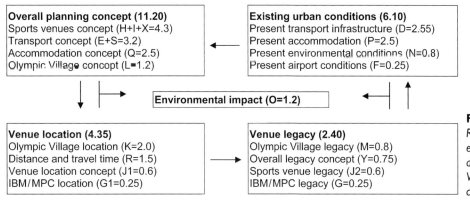

Overall planning concept (11.20)
Sports venues concept (H+I+X=4.3)
Transport concept (E+S=3.2)
Accommodation concept (Q=2.5)
Olympic Village concept (L=1.2)

Existing urban conditions (6.10)
Present transport infrastructure (D=2.55)
Present accommodation (P=2.5)
Present environmental conditions (N=0.8)
Present airport conditions (F=0.25)

Environmental impact (O=1.2)

Venue location (4.35)
Olympic Village location (K=2.0)
Distance and travel time (R=1.5)
Venue location concept (J1=0.6)
IBM/MPC location (G1=0.25)

Venue legacy (2.40)
Olympic Village legacy (M=0.8)
Overall legacy concept (Y=0.75)
Sports venue legacy (J2=0.6)
IBM/MPC legacy (G=0.25)

Figure 7.2
Re-interpretation of the evaluation weightings derived from the IOC Working Group (for codes see Table 7.2)

interventions. It seems cities with superior infrastructure and environmental foundations have advantages in the bid. Issues associated with the venue location (venue proximity and convenient access) are ranked third. The final category of venue legacy includes evaluation of the post-event viability of Olympic facilities. The environmental impact is partly independent but also interwoven with many other criteria in the whole evaluation system.

Technical manuals on Olympic infrastructure

Although many impacts are related to urban planning, design of individual venues requires compliance with the technical rules of the IFs and the IOC. Each sports discipline has strict specifications in terms of dimensions, capacity, surface materials, illumination levels, thermal comfort standards, etc. These technical rules and specifications are enshrined in a series of manuals drawn up by the relevant IF and endorsed by the IOC. Table 7.3 gives a brief summary of Olympic facility design benchmarks, although the whole package of technical specifications for each venue type is far more detailed and sophisticated. These rules lie between design norms and guidelines; some of their components, such as the height of the playing surface, flooring materials of the playfield and the temperature of the sports environments, are subject to strict implementation to ensure correct competition. Other features, such as the seating capacity and level of logistic services, are negotiable. Technical rules are also amended by each IF in line with the development of sports apparatus, training skills and the emergence of new records, interests or choreographies.

Interestingly, in comparing the basic venue-capacity standards laid down by the IOC and by the relevant IF, the IOC's standard is generally lower. Felli (2002) pointed out on behalf of the IOC:

> We [the IOC] said we should follow up the technical requirements for the International Federations, to have the best conditions for athletes and officials. But, IFs now all want the best stadiums for themselves. When they go to the World Championships, they always have the best stadium in the city. At the Olympic Games, with the 28 sports all going on at the same time, they cannot all have the best stadium. We have to work with them to make sure they understand that, and do not ask for too much.

The specifications given in Table 7.3 are taken from the IOC standard for the 2012 Games; note that values are liable to change.

Other documents and dossiers

In addition to the documents above, there are also other materials deserving attention, such as the Report of the IOC Olympic Games Study Commission, which reflects the IOC's thoughts on the potential future reform of the Olympic Games. Others, such as the Olympic Agenda 21 and the IOC Manual on Sports and Environment, reassert the commitment of Olympic development to environmental and sustainability goals. There is also a range of development guidelines produced

Table 7.3 Technical information for Olympic venues

Sharing code	Sport	Competition venue no.	Training site no.	Venue special feature	Minimum capacity	Olympic days no.
	Archery	1	1		4,000	6
A	Athletics (ceremony)	2 (1 warm-up)	3–6	Track surface is synthetic Warm-up venue close to main stadium	60,000	8–10
	Marathon	1 urban course			0	1
	Race walking	1 urban course			0	1
B	Badminton	1	1 (8 courts)	Wood court flooring Height of hall (>12m) Illumination (>1,200 lux)	5,000	8
G	Baseball	2	4		8,000	varies
	Basketball	1	3	Ref. badminton	P: 8,000 F: 12,000	16
	Boxing	1 (2 rings)	1 (12 stalls)		6,000	15
	Canoeing slalom	1	1		8,000	5
C	Canoeing flatwater	1 Regatta course	1		10,000	5
	Cycling track	1	1	Track surface (smooth)	5,000	6
	Cycling road	1 circuit	2		1,000	2–3
	Cycling mountain	1 natural course			2,000	2
	Equestrian (jumping/ dressage/cross country)	1	11 areas		12,000	3
	Fencing	2 (1 warm-up) (4 pistes each)	1 (24 pistes)		P: 2,000 F: 4,000	9–11
A (final)	Football	4	24		P: 20,000 F: 50,000	Men: 18 Women: 14
D	Gymnastics artistic	1	13	Height of hall (>15m)	12,000	8
B	Gymnastics rhythmic	1	6	Illumination (>1,200 lux)	5,000	4
D	Gymnastics trampoline	1	2	Close warm-up venue	5,000	2
	Handball	2	4		P: 5,000 F: 8,000	11
	Hockey	1 (2 fields)	2 fields	1st 8,000 2nd 5,000		15
E	Judo	1	16 mats	Temperature 18–20°C	6,000	7
B	Modern pentathlon	1 Shooting/fencing			3,000	2
F		1 Swimming			12,000	
G		1 Ride/run			10,000	
C	Rowing	1 Regatta course	1 min.		20,000 –30,000	8
	Shooting	1 (also for training)		Illumination (>1,500 lux)	3,000	9
	Sailing	1 (5 areas)	–		0	11
	Softball	1	2 fields		8,000	9
F	Swimming	10 lanes	32 lanes	Strict dimensions	12,000	16
F	Diving	1 pool (also for training)		Water temperature 26°C	5,000	
	Water polo	2	4 pools	Illumination (>1,500 lux)	5,000	
F	Synchronised	1	4 pools		5,000	
H	Table tennis	1	2	Court flooring (wooden) Temperature <25 °C Illumination (>1,500 lux)	5,000	10–12
H	Tae kwon do	1 (2 fields)	3		5,000	4
	Tennis	3 min. (also for training)		Court surface (approved) Illumination (>1,000 lux)	10,000 5,000 3,000	10–12
	Triathlon	1	1		2,000	2
	Volleyball indoor	1	4	Ref. badminton	12,000	16
	Volleyball beach	1	2		12,000	1
E	Weightlifting	1	2		5,000	10
	Wrestling	1	2		6,000	16

Source: IOC, 2004; ASOIF, 2003. Sharing code refers to possible common sharing of a venue; P=Preliminary rounds; F=Final rounds.
*issues linked to Olympic urban development.

by the IOC to help with the design process for specific facilities. They are not compulsory and entail certain flexibility for local practice, but are seen as generic benchmarks for evaluation of outcomes.

The Report of the IOC Olympic Games Study Commission

Over the last 25 years, the Olympic Games have experienced unparalleled growth, but this has increased organisational complexity and capital expenditure. The final report of the IOC Coordination Commission for the Sydney Games pointed out that measures would have to be taken to control the further growth of the Games. Now, unlike in the 1980s when the IOC sought to save the Games from decline, the pressure is to reduce excessive Games' development.

The Olympic Games Study Commission was established in 2002 to analyse the current scale and scope of the Olympic Games, and to propose solutions on how to maintain the position of the Games as the world primary sporting event, while at the same time balancing the need to keep resource requirements for the Games under control. The report was submitted to the 115th IOC session in Prague, and because many of its recommendations related to urban infrastructural issues, it seems these will have an impact on Games preparation and operation in the future. The report focused on several principles concerning Olympic development (some already mentioned) and all relevant to the theme of this text on Olympic sustainability. Issues raised were:

* the Games (and their incurred urban developments) should remain in one host city to maintain its inherent nature;
* the number of venues should be minimised by encouraging the multiple use of venues for various competitions, and tactical incorporation of temporary facilities and overlays;
* venue capacities and service requirements should be flexible and adaptable to local conditions;
* venues should be clustered wherever appropriate to avoid duplication of infrastructure and operational costs, without losing sight of the necessity of adequate after-use;
* the number of training sites in the current standard can be reduced;
* the Main Press Centre and the International Broadcasting Centre should be adjacent to one another;
* certain Olympic-specific equipment and overlays that are needed at every Games should be reused and recycled. (e.g. flag poles, signage, etc.).

The Olympic Agenda 21 and the IOC Manual on Sports and the Environment

Agenda 21 emanated from the United Nations Earth Summit in Rio de Janeiro in 1992. It provided a global action plan that has been adopted in many countries and international organisations to help promote environmental sustainability. Within this framework, the IOC drew up the Olympic Movement Agenda 21 and validated it at the session in Seoul in 1999. Released slightly earlier was an educational dossier for an environmental awareness campaign within the global sports community: the IOC Manual on Sport and the Environment.

Each of these documents called upon all sports activities to take place with due respect for the environment and in the spirit of sustainable development, and pledged the commitment of the Olympic Movement in this regard. In particular, the documents amplified the critical position of sports facilities when they impose upon human settlements, natural surroundings and resource consumption, at both global and local scales. Environmental considerations were outlined as generic guidance to all sports-related infrastructure developments, including: the avoidance of unnecessary and over-sized venues; long-term viability and functional versatility; the tactical determination of site location, architectural form, material application and construction process to control the environmental consequences; the minimisation of energy demand, waste and pollution; and the promotion of green technology. Most of this content has now been organically integrated into the Bidding Manual and the IOC's criteria for host city selection.

The IOC Olympic Village Guide and the IOC Media Service Guidelines

These guides are similar to the technical manuals on competition venues. They specify the preparation of the Olympic Village and the media premises (the Media Village, the Main Press Centre and the International Broadcasting Centre) in terms of development objectives, basic composition, surface area of each functional space and necessary equipment to support the living and working environmental standards. According to these guidelines, the host city should prepare the Olympic Village to be capable of housing at least 15,000 people with athletes and officials in a ratio of approximately 2:1. In addition, the host city should prepare accommodation with the same capacity or higher for media representatives, either by the means of a Media Village or appointed hotels.

Summary of Olympic infrastructural requirements

This chapter has outlined the background to the infrastructural requirements that are imposed by the IOC and IFs on a host city aiming to stage a Summer Games. These requirements are of two types: one being mandatory standards enshrined in Olympic rules and technical manuals that 'must' be followed by an organising committee; the other is recommendation-based policy in IOC guidelines and special reports that are preferred to be adopted by the host city. Theoretically, and also found in practice, a host city has certain flexibility for a self-interpretation of the requirements of the second type. In recent years, however, with the intensification of the Olympic bid process, the boundary between the two types of requirement has been blurred. As the benchmarks for selecting a host city have been raised, some features that were 'preferred' in the past have now become almost obligatory. Some of these issues fall clearly in the area of environmental matters; this bodes well for the future in helping develop sustainable events, and the reports of the IOC Evaluation Commission and working groups have shown the significance of following the IOC's policies in achieving a successful bid.

For the process of choosing and developing the criteria and weighting issues for the sustainability evaluation framework presented later in this book, it is clear that the infrastructure requirements of the IOC and the IFs must be fully taken into account. Potential conflicts might arise in certain circumstances; for example, the principle of using existing venues as much as possible may be impossible if aiming for venue clustering. Also, concerns for competitor convenience during the Games may not match with the city's strategies for post-Games legacy. It should be remembered that the evaluation methods employed by the IOC and IFs are based on their interest in promoting the Olympic Movement and running a successful event, rather than local long-term environmental sustainability even though it is claimed to be an important consideration. This suggests that the IOC and IFs' infrastructural requirements and preferences should be valued but not set as exclusive preconditions.

Some IOC evaluation criteria, such as the 'three-step' principle for venue selection and the encouragement of venue versatility, are generically valid in all circumstances and can be incorporated in the evaluation; others, however, need further discussion. For example, the setting of venue capacities can be considered with reference to historical experience; and Olympic urban integration and promotion of sustainable urban form should be analysed incorporating understanding of sustainable development rather than simply following a site-concentration mode.

Modern Olympic urban development is a complicated, though systematic, engineering process and a formidable task for any host city. It is useful at this point to summarise the overall need for infrastructure in hosting a Summer Games. A city needs to prepare: 31 to 38 competition venues and 80 to 90 training sites for the 28 Summer Olympic Sports; one or more Olympic Village complexes housing up to 15,000 athletes and NOC officials; MPC and IBC facilities; accommodation for more than 15,000 media representatives; at least 40,000 hotel rooms of 3-star standard and above; and supportive infrastructure such as transport, logistics, telecommunications and cultural dimensions to help with the running of the event.

Overall, the development should encompass the following characteristics: take place within the boundary of the host city; comply with the technical rules and specifications laid down by the IFs and the IOC; conform to the city's long-term masterplans and sustainability principles; be well balanced with versatile building, temporary overlays and post-Games adaptation in design; have reasonable scale and expenditure cost; be convenient for access and in suitable proximity; and showcase the environment-friendly technology at large.

In the following chapters sustainable outcomes at urban scale are analysed before moving to the development of an evaluation framework for the Olympics as a whole.

Sustainable Olympic urban development

Introduction

The subject of sustainable development is a key contemporary research and policy issue with particular impacts on cities. The Olympics and similar-scale initiatives provide opportunity for change, but evaluation techniques and rating methods are essential to help select appropriate measures to achieve goals in a controlled manner.

This chapter has three main components. First, the background to sustainable development assessment techniques is discussed; second, a preliminary general evaluation framework for Olympic development is constructed (involving the identification of a range of environmental symptoms to be responded to by Olympic intervention); and third, the main issues to be developed within the advanced framework are identified and organised. It becomes clear that although issues must be addressed on all levels and scales, overarching urban components are the most important and also those with which the evaluation proposal must engage for success.

Evaluation frameworks for sustainable development

The complexity of sustainable development as a multi-dimensional, cross-disciplinary process, and its built-in contradictions, make the issues of assessment and evaluation difficult. Environmental evaluation techniques that have been developed over recent years have often focused at the individual building level; this contrasts however with the concept that sustainable development requires communities of several thousand to operate effectively, and that more engagement at urban and regional levels is necessary. Examples of this focus are the 'eco-towns' now being planned for development in the UK with sizes of this magnitude (CLG, 2008). The evaluation tools and development described in this and the following chapter must therefore take account of such focus. If systems can be developed to work at such scale they will aid in optimising design of future communities and particularly Olympic development.

In this first section the aim is to consider evaluation frameworks rather than specific individual tools; there are several advantages to such frameworks:

- they bridge the gap between theoretical principles of sustainable development and tangible planning and design solutions in such a way that complexities of the problem can be explored;

- they provide an effective approach that is able to integrate and synthesise both the various dimensions of the system investigated (a society, a city or a building unit) and different points of view in a holistic manner (Mitchell, 1999; Deakin et al., 2001);
- they promote a set common terminology and values that allow dialogue between stakeholders from different disciplines who engaged with the decision-making process (Brandon and Lombardi, 2005);
- they embrace a value-based judgement and accounting procedure to enable sustainable development to take place in a more measured and accurate way (Pitts, 2004);
- they help the decision makers to understand the challenge more thoroughly by indicating current situation and potential targets, demonstrating whether progress has been made and plotting the future trend.

The following section outlines the fundamentals of evaluation techniques and their development in recent years with a focus on those employed within the built-environment sector. Arising from this, an appropriate framework that can be used to assess Olympic urban development is explored.

Evaluation frameworks for Olympic urban development

Evaluation, in the context of built environment, has been defined as 'a technical–scientific procedure for expressing a judgement, based on values, about the impacts of a policy or of an action on the natural and built environment, or for assessing the effects of these impacts on the community' (Bentivegna, 1997). Evaluation techniques are used in two ways within the built environment: one takes the development activity as object with a focus on the process and impacts of a decision, while the other places the community as object with a concentration on the effects and results of the development activity. These techniques are described below.

Development Activity Evaluation – Systems in this category are widely applied at the building, neighbourhood and district scale. They assess the performance of a specific project or programme in certain dimension of sustainability (e.g. environmental, economic or social impacts), or trace a dynamic process across a wide range of urban activities, from energy and material flows associated with individual buildings, to resources-use patterns of a settlement compared to a set of environmental thresholds (Breheny, 1992; Selman, 1996). Examples include ATHENA (a tool for the life-cycle impact assessment of building components); BREEAM (Building Research Establishment Environmental Assessment Method); SAP (Standard Assessment Procedure for the energy rating of dwellings); and LEED (Green Building Council's Leadership in Energy and Environmental Design rating system). These tools are also used to test and compare alternative development options, sometimes combined with complex computer-based models to simulate the process of procurement and operation of building units. However, some of these frameworks focus only on the environmental impact and ecosystem integrity of the development and less successfully address socio-economic and institutional issues.

Community Impact Evaluation – Systems in this category are normally applied at large scales such as city-region or a whole country. They are used to qualify or evaluate whether the status of the society that arises from urban development process is, in social terms, sustainable (Deakin et al., 2002); to monitor the change during a period to assess whether progress has been made towards the sustainability goal; or to justify any decision that should be made now or in the future (Brandon and Lombardi, 2005). Examples in this category include various forms of sustainable indicators developed by the United Nations and other organisations; different local versions of Quality-of-life Indices used by many governments; and series of comprehensive urban models such as the Australian SRP (Sustainable Regions Programme) and SPARTACUS (System for Planning and Research in Towns and Cities for Urban Sustainability). These frameworks were designed to examine the outcome of development initiatives rather than the strategy and details of the implementation. Normally they are more inclusive and encompass a wider range of issues in economic, social and institutional contexts, which illustrates the growing inter-disciplinary nature of the evaluation exercise.

In considering the proposed evaluation framework for Olympic development and the urban nature of its impact, the aim is to guide the design and planning related to Games' preparation; it therefore aligns with the 'development activity' category above. Another important feature of the evaluation procedure is 'judgement based on values', that is, a need to quantify qualitative data in some way so that they can be judged and explicitly compared (Bentivegna, 1997). However, not all the components of evaluation are expressed physically nor do they have absolute values that can be measured directly. When dealing with social issues or human behaviour, 'indicators' are often used to interpret information into a measurable attribute. Indicators are important for the evaluation process because they also help in simplifying complex phenomena and refining usable information. However, indicators (or an index) can only work credibly if a meaningful relationship can be established between the data measured and the subject to be assessed.

It is important here to distinguish between measurement and assessment. Measurement involves the identification of variables related to sustainable development and the utilisation of technically appropriate data collection and data analysis methods (in part, this is the identification of indicators). Assessment, however, involves the evaluation of performance against a criterion or a set of criteria (in part, this is a processing of the indicators). Both performance and criteria can be defined by value-based judgement, but not from empirical verification. Therefore, an evaluation procedure encompasses both measurement and assessment activities, and an effective evaluation framework can only be achieved when appropriate identification of its indicators and criteria have taken place.

Two further terms require clarification: 'evaluation framework' and 'assessment method'. These seem to be synonymous in some contexts, but they have quite different connotations in this text: assessment method refers to a goal-orientated approach – a way to digest information and pass judgement; whereas evaluation framework refers to a structure or a platform for the organisation and accommodation of assessment methods. Some evaluation frameworks, such as BREEAM and LEED mentioned above, have one dominating assessment method (a multi-criteria-analysis), some others, such as BEQUEST (Building Environmental Quality Evaluation for Sustainability through Time), use a multi-model framework to link different assessment methods into one single procedure (Curwell et al., 1998).

Assessment methods currently in use belong to a wide range of scientific disciplines and technical fields, such as economics, social science, engineering and environmental studies. Each of them can generally only deal with one, or a few, of the many components required for achieving sustainable solutions, and none is able to tackle all the sustainability issues in a comprehensive manner (Mitchell, 1996; Brandon et al., 1997). The fundamental contradiction between the inclusiveness of sustainability goals and the limitation of individual assessment methods requires the establishment of an evaluation framework that enables the integration of different assessment methods in a logical structure, with a multi-disciplinary and multi-hierarchical approach. As discussed in previous chapters: Olympic-scale development is a systematic practice involving various social, economic and technological activities ranging from urban and regional scale down to that of the individual building or component. It can only be evaluated by using a multi-layered framework and not by using any single assessment method.

To establish such a framework, embracing all the factors raised by Olympic development, in a way that can be used in planning and design for sustainable legacies, is a formidable task. It requires wide expertise and knowledge, access to extensive data resources, and collaboration with stakeholders; the authors acknowledge that the ultimate goal may be unattainable; however, even the establishment of a systematic framework and basic structure has demonstrable value in a field where few other options yet exist. The authors are aware that a version of BREEAM is being developed for the London Olympics but no details were available at the time of writing and therefore no examination of it can be presented.

Evaluation framework proposal

Figure 8.1 illustrates the schematic of the authors' proposed framework and suggests a disaggregation process whereby the fundamental goal is divided into significant issues or components. These components are subject to continued subdivision until tangible issues that are amenable to indicator and criteria construction are identified and made available for measurement. During this process, components are treated in three different ways.

Issues shown in the white boxes (A, D1 and D3.1) represent essential issues for attaining sustainability, but cannot be proceeded with for assessment either because the subject falls out of the environmental scope of this analysis, or the resources required are not available (e.g. data is embargoed or there are other limitations). Although such components are ruled out from further analysis at present, they are retained in the evaluation framework for potential progress at a later point.

Issues in dark grey boxes (such as B, D2 and D3.2) indicate that one or more third-party assessment methods can be used. This allows the framework developed here to concentrate on integration and the addressing of specific Olympic planning and design issues that are seldom considered by other generic evaluation systems.

Issues marked as light grey boxes in Figure 8.1 represent the kind of evaluation development undertaken in this book: the identification of single or multiple indicator-criteria set(s) for effective assessment. In addition, extension points in each layer symbolise new issues (and subdivided components) added to the

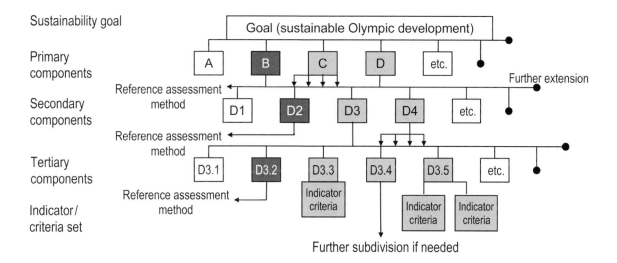

Figure 8.1
Schematic of the proposed evaluation framework

framework as required. The aim is for the evaluation framework to have a high degree of flexibility and to allow amendments and changes to weightings and benchmarks over a period of time.

Within this book certain boundaries of development have to be defined for the proposed framework while avoiding exclusion of any future component. It enables the integration of different assessment methods and allows for the evolution of knowledge over time. In the following, the discussion concerns the structure and formalisation of the framework.

Evaluation systems

A review of a selection of current evaluation systems follows in order to set a backdrop for the development of the proposed Olympic framework. There are more than a hundred accounting systems currently used for the evaluation of planning, design, construction and operation of sustainable development processes. Most of these systems are based upon single-theme assessments, and those that try to integrate environmental, social and economic factors in a more comprehensive tool are perhaps somewhat experimental and fragile at present. There is a serious lack of understanding regarding the complex dynamic interactions and interdependence between assessed activities, and the impacts of Olympic urban development on a host city's social structure is not yet very clear. These problems could cause a multi model approach to lose focus and become more a loose-structured toolkit; however, for those systems developed to examine the performance in a specific realm, such as planning and design, the use of a mono-assessment method has advantages of ease of use and understanding.

An assessment method makes up the soul of an evaluation framework and also provides a means of classification. The early assessment methods for environmental appraisal can be traced back to CBA (Cost-Benefit Analysis); these methods were originally applied in the economic field but adapted to assess environmental issues as non-market goods. Many variations were developed in which the common feature

Table 8.1 Survey of significant relevant evaluation frameworks

Evaluation frameworks for built environment	Evaluation frameworks for Olympic construction
Cost-benefit analysis	
Ecological footprint	Cost-benefit analysis has been widely applied in potential
Eco-points	Olympic cities, either by government or by other
Economic impact assessment	involved groups, to evaluate the viability of a bid. Well-
ENVEST	known cases include the ARUP London Olympics 2012
Financial evaluation of sustainable communities	Cost and Benefits and the Benefit of Beijing 2008 Games
Hedonic analysis	by Beijing Municipal Council, etc.
Mass Intensity Per Service Unit (MIPS)	
Planning balance sheet analysis	
Risk assessment methods	
Travel Cost Theory (TCT)	
Life-cycle assessment	
Eco-effect	Stadium Australia Life Cycle Assessment (SALCA)
Eco-quantum	
Life cycle impact assessment of building components (ATHENA)	
Life Cycle Analysis (LCA)	
LISA Project	
Expressed preference method	
Achieving Excellence Design Evaluation Toolkit (AEDET)	Economic impact of Olympic Games (EIOC)
Assessing the Sustainability of Societal Initiatives and Proposed Agendas for change (ASSIPAC)	IOC Olympic marketing survey system
Community Impact Evaluation (CIE)	
Contingent valuation method	
Meta Regression Analysis (MRA)	
Social impact assessment	
Semantic Differential (SD)	
Checklists	
Eco-profile	IOC environmental guidelines for the Summer
BRE environmental profiles	Olympic Games
Green guide to specification	Greenpeace Olympic environmental guidelines
BRE sustainability checklist for developments	
Multi-criteria analysis	
Analytic Hierarchy Process (AHP)	Assessment System for Green Building of Beijing Olympics
Building Environmental Performance Assessment Criteria (BEPAC)	(ASGBBO)
BRE Environmental Assessment Method (BREEAM)	IOC OlymLogic (Decision Matrix)
Building Environmental Assessment and Rating System (BEARS)	
Environmental Impact Analysis (EIA)	
Green Building Challenge (GBC)	
Leadership in Energy and Environmental Design (LEED)	
National Australia Building Environmental Rating System (NABERS)	
Project Impact Assessment (PIA)	
Regime analysis	
Strategic Environmental Assessment (SEA)	

Table 8.1 (continued)

Evaluation frameworks for built environment	Evaluation frameworks for Olympic construction
Multi-model framework	
Building Environmental Quality Evaluation for Sustainability Through Time (BEQUEST)	N/a
BRE environmental management toolkits	
Quantitative city model	
System for Planning and Research in Towns and Cities for urban sustainability (SPARTACUS)	
Sustainable Cities Network (SCN)	
Computer modelling and simulation	
Building Energy Environment (BEE 1.0)	PrimaSoft: Olympic Organiser Deluxe (OOD)
Building for Economic and Environmental Sustainability (BEES)	Spreadsheet of Assessment System for Green Building of Beijing Olympic (ASGBBO)
DOE-II	
Eco-Instal	
Eco-ProP tool	
EcoTech	
Standard Assessment Procedure (SAP)	
The LT method	
UMBERTO	
Indicator set	
Eco-indicator'95	N/a
Quality-of-life index	
Sustainable Regions Programme (SRP)	
UN sustainable indicators	
CIRIA environment indicators for civil engineering industry	
World Bank: Monitoring Environmental Progress (MEP)	
OECD environmental indicators	

was the definition of a credit system to value the loss and gain caused by development in terms of social and environmental effects. Well-known examples include the concept of 'community capital' (Hart, 1999), the 'polluter pays' principle (Constanza, 1991), and 'ecological footprints' (Wackemagel et al., 1993).

After the UN Conference on Environment and Development in 1992, the importance of social and economic sustainability (as well as environmental issues) increased in the assessment. This in turn led to the development of methods taking into account activities up to urban scale, and social science techniques such as the 'Expressed-Preference Method' were added to evaluate users' satisfaction with the built environment. Examples of this group include CVM (the Contingent Valuation Method), TCM (the Travel Cost Method) and AEDET (the Achieving Excellence Design Evaluation Toolkit).

The concept of sustainable development as a process rather than a product boosted the development of life-cycle assessment techniques and the tracing of energy and material flows over the lifespan of development projects. In addition, supporting methods, such as sustainability checklists, and more sophisticated computer modelling and simulation techniques, have been found useful to aid decision-making processes.

Cost-benefit analysis has been further explored to combine market and non-market valuation. Agenda 21 (UNCED, 1992) proposed the establishment of a system of accounting that could integrate national economic and environmental values so that progress towards sustainability could be measured through a unified monetary regime (the concept of greenhouse gas emission trading also arose from this consideration). Due to the fact that environmental impacts are quite difficult to assess in economic terms within a market framework, an alternative MCA (multi-criteria analysis) has attracted increasing attention for built-environment evaluations.

In general, MCA is designed to manage decision processes characterised by many assessment criteria, alternatives and actions (Brandon and Lombardi, 2005). It encompasses weighting and ranking systems that can value the environmental impacts in non-monetary terms. The main advantage of MCA is that it makes it possible to handle a wide range of data, relations and objectives, often in conflict, so that the problem can be examined from multiple angles. For instance, one of the well-known methods based on the MCA concept, the AHP (Analytic Hierarchy Process), can be used to deal with the complex judgement associated with both qualitative and quantitative parameters, which are generally present as specific real-world decision problems. Quite a number of evaluation systems that have been implemented were developed based upon the MCA method, such as BREEAM, GBC (Green Building Challenge) and SEA (Strategic Environmental Assessment). In this text, the MCA method is used to shape the proposed framework for evaluating Olympic urban development. Table 8.1 lists a survey of main evaluation frameworks, both in the environmental sustainability field and the Olympic development field; arranged by assessment methods.

Construction of the evaluation framework

From the discussion above it can be seen that there is a wide variety of evaluation approaches for sustainable development in planning, design and construction; though little agreement neither concerning the theoretical structure to be used nor on a homogeneous vocabulary. The proposal here takes the assessment methods as the key determinant; these are different when the analytical focus is on design and planning or the overall development output, compared to natural resources consumption or the impact on neighbourhoods. The organisation of the overall framework has been devised to comply with the assessment methods it employs.

Weighting and rating are important within the methods and a methodological procedure was used to develop indicators (PICABUE), which has been adopted by frameworks based on multi-criteria assessment (MCA) (Mitchell et al., 1995, 1997, 2002). This approach helped construct and define the proposed evaluation framework for Olympics; see Figure 8.2.

The purpose of the evaluation framework is to guide the design and planning process of Olympic preparation. The principles of sustainable Olympic development (particularly at urban scale), against which the performance objectives of this framework can be set, have been defined as those which maintain and improve the

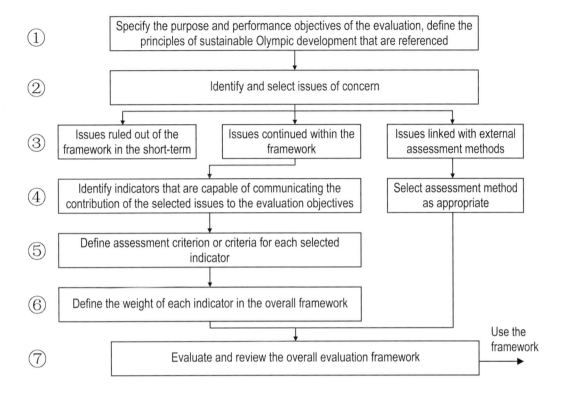

sustainability of the built environment of the host city. All evaluation content should be focused on this fundamental task.

Figure 8.2
The process for constructing the proposed evaluation framework

Identification of the issues of concern is a crucial step in shaping the overall framework. In this proposal, the method used is based on a 'driving force – pressure – state – impact – response' (DPSIR) model (an analytical procedure to generate societal actions and design responses from human activities and patterns that impact on the built environment). It was first introduced by the United Nations Commission on Sustainable Development in 1992, and has been used to construct several evaluation systems including the indicator inventory of the World Bank and the OECD. In this exercise, because the task is to identify the issues associated with Olympic initiatives, the model can be adapted and simplified to the following chain:

Symptom – Driving force – Response   Olympic Initiatives (SDROI) model

Issues of concern

The analytical process is used to identify issues to be included in the evaluation framework. The first step is to identify the 'target' as the input information. To enable this, it is essential to review the main environmental problems that can be confronted by Olympic intervention, and explore their influence on the decision-making process. In the following discussion, environmental imperatives are defined as the key drivers for planning response; economic and social factors are considered in due course.

Concepts of sustainable development are often based on awareness of environmental degradation and the concerns of climate change. A range of environmental problems exists in modern societies at many levels, and it is suggested that the earth's systems and its built environment are already at a point of unsustainability. The profligate use of resources and energy associated with building and urban development are both results of, and contributors to, the problem. The underlying hypothesis is that by alleviating some of the problems identified a city can move towards a greater degree of sustainability. Clearly the potential of Olympic intervention to solve urban problems is limited and far from straightforward; however, there is potential to encourage Olympic schemes to leverage longer term as well as immediate strategies.

In this proposal, 11 issues are identified as major environmental concerns experienced by large cities. The selection of these issues is based on a variety of well-cited publications, including the BRE Sustainable Development Checklist (Brownhill and Rao, 2002) and the United Nations Environment Programme (UNEP)'s Global Environment Outlook (UNEP, 2003, 2004).

Global warming

In recent decades, the evidence for climate change has grown, with the most prominent phenomenon known as global warming. Both computer simulation and data from measurement has indicated that global mean temperatures are increasing (IPCC, 2007). Some commentators regard global warming as a greater threat to humanity than terrorism (Roaf et al., 2005).

Global warming is the consequence of additional gases liberated into the earth's atmosphere as a result of human activities causing the so-called greenhouse effect. The most problematic gas is carbon dioxide (CO_2); other gases such as methane (CH_4), CFCs and HFCs are more damaging but are produced in smaller quantities. The increase of greenhouse gas concentration is now generally understood to be caused by the burning of fossil fuels, which accounts for about 80 per cent of anthropogenic emission; the remaining 20 per cent being due to deforestation, industrial processing and agriculture. Buildings, construction and associated processes are directly and indirectly responsible for a high proportion of the total energy consumption and hence CO_2 emissions. In the UK, for instance, about 46 per cent of the total energy is used in constructing and servicing buildings (heating, lighting, cooling and ventilation) and associated activities. Approximately 35 per cent is from transport energy use, which is growing partly as a result of planning and urban design decisions.

Clearly it is important to address climate change in Olympic development. There are three objectives: to reduce greenhouse gas emissions in the procurement of Olympic facilities, including the means of manufacture, processing, transport and construction; to reduce greenhouse gas emissions from the daily operation of Olympic facilities; and to reduce greenhouse gas emissions from the daily transportation of goods and people between Olympic facilities and the rest of the city.

In pursuing these goals, there are two main components: one is the reduction of energy demands through tactical planning and design (for instance, selection of materials with low embodied energy, encouraging reuse and recycling, use of energy-efficient options for creating thermal and visual comfort, and addressing the energy used in motorised transport). The other is the promotion, exploitation and application of new and renewable energy resources in venues and vehicles. Though renewables have enormous potential to satisfy demands, technical and financial constraints, as well as local availability and acceptance, means that expansion of use may be over a longer timescale.

Ozone depletion

The ozone layer in the stratosphere is crucial to the earth's ecosystem through its absorption of potentially damaging and harmful ultraviolet radiation (UV) from the sun. Damage to the ozone layer can be caused by chlorofluorocarbons (CFCs), some hydrochlorofluorocarbons (HCFCs) and halons. Many of these substances have been used in the building industry as foam-blowing agents, in refrigerators and air conditioners, and in fire extinguishers. Once discharged into the atmosphere, these chemicals take about 20 years to migrate to the stratosphere, where under the catalyst of sunlight, they release chlorine atoms to destroy ozone.

In 1987, the Montreal Protocol was signed by many nations to ban the use of ozone-depleting chemicals, and according to the schedule, CFCs and HCFCs should be entirely phased out by 2030. Because of the time-lag effect, the ozone 'hole' found over the Antarctic should recover over the coming century. In order to minimise ozone depletion, Olympic venues should avoid use of all ozone-depleting chemicals listed in the Montreal Protocol, as well as those products or synthetic materials that involve ozone-depleting substance in their manufacturing process, such as polyvinyl chloride (PVC) for window frames, insulations, rain pipes and gutters, and chlorine filters for swimming pools.

Air pollution

Air pollution is a common environmental hazard in large towns and cities. According to the World Health Organisation, there are three main categories of pollutants: suspended particulates, oxides of sulphur (particularly SO_2) and oxides of nitrogen (particularly NO_2). Long-term exposure to high levels of these pollutants affects fauna and flora directly, contributes to a wide range of human health problems, and leads to the deposition of acid rain and smog.

Suspended particulates are made up of soot, smoke, dust and liquid droplets. One source is topsoil erosion and vegetation damage, resulting in dust and sandstorms, which may be caused by overgrazing, over-ploughing and desertification of urban hinterlands. Cities close to deserts are particularly at risk. In relation to Olympic cities, Beijing has experienced severe springtime sandstorms arising from the Mongolian Plateau, and these can even reach the Korean peninsula and Japan at times. Beijing's particulate problem is also characterised by smoke due to heavy dependence on coal as the primary energy source for both industrial and domestic use. Oxides of carbon, nitrogen and sulphur are often associated with the combustion of fossil fuels used in buildings and in motor vehicles.

Different solutions may be possible according to the type and scale of air pollution problem. For cities suffering from particulate and sulphur pollution arising from combustion, a solution might be to encourage modification of energy sources, improving the ratio of new and clean energy (such as natural gas and renewables) for the industrial and domestic use. For cities suffering from dust and sandstorms, Olympic projects could help support the ecosystem in the surrounding area. In cities experiencing motor vehicle-induced pollution, the reduction in traffic intensity and congestion would itself be a valuable outcome. Public transit networks should be boosted wherever possible by Olympic development. Olympic planning should also enlarge rather than reduce the green areas of the city and vegetation can act as filters in the urban environment to reduce levels of CO_2, NO_2, dust and aerosols. Urban green areas such as large Olympic parkland may be particularly important for cities such as Beijing and Mexico City, which have high levels of more than one pollutant.

The heat island effect

This phenomenon is caused because large areas of built structures and paved surfaces absorb, rather than reflect, the sun's heat. The heat island intensity is associated with urban size and population density: larger and denser settlements generate higher temperatures than smaller and lower-density counterparts. Various factors including the amount of building, HVAC usage, albedo of materials, topographic features, vegetation coverage and streetscape, all impact on the heat capacity of the city area and the ease or difficulty of heat dissipation. The issue has been prevalent in large cities for some time, but is becoming more problematic with global warming. A study found that in London the number of nights with intensive heat island effect (more than 4°C warmer than the surrounding countryside) has been climbing steadily since the 1950s (Roaf et al., 2005) and in Athens the heat island temperature increase has been estimated as high as 10°C (Santamouris et al., 2001).

The heat island effect can be mitigated in a number of ways through climatic design techniques, in terms of using the natural wind, and increasing the albedo of constructed surfaces. Passive cooling strategies are particularly important for venues of summer sports. Urban green space and large areas of water can also ameliorate the microclimate by evaporation, which can absorb significant amounts of ambient heat. Large centrally located Olympic parklands such as those of Helsinki and Munich have been proved to benefit the microclimate conditions and the alleviation of urban heat island effects and should be encouraged.

Waste and sewage treatment

It has been estimated that over 10 billion tonnes of various waste is produced worldwide each year from industrial and domestic processes. And yet, for many cities the infrastructure for safe disposal of waste and sewage is often lacking. In developing countries as a whole, only 60 per cent of urban solid waste is collected and less than 50 per cent of the urban population is served (UNEP, 2002). In developed countries, waste disposal is dominated largely by incineration and landfill, representing a waste of natural resources and a range of consequent environmental problems.

Waste disposal issues have implications for Olympic development. For the design and construction of Olympic facilities, reuse of existing structures and on-site recycling and reclamation of salvaged materials should be encouraged. Waste classification and management systems should also be integrated into all Olympic venues and villages. The improvement of waste and sewage disposal systems and capacities of the host city may also be part of Olympic development, as in the cases of Rome, Tokyo and Barcelona.

Water use

Water is a scarce resource in many parts of the world. It has been estimated that more than two billion people are affected by different levels of water shortage in over 80 countries (UNEP, 2003). In recent years, climate change has led to increasing droughts and floods, exacerbating the problem of water supply at a global level.

Many Olympic venues are significant water consumers. Large athletic stadiums, such as Sydney's main stadium, consume 50 to 100 million litres of water annually, mostly for turf irrigation and lavatory flushing. Facilities such as aquatic arenas, regatta courses and white-water course venues all directly rely on vast amounts of water to function. Water conservation should therefore play an increasing role in Olympic infrastructure design. The most basic change is to introduce appliances with high water efficiency and metering utilities to reduce and control consumption. Greywater recycling and rainwater collection should be encouraged for non-potable use. Sustainable urban drainage systems (SUDS) should be considered as a matter of course in developing Olympic parklands and venue precincts. Ground surfaces should enable a level of permeability to reduce water runoff and replenish groundwater. In addition, the impacts of construction processes on local water sources should be minimised.

Noise pollution

Noise is an almost all-pervasive pollution found in the urban built environment, yet it is controllable and one that responds to abatement technology. For Olympic development, the ability to alleviate existing noise problems in a host city is limited; however, design improvements can help in new and refurbished Olympic projects to minimise the creation of new nuisance, for example.

Urban greenery and public amenities

Public open spaces and urban green areas have been recognised for their social benefits, environmental merits, ecological significance and aesthetic value. The perception that urban open space enhances quality of life can be traced back to the early modernist movement as a reaction to nineteenth-century overcrowded industrial towns, where residents had little or no public open space.

Urban open space and urban green space are two different concepts, the latter being more important from an ecological standpoint. Large areas of urban green land can provide a buffer to traffic noise and fumes, trap dust and pollutants, release moisture and oxygen, and cool the ambient air; all contributing to the amelioration of poor microclimatic conditions. Research shows that one hectare of mixed green land can consume one tonne of carbon dioxide and release 0.73 tonnes of oxygen to the air on a sunny day (Shen and Xiong, 1996). Very fragmented green areas, however, do not have as beneficial an effect as concentrated ones. For city residents, urban green space is perhaps the only convenient way to achieve beneficial contact with nature: a survey conducted by the European Commission showed a direct correlation between the accessibility of public parks and citizens' satisfaction with the urban environment (Tarzia, 2003).

Olympic urban development provides a chance to improve the local capacity of green space and public amenity by introducing one or more Olympic theme parks. The size and distribution of these parks, as important parameters of the Olympic masterplan, should be based on the study of the conditions of a host city. Such a study was undertaken in Munich, where Olympic planning resulted in 3km² of parkland at the heart of the city and considerably changed the city's green space impact.

Traffic congestion

Traffic congestion is often witnessed in a well-mobilised society. It occurs when traffic demands approach or exceed the available capacity of the urban transportation infrastructure. According to a study from the Texas Transportation Institute (TTI) in 85 urban areas in the United States, congestion not only brought inconvenience to daily life, but also economic loss and air pollution (Schrank and Lomax, 2005). This study found that larger, culturally and economically vibrant cities tended to have worse congestion than smaller and declining cities. It also found that public transportation services contribute significantly to the alleviation of congestion, particularly in very large conurbations.

During the Olympic Games, the sudden increase in travel demands may lead to severe congestion. It is clearly important to plan effectively to reinforce public transit services in anticipated congestion corridors, and to adjust, where possible, urban road capacity to match Olympic traffic demand. Road management systems (such as toll lanes, congestion charges and incident reaction programmes) can be used as complementary measures. In addition, the adjustment of working patterns within the city to reduce travel peaks should be further explored.

Urban sprawl

The increase of mobility and communication technologies has enabled the separation of home and work, and triggered the phenomenon of suburbanisation. One of the results of this process is urban sprawl. Urban sprawl is not the same as urban expansion; it refers particularly to urban expansion in which the growth in urban land consumption is not proportional to the change in urban population. Although there is evidence that the trend of suburbanisation has slowed in recent decades, urban sprawl is still evident. According to Beck et al. (2003), since the 1980s the

United States alone has converted approximately 110,000km^2 of rural land to urban area. Much expansion has also occurred at the same time as urban depopulation.

Urban sprawl results in a range of negative consequences. It threatens agricultural land and rural ecosystems, and the expansion of impervious surfaces such as roads and roofs causes the degradation of local water resources by increasing the water run-off volumes. Urban sprawl also increases travel, in particular journeys using private vehicles. Reduced rates of walking and cycling have been found in more sprawling cities (Ewing et al., 2000).

Since urban sprawl is characterised by dispersed low-density development and suburbanisation, the encouragement of a more compact urban form and the repopulation of inner-city areas are solutions to be encouraged to tackle the problem. For Olympic host cities, Olympic projects may be conceived that either infill vacant plots in already built-up areas, thus changing the community density, or follow a transit-orientated development in helping control urban expansion orientation.

Neglected urban areas

Several agents can generate run-down urban areas. In the developed world, suburbanisation processes can give rise to 'desolate inner cities surrounded by an outer ring of prosperous suburbs' (Rudlin and Falk, 1999). During periods of decline, the development of modern motor networks affected traditional transport hubs and systems.

In cities of the developing world, the boom of manufacturing accelerated the speed of urbanisation. Rural-to-urban migrants flooded into cities at a faster rate than the capacity of the government to provide even the most basic infrastructure. Concurrently, large numbers of the original urban residents were evicted from traditional blocks as their neighbourhoods were demolished to allow building of higher value properties. These displacements produced a new class of urban homeless and eventually slums in the least favoured areas; Olympic urban development has a risk that it may actually encourage this effect. Some urban run-down areas may also include undeveloped vacant zones (caused by leapfrog development and land speculation), and environmentally degraded and contaminated areas (including rubbish tips and landfill sites). These areas reduce the urban integrity and aggravate the sprawl.

The origins of urban slums and run-down areas may vary, but their remedies seem often to share a common theme: surgical clearance followed by new development. In recent decades, the growth of modern service industries in Western cities has also helped to stimulate the inward reinvestment and urban renaissance. To optimise benefits in Olympic host cities, the development of Olympic projects should be combined with long-term land use modification and regeneration schemes, such as at the main Olympic sites of Munich and Sydney, which were deliberately placed on previously contaminated landfill sites.

Summary of issues

Clearly, a range of environmental problems confronts many world cities at the current time, but there is potential to alleviate them through Olympic intervention.

Some of the environmental issues, for instance global warming and ozone depletion, have an international dimension, whereas others are based on regional or local issues, varying in seriousness and scale. It is clear that environmental problems rarely exist alone, but generally interlace and interact during the development of the city, as shown by Figure 8.3.

Overall urban form (sprawl) is at the core of the matrix to which other phenomena are linked, though rarely in only the simplified ways shown. To achieve sustainable development goals, it seems clear that urban form is a fundamental issue. In the proposed evaluation framework, therefore, issues associated with land use, site selection and urban integration, and impacts on the existing urban form, are given greater weighting. Of course, there is a possibility that in tackling one problem another may be created: Roaf et al. (2005) have provided the example that the growth of the 'café culture' in the UK has help to rejuvenate inner cities but also increased street noise (most apparent in non-traffic zones). This emphasises the benefits of a multi-criteria accounting procedure to assess the environmental performance of development in a comprehensive manner.

Olympic development impacts

Figure 8.3
The matrix of urban environmental problems with some causal links

Table 8.2 illustrates the usage of the SDROI (Symptom – Driving force – Response – Olympic Initiatives) analytical procedure to identify issues of concern in Olympic urban development. In this, the environmental symptoms discussed above are

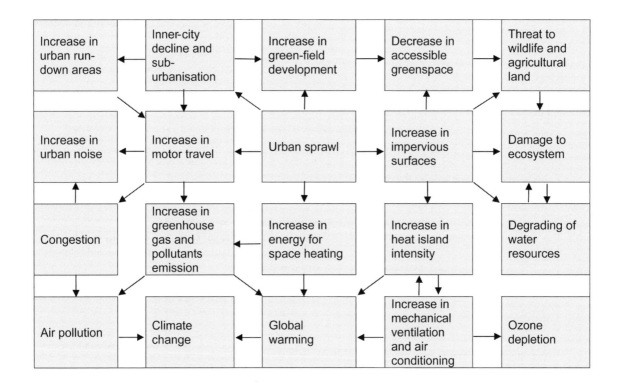

Table 8.2 Olympic initiatives to address issues of concern

Symptom (S)	Driving force (D)	Response (R)	Olympic initiatives (L)
Global warming (S1)	Inefficient use of energy and resources in venue procurement (D1)	Reduce energy and resource consumption in venue procurement process (R1)	Full use of existing facilities (L1.1)
			Full use of existing structure in venues' refurbishment (L1.2)
			Selection of structures with low embodied energy (L1.3)
			Selection of materials with low embodied energy (L1.4)
			Improve on-site materials recycle and reduce the waste from the construction process (L1.5)
			Design for use recycled materials from off-site sources (L1.6)
			Use of materials that are locally produced (L1.7)
			Design for an easy disassembly, re-use or recycling (L1.8)
			Establishment of on-site waste management system (L1.9)
	Inefficient use of energy in venue operation (D2)	Reduce energy use in venue operation (R2)	Design for maximum passive solar gain potential (L2.1)
			Design for maximum use of day lighting (L2.2)
			Design for maximum use of natural ventilation (L2.3)
			Design for use of passive cooling strategies (L2.4)
			Design for minimising building envelope heat loss (L2.5)
			Design for wind and rain protection for athletes and spectators (L2.6)
			Design for minimisation of glare in venues (L2.7)
			Design/use of high efficiency/managed lighting system (L2.8)
			Design for appropriate illumination level and quality (L2.9)
			Design/use of high efficiency well-managed HVAC systems (L2.10)
			Design for use CHP/DH or other high efficiency heating system (L2.11)
			Other features to minimise energy use in venue operation (L2.12)
			Establishment of overall energy management system (L2.13)
			Regular assessment of the overall energy load (L2.14)
		Use renewable energy in venue operation (R3)	Plan for use of energy that generated from on-site renewable systems (L3.1)
			Plan for use of energy generated from off-site renewable resources (L3.2)
	Inefficient use of energy in transport between venues and city (D3)	Promote public transit between venues and city (R4)	Proximity of site to public transportation node (L4.1)
			Locate sites in the overall urban fabric to trigger/support public transport (L4.2)
		Reduce private motor travel between venues and the city (R5)	Selection of sites for easy accessibility (L5.1)
			Proximity of sites to large residential community (L5.2)
			Proximity of sites to commercial, entertainment and cultural facilities (L5.3)
			Proximity of competition sites to Olympic Villages (L5.4)
			Plan for mixed development (L5.5)
			Planned support for pedestrians (L5.6)
			Planned support for bicycle users (L5.7)
			Planned policies controlling the use of private vehicles (L5.8)

Table 8.2 (continued)

Symptom (S)	Driving force (D)	Response (R)	Olympic initiatives (L)
Global warming (S1)	Energy and resources used in venues during the post-Games period (D4)	Improve venues' viability in long-term use (R6)	Plan for compatibility with the city's long-term masterplan (L6.1) Plan for post-Games use of each venue (L6.2) Location of sites for easy daily use by local community (L6.3) Plan for appropriate development scale based on local needs (L6.4) Design for versatility of venues (L6.5)
		Improve the flexibility and adaptation of venues (R7)	Design for flexibility and easy adaptation of venues (L7.1) Design to include appropriate temporary structures and overlays (L7.2)
		Minimise waste resulting from demolition and redevelopment of venues (R8) ref. R22	
	Deforestation and degradation of rural land (D5)	Reduce the intrusion into agricultural and rural land (R9)	Selection of sites for infill development (L9.1) Selection of low ecologic value land or Brownfield development (L9.2) Plan for minimisation of the impact on agricultural and rural landscape (L9.3) Establishment of wildlife corridors (L9.4) Location of sites in the overall urban fabric to contain sprawl, ref. S10
		Use timber or bio-based products from sustainable labelled resources (R10) (L10.1)	
		Minimisation of emission of acidifying chemicals (R11), ref. D8, D9	
Ozone depletion (S2)	Use of ozone depleting substance (ODS) in venue procurement and operation (D6)	Ban ODS in venue procurement (R12)	Selection of materials according to Montreal Protocol (L12.1)
		Reduce ODS in venue operation (R13)	Use substitutes for chlorine in swimming pools (L13.1) Use HVAC system with ODS-free refrigeration (L13.2) Reduce the use of HVAC, ref. L2.3, L2.4, L2.10 Use ODS-free extinguisher (L13.3)
Air pollution (S3)	Sandstorm and dust caused by topsoil erosion and vegetation damage (D7)	Recover the ecosystem in surrounding land and enlarge the vegetation coverage to help remove air-borne pollutants and particulates (R14)	Introduction of Olympic parkland with appropriate location and size (L14.1) Improvement of urban green spaces through Olympic 'beautification' (L14.2) Design for sustainable drainage system to reduce water run-off (L14.3) Measures to enhance or sustain ecological value of the site (L14.4) Measures to minimise impact of construction process on soil erosion (L14.5) Design for main roads/tram lines to be flanked by tree belts or shrubs (L14.6) Reduce intrusion of ecosystem, ref. R9, R10
	Sulphur oxide pollution caused by dependence on coal as a primary energy resource (D8)	Use new and renewable energy in Olympic projects (R15)	Use 'clean' energy such as natural gas and nuclear resources (L15.1) Use renewable energy in running venues, ref. R3
		Reduce energy consumption in venue procurement and operation (R16)	Ref. R1, R2

Table 8.2 (continued)

Symptom (S)	Driving force (D)	Response (R)	Olympic initiatives (L)
Air pollution (S3)	Sulphur and nitrogen oxide pollution caused by car fumes (D9)	Reduce traffic intensity (R17)	Ref. R4, R5
		Reduce traffic congestion (R18)	Ref. S9
		Use 'greener' fuel for motor travel (R19)	Use green fuel such as natural gas, biofuels and eco-friendly vehicle fuels(L19.1)
Heat island effect (S4)	Intensive built areas absorb and release heat to ambient environment- problem is made worse by global warming and the wide use of air conditioning (D10)	Use climatic design techniques in planning and design of Olympic projects (R20)	Selection of surface materials with high albedo (L20.1)
			Deduce the use of HVAC ref. L2.3, L2.4, L2.10
			Control the density of Olympic cluster, avoid extreme high rise, high dense settlements (L20.2)
			Plan the site according to the wind orientation and streetscape (L20.3)
		Use larger green space to ameliorate the microclimate (R21)	Plan for Olympic green space and parkland ref. L14.1, L14.2, L14.6
Waste and sewage treatment problem (S5)	A range of environmental problems caused by the inadequate capacity for waste and sewage treatment systems in the host society (D11)	Minimise waste from venue procurement and redevelop-ment (R22)	Minimise waste resulting from energy and resources generation, ref. R1
			Reduce the demolition of venues, ref. R6, R7
		Minimise waste from venues' operation (R23)	Design for waste classification and management system in venues (L23.1)
			Minimise waste resulting from energy and resources generation in venue operation, ref. R2, R3
		Improve the waste and sewage systems in the host city (R24)	Upgrade waste and sewage disposal infrastructures particularly using more advance techniques (L24.1)
		Remedy of previous landfill site (R25)	Select contaminated land or landfill site for Olympic project development, ref. R40
Water scarcity (S6)	Inefficient use of water and potable water use in venue procurement and redevelopment (D12)	Reduce water use in venue procurement and redevelopment (R26)	Selection of materials with low embodied water (L26.1)
			Reduce the overall materials usage, ref. L1.1, L1.2, L1.5, L1.6, L1.8, L1.9
			Use of high-efficiency water-appliances on construction site (L26.2)
			Establishment of water management system on construction site (L26.3)
	Inefficient use of water and potable water in venues' operation (D13)	Reduce water and potable water use in venues' operation (R27)	Use of high-efficiency water appliances in all venues (L27.1)
			Establishment of water management systems in all venues (L27.2)
			Design for a split grey water and potable water system (L27.3)
			Establish grey water and rainwater collection and recycle system for non-potable use (L27.4)
			Regular assessment of overall water loads (L27.5)
			Design for sustainable drainage system for Olympic sites, ref. L14.3

Table 8.2 (*continued*)

Symptom (S)	Driving force (D)	Response (R)	Olympic initiatives (L)
Water scarcity (S6)	Intrusion of local water resources (D14)	Reduce untreated effluents from site (R28)	Reduce untreated effluents sent off during the site construction (L28.1) Avoid untreated effluents resulting from venues' operation drain directly to water course (L28.2) Establishment of on-site passive treatment system (28.3)
		Avoid intrusion of local water system (R29)	Plan for minimisation of impact on local water course (L29.1) Ref.R9, R10, R11, R14
Noise pollution (S7)	Noise pollution caused by traffic, industrial equipment, human activity, domestic air conditioning, etc. (D15)	Reduce traffic noise (R30)	Reduce traffic intensity and congestion, ref. S9 Plan for traffic barrier by roadside and green open space, ref. R14 Design to include physical traffic barrier on road infrastructures (L30.1) Avoid intrusion of new transport route into main residential quarter (L30.2)
		Reduce human activity noise (R31)	Zoning venues and Olympic Villages to avoid intra-disturbance (L31.1)
		Reduce air-conditioning noise (R32)	Ref. L2.3, L2.4, L2.10
		Promote acoustic benefits through design techniques (R33)	Design for optimum acoustic features in all venues (L33.1)
Shortage of urban open-space and parkland (S8)	Land speculation and cost-benefit analysis results in urban parks being marginalized (D16)	Introduce more urban green spaces and parklands (R34)	Avoid occupation of current urban parklands (L34.1) Ref. L14.1, L14.2
Congestion (S9)	Traffic demands close to, or exceeds the available capacity of urban transportation infrastructure (D17)	Reduce traffic demands (R35)	Ref R4 Plan to promote an inner city renaissance (L35.1)
		Improve capacity of transportation network (R36)	Reinforce the urban road network infrastructure (L36.1) Promote public transit system, ref. R5
		Reduce congestion using management measures (R37)	Introduce congestion charges or controlling measures to special area (L37.1) Reinforce the urban traffic management and information systems (L37.2)

Table 8.2 (*continued*)

Symptom (S)	Driving force (D)	Response (R)	Olympic initiatives (L)
Urban sprawl (S10)	Inner-city decline, suburbanisation and the separation of living and working cause low density, dispersed urban form (D18)	Encourage a more compact urban form (R38)	Control the density of Olympic cluster, avoid over dispersed, low density settlements (L38.1) Plan to promote a decentralised concentration urban form (L38.2) Plan to promote inner-city renaissance, ref. L35.1 Plan to promote infill development, ref. L9.1 Avoid intrusion of ecosystem, ref. R9, R10
		Steer the expansion orientation of the city (R39)	Plan for compliance with the city's long-term master plan, ref. L6.1 Plan to promote transit-orientated development (L39.1) Plan to promote self-sufficient satellite development (L39.2) Reinforce urban green belt (L39.3)
Run-down urban areas (S11)	Urban run-down areas generated because of inner-city decline, shift of transport hubs, social displacement and hence slums, and natural or man-made land contamination (D19)	Apply an appropriate surgical clearance with new development (R40)	Selection of environmentally vulnerable sites (L40.1) Selection of former landfill sites (L40.2) Selection of former contaminated sites (L40.3) Selection of appropriate measures for decontamination (L40.4) Selection of declining zone for redevelopment (L40.5) Selection of former mineral extraction sites (L40.6) Plan to promote inner-city renaissance, ref. L35.1 Selection of vacant site within the urban built area, ref. L9.1

considered as remedial objectives to be responded to by the various design and planning initiatives associated with the Games' preparation process. Each of the initiatives is given an identification code to aid implementation; the more frequently an issue occurs, the more important it tends to be in the overall development with a greater weighting in the evaluation system.

If certain overlapping components of the table are neglected, 98 issues remain on the list; these cover the prime activities for delivering the sustainable development goals of Olympic intervention. However, this process produces an extensive but rather fragmented list for which it is neither practical nor desirable to define indicators in all cases. A refining process has been applied to select, synthesise and re-categorise eventual indicators in which the issues are reorganised according to the design-orientated hierarchy set out by Table 8.3, and all issues are summarised under nine headings.

Taking the components of Table 8.3 it is possible to develop the upper levels of an evaluation framework according to the major issues – this is shown in Figure 8.4.

Table 8.3 Re-structuring of issues of concern for the evaluation framework

Recode	Assessment components	Coverage
A	**Strategic development objectives**	
A1	Compatibility of Olympic urban development with the city's long-term master plan	L6.1
A2	Full use of existing facilities	L1.1
A3	Introduction of Olympic parkland with appropriate location and size	L14.1
A4	Appropriate development components and scale for supportive infrastructure based on local needs	L24.1, L36.1
B	**Masterplan and site selection**	
B1	Contribution of overall Olympic master-planning to a sustainable urban form	L9.1, L9.3, L35.1, L39.2, L39.3, L38.2
B2	Contribution of overall Olympic master-planning to public transport	L4.2, L39.1
B3	Contribution of overall Olympic master-planning to mixed development	L5.2, L5.3, L5.4, L5.5, L6.3
B4	Selection of Brownfield or problematic land	L9.2, L34.1, L40.1, L40.2, L40.3, L40.4, L40.5, L40.6
B5	Appropriate form of development: grain, layout, density and scale	L20.2, L20.3, L38.1
C	**Energy consumption**	
C1	Reduce energy for heating	L2.1, L2.5, L2.11
C2	Reduce energy for lighting	L2.2, L2.8, L2.9
C3	Reduce energy for cooling and ventilation	L2.3, L2.4, L2.10
C4	Application of new and renewable energy	L3.1, L3.2, L15.1
C5	Other features to reduce energy load in venue operation	L2.12
C6	Establishment of energy management system in all venues	L2.13
C7	Assessment of GHG emissions from all energy used for annual venue operations	L2.14
D	**Water conservation**	
D1	Minimisation of impact on local water resources	L14.3, L28.1, L28.2, L28.3, L29.1
D2	Reduce water and potable water consumption	L26.2, L27.1, L27.3, L27.4
D3	Establishment of water management system for venues	L26.3, L27.2
D4	Assessment of water consumption for annual venue operation	L27.5
E	**Materials and structures**	
E1	Selection of materials and structures with low embodied environmental impacts	L1.3, L1.4, L26.1
E2	Encouragement of structure re-use and materials recycle	L1.2, L1.5, L1.6, L1.8
E3	Selection of materials that are locally produced	L1.7
E4	Selection timber and bio-based products from sustainable sources	L10.1
E5	Selection of ODS-free materials	L12.1, L13.1, L13.2, L13.3
E6	Selection of façade surface materials with high albedo	L20.1
F	**Transportation**	
F1	Plan for easy access	L4.1, L5.1
F2	Planned support for pedestrians and bicycle users	L5.6, L5.7
F3	Control the use of private vehicles	L5.8, L37.1
F4	Establishment of Olympic traffic management and information system	L37.1
F5	Minimisation of traffic pollution in planning new transport infrastructure	L14.6, L30.1, L30.2
F6	Use of eco-friendly fuel for vehicles	L19.1
G	**Post-Olympic usage**	
G1	Post-Games usage plan for each venue	L6.2
G2	Versatility of venues	L6.5, L7.1
G3	Appropriate venue scale, temporary structures and overlays	L6.4, L7.2
H	**Functionality**	
H1	Compatibility of venues with IF's technical requirement	complementary
H2	Plan for well being of athletes and spectators	L2.6, L2.7, L31.1, L33.1
J	**Environmental impacts**	
J1	Enhancement of ecological value of development sites	L14.2, L14.4
J2	Establishment of wildlife corridor in development sites	L9.4
J3	Minimisation of soil erosion in construction site	L14.5
J4	Design for waste classification and management system in venues	L1.9, L23.1

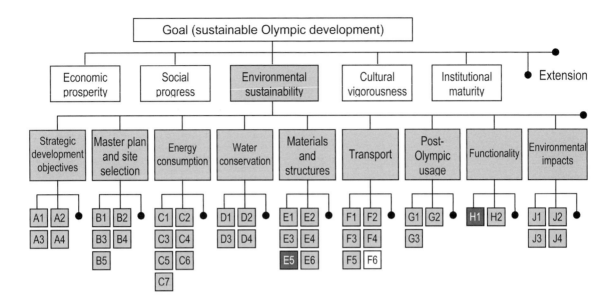

Summary

This chapter has attempted to provide a basis for analysing sustainable development within the Olympic urban context, and has established some guiding principles for the evaluation framework. The growth, decline and adaptation of cities over time means that the Olympics and other large-scale events can intervene to trigger the desirable urban transformation.

In order to help organise this quest for sustainability, evaluation techniques have been assigned an important and integrating role by design professionals. Evaluation frameworks necessarily employ a trans-disciplinary language for the built environment, and bring together the diversity of interests necessary to assess development performances and impacts. The techniques and frameworks make sustainable development more tangible, practical and predictable. This chapter has considered the basis of several contemporary assessment methodologies; their potential for success and their limitations; and thus the ability to construct the proposed framework for evaluating Olympic development.

In the latter part of the chapter, the construction of a framework based on multi-model and multi-criteria assessment techniques was initiated. A range of issues was identified using the SDROI analytical procedure and reassembled in Table 8.3. Each of these issues and objectives plays an important role in the successful delivery of sustainable changes in Olympic host cities while preparing for the Games; in the following chapter this basic framework is built upon to define indicators, assessment criteria and weighting for each selected issue.

Figure 8.4
Schematic of the upper hierarchies of the proposed evaluation framework (for legend see Figure 8.1)

CHAPTER 9

Proposed evaluation framework for the Olympic city

Introduction

The task of this chapter is perhaps the most significant of the book: to define indicators and assessment criteria in the evaluation framework for all the issues previously identified, and to determine their weighting within the overall system. These processes are the steps 4, 5 and 6 shown in Figure 8.2.

In Table 8.3 these issues were categorised under nine headings; each of these major themes is now dealt with below. For each issue, one or more indicator(s) are designed to ascertain specific performance levels of the Olympic scheme in terms of environmental sustainability. A set of criteria and benchmarks is proposed to convert the information into an assessable outcome. As with most evaluation systems, scores are awarded for each indicator where specific performance levels are achieved, so that the overall quality of a development can be determined by summing the scores obtained.

In some assessments, such as LEED (the Leadership in Energy and Environmental Design rating system), different issues are judged by using a discrete and hetero-geneous set of credits but without any very sophisticated attempt to weight them in a final analysis. In AEDET (the Achieving Excellence in Design Evaluation Toolkit), issues are examined by a homogeneous set of credits and their importance is reflected by multiplying weighting factors. In the accounting framework proposed here, the second style is adopted and the overall performance of each issue is scored between one and five to represent a gradation from 'poor practice' to 'excellent practice'.

As with most evaluation systems, criteria are of two basic types: those that can be expressed as quantitative values; and others that are best described in qualitative form. For ease of use it would be convenient to express as many parameters as possible in a numeric form, but in practice this may lead to spurious results and should be applied with caution. For those indicators with qualitative-based criteria, an accounting procedure is introduced to convert information into a quantitative measure. First the performance of a subject is assessed against each criterion by applying a ternary credit scale (good, medium and poor), then a synthetic 'assessment index' ($\triangle$) is produced to integrate the whole evaluation into a standardised numeric scale for scoring. The standard accounting procedure is demonstrated in Figure 9.1.

Indicator code	Score:	5–1 (according to the value of Δ)		
Indicator description ...				
5 Δ > 0.8	**4** 0.6 < Δ ≤ 0.8	**3** 0.4 < Δ ≤ 0.6	**2** 0.2 < Δ ≤ 0.4	**1** 0 < Δ ≤ 0.2

Assessment criteria	*Credits gradation (C)* ⟶	Good	Medium	Poor
1 Criterion description 1 ...		2	1	0
2 Criterion description 2 ...		4	2	0
... ...		2	1	0
N Criterion description N ...		2	1	0
Maximum credits available:	A	**Credits awarded:**	$B = C_1 + C_2 + ... + C_n$	
Indicator code		**Assessment index (Δ):**	$Δ = B / A$	

In Figure 9.1 the three values shown are 2, 1, 0 to assess performance against a particular criterion; these values can be varied to reflect a different weighting for a criterion, for instance: 4, 2, 0, or 6, 3, 0, or other multiples. The weight of each category and sub-weight of each issue within the category are considered later in the chapter. The AHP method is used to identify the degree to which issues are significant for the overall Olympic sustainability goals. Initial values are a default setting that can be adjusted by multiplying a correctional coefficient to reflect local circumstances.

The strength of the analysis in criteria and benchmarks lies in the combination of assessments based on the theoretical mainstream of sustainable development, the IOC's latest requirements for Olympic infrastructure, and the wealth of empirical information from historical experiences reviewed in previous chapters. Most quantitative judgements have been derived for 'typical' Olympic developments; however, as no development is ever typical and every host city has a certain uniqueness, values should be adjusted after appropriate consultation to derive the local evaluation.

Figure 9.1
Typical format for an indicator in the framework with a series of criteria

Strategic development objectives (Indicators A-1 to A-4)

This group of issues examines the appropriateness of the objectives, components and scale of Olympic urban development in terms of the compatibility with local needs. Decisions at strategic planning level are crucial to achieving overall sustainability goals.

Compatibility of Olympic urban development with the city's long-term masterplans (Indicator A-1)

Cities have very diverse planning and management systems. Those with traditions of strong governmental control, such as Moscow (in the 1980s) or Beijing, have powerful planning authorities responsible for creating local masterplans that

Indicator A-1	Score:			
Consistency of Olympic urban development with the city's long-term masterplans and other local planning consensus.				
5 Δ > 0.8	**4** 0.6 < Δ ≤ 0.8	**3** 0.4 < Δ ≤ 0.6	**2** 0.2 < Δ ≤ 0.4	**1** 0 < Δ ≤ 0.2

	Assessment criteria	Good	Medium	Poor
1	The city's long-term masterplans and other local planning consensus have been fully reviewed, studied and considered when determining the holistic Olympic urban scheme	4	2	0
2	The Olympic urban plan is consistent with the city's established development orientation	2	1	0
3	Most Olympic projects and infrastructure (particularly non-competition venues) have already been identified in urban plans prior to Olympic bid	2	1	0
4	The deployment of Olympic sites is consistent with the city's arrangement for land usage	2	1	0
5	Olympic urban development is consistent with the city's plan for demographic control	2	1	0
6	Olympic urban development is consistent with the city's objects for social equity	4	2	0
7	Olympic urban development is consistent with the city's transport network plan	2	1	0
8	Olympic urban development is consistent with the city's economic and investment strategy	2	1	0
9	Olympic urban development is consistent with the city's environment protection agenda	4	2	0
10	Olympic urban development is consistent with the city's resources management plan	2	1	0
11	Olympic urban development is consistent with the city's plans for culture, media and leisure industries	2	1	0
12	Olympic urban development helps maintain or reinforce the city's spatial identity	2	1	0
Maximum credits:	30	**Credits awarded:**		
Indicator A-1		**Assessment index (Δ):**		

coordinate land use, spatial layout, resource management, economic strategy and infrastructure development across their regions. Cities in more 'market' economies may not have such a counterpart; consequently, the breadth, depth and utility of the masterplans produced by cities may be different.

The proposed evaluation relates to government-initiated documents and guidelines, and also includes local consultative reports and publications undertaken by non-governmental parties with participation of the general public. For example, London Business School analysed the development needed to ensure the city's continued prosperity in the new competitive environment (Thornley, 1999) and Arups produced a series of reports for their own interests in exploring London's Olympic masterplans before the city's bid. These both contributed to local planning knowledge.

A city's masterplans are normally based on a long-term survey of local needs and deficiencies, and should also reflect the debate of local stakeholders. They can be a basis for Olympic urban development in evaluating infrastructure and local interests, however planning is also subject to the requirements of staging the Games.

Use of existing and temporary facilities (Indicator A-2)

General concerns for sustainable development, and the IOC's policies, each encourage the full use of existing facilities to minimise resource consumption and capital expenditure in venue construction and maintenance. New facilities should be considered only when there is a legacy demand in the post-Games period, and temporary venues should be explored for use by one-off events. Historically, the proportion of existing venues has varied among host cities from 30 to 70 per cent (see Table 9.1); the average value is around 40 per cent. Cities with few existing facilities normally have a higher ratio of temporary venues to avoid the costs of building new permanent facilities (which make up a large proportion of overall costs and resource consumption). Entirely temporary venues are still relatively rare and restricted to sports with simple needs.

Indicator A-2	Score:				
Use of existing and temporary facilities					
5 Δ > 0.8	**4** 0.6 < Δ ≤ 0.8	**3** 0.4 < Δ ≤ 0.6	**2** 0.2 < Δ ≤ 0.4	**1** 0 < Δ ≤ 0.2	

	Assessment criteria	Good	Medium	Poor
1	The city's sports resources (as well as shortages) have been fully surveyed, and the potential to adapt existing facilities and to use temporary solutions for Olympic events are carefully studied and assessed	4	2	0
2	The ratio of the newly permanent venues in the overall venue development package is appropriate (within the scope of the host city) **Good**: 40% and below; **Medium**: 41%–50%; **Poor**: 51% and above	2	1	0
Maximum credits:	6	**Total credits awarded:**		
Indicator A-2		**Assessment index (Δ):**		

Table 9.1 Use of existing and temporary venues: Rome to Athens

Games	No. of venues in total	No. of venues in host city	Newly built venues in host city	Existing venues used in host city	Existing venues (%)	Temporary venues in host city	Temporary venues (%)	New permanent venues (%)
Rome 1960	24	17	12	5	29.4	4	23.5	47.1
Tokyo 1964	30	25	14	11	44.0	4	16.0	40.0
Mexico City 1968	22	17	7	10	58.8	0	0.0	41.2
Munich 1972	32	21	13	8	38.1	4	19.0	42.9
Montreal 1976	26	17	10	7	41.2	0	0.0	58.8
Moscow 1980	27	23	11	12	52.2	0	0.0	47.8
Los Angeles 1984	33	23	7	16	69.6	2	8.7	21.7
Seoul 1988	32	23	13	10	43.5	2	8.7	47.8
Barcelona 1992	40	23	11	12	52.2	2	8.7	39.1
Atlanta 1996	32	24	16	8	33.3	5	20.8	45.9
Sydney 2000	37	33	26	7	21.2	3	9.1	69.7
Athens 2004	39	33	22	11	33.3	3	9.1	57.6
Average	31.2	23.3	13.5	9.8	43.1	2.4	10.3	46.6

Complicated temporary structures may not necessarily save cost and resources in procurement and use, but they can reduce the burden of venue operation and management after the Olympics. In this evaluation, temporary structures are assumed to be demountable for reuse. The issues can be examined in two ways: first, to analyse whether the city's sports resources/needs have been fully understood and decisions made on the information gathered; and second, whether the ratio of new permanent venues in the overall package is reasonable. Those cities with higher new build percentages, such as Sydney, Montreal and Athens (2004) all experienced different levels of 'venue excess' after the Games. Accordingly, it is suggested that as an acceptable planning figure, 50 per cent of facilities should be existing or temporary (equating to 12–16 venues with the current scale of the Games). Clearly, with fewer new facilities, lower expenditure and resources should be needed for procuring and sustaining the overall Olympic urban assets.

Olympic parkland – location and size (Indicator A-3)

Olympic Games promote green areas in host cities in two ways. One is through urban beautification campaigns to introduce boulevards, cultivating green verges beside roads and buildings and creating small plazas or gardens for the community use. A more obvious and focused option is to introduce Olympic parkland. Olympic parks normally combine urban amenities, open spaces and green planting. During the Games, they provide celebratory gathering places for local citizens and visitors to experience the festival atmosphere, which is an integral part of Olympism. After the Games, they become a permanent legacy for the city and often act as tourist attractions. It is estimated that 322 million visitors frequented the Munich Olympic park between 1972 and 1988. In Seoul, the Olympic park attracts over six million visitors annually, even with an entrance charge (Preuss, 2000).

Indicator A-3	Score:							
Olympic parklands: location and size								
5 $\Delta > 0.8$	**4** $0.6 < \Delta \le 0.8$	**3** $0.4 < \Delta \le 0.6$	**2** $0.2 < \Delta \le 0.4$	**1** $0 < \Delta \le 0.2$				

Assessment criteria				Good	Medium	Poor		
1	Olympic parklands are introduced as an essential part of Olympic urban development.			2	1	0		
2	Olympic parklands are introduced with appropriate size which can improve the host city's deficiencies in urban parks and large green space.	a	b	c	d	e	f	
		10	8	6	4	2	0	
3	Olympic parklands can be accessed easily by local residents and serve the community at large. (Are the Olympic parks located within or close to the urban centres? Are they well connected with public transportation? Are they free to the public or with minimal charge? Are they to be well maintained and attractive?)			4	2	0		

Maximum credits:	16	Credits awarded:	
Indicator A-3		Assessment index (Δ):	

The importance of Olympic parks has been recognised by all host cities. Even Atlanta with comparatively modest venue development set up its Centennial Olympic Park.

Olympic intervention provides a chance to remedy a city's deficiency in large green spaces, but there is no internationally accepted method to measure a city's condition of parkland. One indicator is the 'urban greenspace per capita', which is a United Nations Sustainable Development Indicator (UNCSD, 2005), although there is a difference between the measurement of urban greenspace and urban parkland. The former is an environmental indicator whereas the latter relates more strongly to social function (Hough, 1984).

For the evaluation here, 'urban parkland per capita' and 'percentage of residents in proximity to urban parks' are taken as indicators, but they need to be used with caution because the statistics may vary widely depending on the definition of urban parks. This needs further clarification to refine multi-city comparisons. In addition, it is difficult to identify appropriate baselines for the measures and is to some degree subjective.

Figure 9.2 analyses the correlation of central city density and urban parks per capita in some major cities and Olympic host cities. Data were collected from the United Nations Cities project (1998) ; although the number of samples is limited, the diagram clearly demonstrates the variety in availability of urban parklands

Figure 9.2
Urban open space per capita and urban density

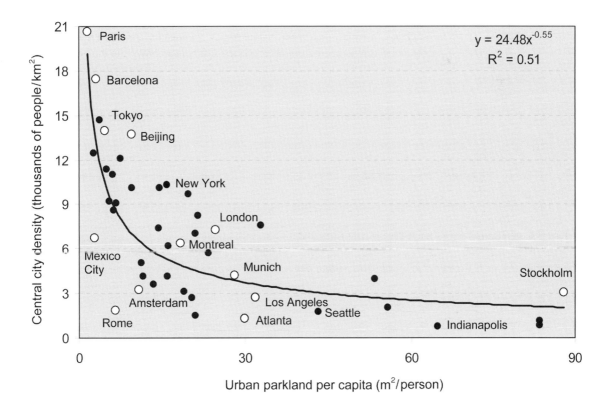

$$y = 24.48x^{-0.55}$$
$$R^2 = 0.51$$

among cities. For instance, Amsterdam and Stockholm have similar urban densities, but a great difference in personal share of parkland asset.

It would be an over-simplification to apply universal benchmarks in judging a city's performance in parkland deployment. Nevertheless, multi-city comparison is valuable as a reference and guide for future decision-making.

Table 9.2 summarises the development of Olympic-orientated parklands in recent host cities from Tokyo to London. The total area of each development ranges from $0.5km^2$ up to more than $10km^2$. Generally, large Olympic parks (more than $2km^2$) have been planned in peripheral urban areas or suburbs where more land can be easily set aside for this purpose. More extensive parklands (more than $5km^2$), such as in Sydney and Beijing, normally contain a large area of natural landscape beside a venue cluster.

Table 9.2 Olympic urban parkland development from Tokyo to London

City	Olympic park area (km^2)	Other park area (km^2)	Total area Olympic-orientated parks (km^2)	Location	Nature
Tokyo	0.664	–	0.664	urban central area	semi-greenspace
Munich	2.830	–	2.830	urban central area	semi-greenspace
Montreal	0.460	–	0.460	urban central area	semi-openspace
Los Angeles	0.538	–	0.538	urban central area	semi-greenspace
Seoul	1.674	0.831	2.505	suburban area	semi-greenspace + greenspace
Atlanta	0.085	–	0.085	urban central area	greenspace
Sydney	1.500	6.100	7.600	suburban area	semi-openspace + greenspace
Athens	–	2.000	2.000	urban peripheral area	greenspace
Beijing	4.050	6.800	10.850	suburban area	semi-openspace + greenspace
London	2.000	–	2.000	urban peripheral area	semi-greenspace

Figure 9.3
Categorisations of assessment for Olympic parkland development

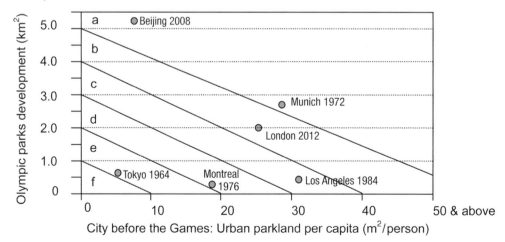

The evaluation examines whether Olympic parklands are developed for cities with low values for urban parkland per capita, and second whether they can be easily accessed by local residents. An evaluation chart has been designed with six zones to score the performance level from 'a', representing good practice, to 'f', representing poor practice (see Figure 9.3). Values of 5km^2 of Olympic park development and 50m^2 per capita of urban parkland are set as maximum scale values and categorisations developed. Several recent Olympic host cities are shown on the chart as examples.

Development components for supportive infrastructure (Indicator A-4)

Olympic intervention also provides a chance to remedy a host city's deficiencies in civic infrastructure. Intra-city comparisons and studies similar to those used for urban parklands can be applied to urban elements in order to determine whether they should be included as essential components of the Olympic development package, and if so at what scale.

The following are urban elements that should be included:

- housing stock with quality requirements (e.g. housing area per capita, distribution and percentage of housing with certain standards, housing market index, etc.);
- hotel stock with certain international standards (e.g. total beds in 4/5-star hotels, distribution of hotels in local area, etc.);
- appropriate traveller/goods-handling capacity of main airport;
- suitable urban road network (e.g. road network density, road length per capita, distribution of major roads in local area, etc.);
- public transit systems (e.g. underground/metro length per capita, commuter-handling capacity of current system, the coverage of urban rail network, etc.);

Indicator A-4	Score:				
Development components for supportive infrastructure					
5 Δ > 0.8	**4** 0.6 < Δ ≤ 0.8	**3** 0.4 < Δ ≤ 0.6	**2** 0.2 < Δ ≤ 0.4	**1** 0 < Δ ≤ 0.2	

	Assessment criteria	Good	Medium	Poor
1	Development of sustainable housing schemes other than directly Olympic related	6	3	0
2	Development of Olympic hotels and accommodation	2	1	0
3	Enhancement of facilities at existing airport	2	1	0
4	Road development external to Olympic venues	2	1	0
5	Development of detailed Olympic transit policies, projects and frameworks	6	3	0
6	Improvements to sewage and waste disposal systems from sustainable perspective	4	2	0
7	Planning and design of new sustainable energy plant	4	2	0
Maximum credits:	26	**Credits awarded:**		
Indicator A-4		**Assessment index (Δ):**		

- efficient disposal capacity of sewage and solid-waste systems (e.g. capacity of local wastewater purification, capacity of landfill, waste-to-energy, solid wastes recycle rate, etc.).
- appropriate capacity of energy grid.

Components that might be considered in Olympic urban development are:

- Olympic-orientated housing schemes other than Olympic Villages;
- Olympic-orientated hotel projects;
- extension of existing airport;
- Olympic-orientated road development;
- Olympic-orientated transit projects;
- improvement of existing sewage and solid-waste disposal facilities;
- new energy plant.

For each urban element, an indicator similar to that for assessing Olympic parklands can be introduced relating to development scale and objective. The hotel stock, airport and transportation infrastructures are also important themes in the IOC's Olympic Bidding Manual. Housing projects also have practical impacts, as they might be used as temporary accommodation for out-of-town Olympic visitors to complement the local hotel network. Seoul, Barcelona and Athens each had substantial development of urban housing. Since the Olympics may impact on the demographics of the host city, development decisions should look at long-term implications.

At the current time, although each of these points should be considered the authors have not found it possible to derive any sophisticated means of assessing indicators for these indirectly related Olympic development components. The credits awarded must therefore be limited to assessing whether adequate and appropriate attention appears to have been paid to the issue in the planning and development of the event. It would also be possible to omit this category from the final assessment and allow it to be balanced by other assessments that consider these topics outside the Olympic planning system.

Masterplans and site selection (Indicators B-1 to B-4)

This section examines the integration of Olympic sites into a host city's urban fabric. The first evaluation concerns whether the selection and planning of Olympic sites contributes to achieving a more sustainable urban form. The second concerns the appropriateness of design parameters of individual sites, including venue scale, cluster density, grain and layout; each being features defined by Olympic masterplans and development briefings.

Contribution of Olympic masterplanning to sustainable urban form (Indicator B-1)

The criteria used to examine this issue are based on the urban sustainability principles discussed earlier. The evaluation is based around the six Olympic

Indicator B-1	Score:			
Contribution of overall Olympic masterplanning to a sustainable urban form				
5 Δ > 0.8 **4** 0.6 < Δ ≤ 0.8 **3** 0.4 < Δ ≤ 0.6 **2** 0.2 < Δ ≤ 0.4 **1** 0 < Δ ≤ 0.2				

	Assessment criteria	Good	Medium	Poor
1	Supports urban containment policy	2	1	0
2	Optimises urban density	2	1	0
3	Rectifies dispersed urban form	4	2	0
4	Defines community centres	4	2	0
5	Encouragement for mixed-use development	2	1	0
6	Brownfield development potential	2	1	0
7	Promotes public transport systems	2	1	0
8	Promotes transit oriented development	2	1	0
9	Generates inner city renaissance	4	2	0
10	Promotes urban greenery and attractive public realm	2	1	0
11	Revitalises urban run-down areas	4	2	0
12	Promotes efficient energy systems (CHP/DH)	2	1	0
13	Creates new urban landmarks	2	1	0
14	Coherence with the IOC planning policy	2	1	0
15	Implementation feasibility	2	1	0

Maximum credits:	38	**Credits awarded:**	
Indicator B-1		**Assessment index (Δ):**	

urbanisation models considered: these models are hereafter referred to as S1 to S6 and shown in Figure 9.4. The integration of Olympic sites into host cities could fit to one of these models and over time aid in developing benchmarks for future comparison and analysis.

Some of the particular criteria deserving of more detailed explanation are covered below.

Criterion: support for urban containment policy

This policy can be interpreted as the encouragement of inwardly focused, reused sites (e.g. brownfield development) for Olympic venues. Forms S1, S2 and S3 comply with this principle subject to land availability in the inner city. Large unused areas are unlikely to be found in the central region of large cities (though Munich was an exception). Seoul and Barcelona showed Olympic sites could be centrally located by demolishing derelict or declining urban estates, outdated industrial premises and slums; this has the possible consequence of population displacement and damage to the traditional urban context. S1 is the most easy to implement, less sensitive to criticism, and generally has a lower cost. S4 and S6 are typical models for peripheral development and involve an organised sprawl; S6 particularly deserves caution in application and S5 involves the creation of a satellite town. If the town has a degree of self-sufficiency, it may help to restrain the sprawl of the main city

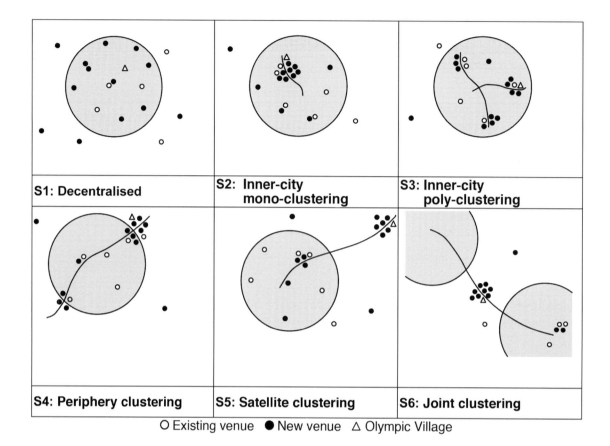

O Existing venue   ● New venue   △ Olympic Village

Figure 9.4

The six theoretical models of Olympic-site integration into the host city

by organically dispersing development pressures; otherwise substantial commuting may occur between the two, incurring environmental and energy costs.

Criterion: rectification of dispersed urban form

Although it is unlikely to modify a city's overall density, Olympic intervention could optimise a dispersed urban form by encouraging higher density development clusters or corridors. Investment may be drawn in through improved infrastructure and transport around Olympic sites with impacts on land value. New and thriving neighbourhoods might be shaped if Olympic venues are clustered at a certain scale in physical and economic contexts. The scattering of venues as in S1 compromises their impact; likewise, for S3, the number of venue clusters should be balanced and scaled to avoid this problem. The promotion of a poly-nucleated urban form by combining and consolidating venue clusters with existing urban centres needs evaluation against the alternative of injecting new development to an area lacking a centre in order to give better overall urban balance. For S2 and S3, unless mass demolition takes place, the land limitations of the inner city may restrain the scale and growth of the new centres. Alternatively, S4 and S6 support new Olympic-induced urban nuclei in a city's periphery, where land may be more available. S4, S5 and S6 generally promote links between old and new urban areas and favour linear transit-orientated development.

Criterion: encouragement for mixed-use development

This policy encourages co-location of housing, retail, employment and public services. S1 might not deliver significant mixed-use development around Olympic venues, yet it provides flexibility to deploy the new venues within existing neighbourhoods, with better local access. None of the other scenarios obviously limit mixed-use development.

Criterion: promotion of public transport and transit-orientated development

Each of the forms S4, S5 and S6 has sites some distance from original centres, and thus require new transport and movement systems. Host cities generally expand their metro or light-rail systems, which also helps to alleviate traffic in the inner city in the longer term. In Tokyo and Seoul, the strong reliance on public transport today is due to the foundation laid by Olympic intervention in the past. For cities with S2 or S3 forms, such as Munich and Montreal, the Olympic impact on public transit appears more moderate. S1 does not guarantee development of new transit systems because of the wide dispersal of venues, a typical case being Mexico City where efforts focused on improving roads and motorways with mass-transit systems lagging behind other infrastructure.

Criterion: generator for inner-city renaissance

S2 and S3 favour inner-city renovation schemes and new central development. Most cities following these models, such as Munich, Moscow and Barcelona, experienced urban revival during and after the Olympic cycle, and an increase in inner-city population and investment. S1 also involves some new urban development within the city's central mass and may therefore foster a degree of urban revival. S4, S5 and S6 each encourage development outside, or at the margin of, the city's central mass, making impacts on the inner city rather difficult to assess. Atlanta and Sydney experienced an increase (at least in the short term) in occupancy rates of central area office and commercial estates (McKay and Plumb, 2001); comparatively, Munich and Barcelona had a broader-based urban change. In Atlanta, however, the growth of the CBD was reported to be concurrent with a decline in poor communities in the inner city (Stone, 2001).

Criterion: promotes urban greenery and attractive public realm

This issue has already been discussed: generally, cities adopting out-of-town clustering (S4, S5 and S6) find it easier to develop large Olympic parklands.

Table 9.3 summarises the performance of the six Olympic urban models against the main sustainable-development criteria discussed above, and cross-referenced

Table 9.3 Comparison of Olympic urban models in creating sustainability-orientated impacts

Criteria	S1	S2	S3	S4	S5	S6
Supports urban containment policy	4	5	5	1	3	1
Optimises urban density	1	3	4	3	0	0
Rectifies dispersed urban form	2	4	5	4	3	0
Defines community centres	0	5	4	5	5	5
Encouragement for mixed-use development	3	4	4	5	5	4
Brownfield development potential	5	5	5	3	1	2
Promotes public transport systems	1	2	4	5	5	5
Promotes transit-orientated development	0	1	3	5	4	5
Generates inner-city renaissance	3	5	5	2	0	0
Promotes urban greenery and attractive public realm	1	3	3	5	3	5
Revitalises urban run-down areas	4	5	5	4	1	4
Promotes efficient energy systems (CHP/DH)	0	5	4	5	5	5
Creates new urban landmarks	2	5	4	5	2	4
Coherence with the IOC's planning policy	2	5	5	5	2	4
Implementation feasibility	5	2	3	5	4	5
Overall score	33	59	63	62	43	49

(0 = low potential; 5 = high potential)

against the IOC's apparent planning preferences, and also their feasibility of implementation. A 5-credit-based evaluation technique is applied for comparison: a '5' is given to an urban model having a very strong potential to support the principle examined, whereas a '0' is given to those with very low or no potential.

Each Olympic urban model has both strengths and weaknesses and the favoured model must obviously take into account a host city's situation. Nonetheless, it can be concluded that S3 and S4 are superior in general for the process of creating a more sustainable urban form; they are also the most common forms found in Olympic cities so far. S2 has some good impacts but a poor outlook in terms of feasibility; S5 and S6 have many uncertainties in a number of planning issues and should be considered with caution. S1 has the lowest compatibility with the sustainability criteria and also clashes with IOC planning preferences. It should be pointed out that a low score indicates a lower potential to trigger sustainability-orientated Olympic impacts and does not necessarily mean such planning will cause environmental problems.

Key outcomes

S1 is suitable for a city having good infrastructure with no obvious environmental deficiencies to be redressed by planning, but could benefit from modest adjustments to balance overall development. S2 and S3 are suitable for a city suffering from inner-city decline, suburbanisation and sprawl. They help to re-nucleate an evenly dispersed urban form and introduce large green and public spaces to the city's central mass.

S4 is suitable for cities experiencing considerable population growth with development pressures and expansion needs. It can help to define development orientation and linear transit-orientated forms. S5 is suitable for large conurbations where internal development pressures need to be organically dispersed and multi-hierarchy settlements need to be reinforced in the region. S6 is suitable for strategic development and coordination of two closely located urban areas.

Reclamation and reuse of brownfield and problematic land (Indicator B-2)

Land modification is a common environmental initiative undertaken in recent Olympic development and this indicator has been devised to reward the reclamation of brownfield (previously used) land and problematic land. 'Problematic land' refers to land requiring rehabilitation in social, economic and ecological terms and includes run-down areas, decaying or derelict estates, environmentally vulnerable sites and contaminated sites caused by natural or human impacts. Credits are given according to the percentage of brownfield and problematic land use within Olympic development. If the scheme involves the release of brownfield land for post-Games projects, those areas can also be counted in the total.

The method of remediation of contaminated sites is as important as the fact that the land is being reclaimed, because it has strong environmental consequences. Two of the most commonly used methods are 'dig and dump', which involves removal of soil and wastes to a landfill site elsewhere; and 'cover layer', which is to cap and seal the contaminated material. Both methods raise environmental concerns: the former clears one site by moving the problems elsewhere, and the latter only quarantines the contaminants, which still have the potential to leach out into water sources over time (CIRIA, 1998). In recent years, innovative *in situ* decontamination techniques have been developed, including biological deconta-mination, soil vapour extraction and soil washing. These methods generally have less long-term environmental impacts and should be encouraged.

Indicator B-2	Score:			
Reclamation and reuse of brownfield and problematic land				
5 Δ > 0.8	**4** 0.6 < Δ ≤ 0.8	**3** 0.4 < Δ ≤ 0.6	**2** 0.2 < Δ ≤ 0.4	**1** 0 < Δ ≤ 0.2

	Assessment criteria	Good	Medium	Poor
1	Percentage of overall land inventory for Olympic urban development from the reclamation of brownfield land and problematic land: **Good**: 50% and above; **Medium**: 30%–50%; **Poor**: 30% and below	2	1	0
2	Percentage of contaminated land treated by using sustainable decontamination methods (i.e. avoidance of 'dig and dump' or 'cover layer' methods): **Good**: 75% and above; **Medium**: 30%–75%; **Poor**: 30% and below	2	1	0
Maximum credits:	4	**Credits awarded:**		
Indicator B-2		**Assessment index (Δ):**		

Appropriate form of development: grain, layout and density (Indicator B-3)

The form of development affects the viability of Olympic sites and their integration into the host city. Grain is a term used to describe the pattern made by the buildings and streets forming a development. The grain and division of urban blocks can determine whether they are pedestrian-friendly or vehicle-orientated communities; the layout of streets and footpaths and the orientation of buildings impact on the movement patterns within the area; the density of development affects the population capacity and the requirement for public amenities; and the scale of development directly influences resource consumption and post-Olympic adaptation. All these parameters contribute to the nature of the built environment created and also impact on the microclimate of the Olympic sites.

Indicator B-3	Score:				
Appropriate form of development: grain, layout and density					
5 $\Delta > 0.8$	**4** $0.6 < \Delta \leq 0.8$	**3** $0.4 < \Delta \leq 0.6$	**2** $0.2 < \Delta \leq 0.4$	**1** $0 < \Delta \leq 0.2$	
Assessment criteria			Good	Medium	Poor
Grain					
1	The grain of the development is appropriate to needs (e.g. supports sports venue design in terms of orientation, circulation and zoning for crowd control and security)		4	2	0
2	The grain of the development is appropriate to the surrounding context (e.g. matches or merges into the surrounding grain)		2	1	0
Layout					
3	Public spaces are linked by routes that can be used by pedestrians		2	1	0
4	Routes within the development are well-connected into existing urban road network		2	1	0
5	Primary pedestrian and vehicular routes are designed to be separate but coherent within the development		4	2	0
6	Public squares, streets and spaces are designed to give a sense of enclosure through the use of buildings, structural elements, vegetation, etc.		2	1	0
7	Route nodes and public spaces are designed to enable users to orientate themselves within the development, through use of paving, elevations, buildings, visual landmarks, etc.		2	1	0
8	Works of art, signage systems and other memorial structures are beneficially incorporated into the development and are suitable for post-Games period		2	1	0
9	The development is well zoned (taking account of the 'asymmetries of the competition cycle', particularly in the Olympic Villages)		2	1	0
Density					
10	Residential density of the Olympic Village: **Good**: 250 pph and above; **Medium**: 101–249 pph; **Poor**:100 pph and below		2	1	0
11	The development supports Transit-Oriented-Development, i.e. follows a clear strategy of increasing development densities with access to public transportation		2	1	0
12	If development density contrasts significantly with the surrounding areas, measures are taken to merge the development into surrounding environment		2	1	0
Maximum credits:		28	**Credits awarded:**		
Indicator B-3			**Assessment index (Δ):**		

In order to make the form of a development consistent with surrounding urban context, the grain and layout of neighbouring blocks need to be studied to provide input information. Yet, as much Olympic urban development is centred on sports venues, the particular requirements of the venue, in terms of shape, dimension and orientation, should be considered as the primary issue to enable fulfilment of its function. For instance, pitch orientation must be suitable for the events to be staged. This depends on the location of the stadium, the time of the year in which the designated sports will be played and specific local environmental conditions, such as wind direction. Sunlight/shade and wind patterns should not disturb athletes (nor spectators if possible), and design should take these features into account. The best orientation in the northern hemisphere for most athletic and pitch events is for the longitudinal axis of the pitch to run between 45 degrees west of north and 20 degrees east of north. Sometimes an optimum is difficult to achieve when wind conditions are included; however, special design features for the roofscape and wind-shields may compensate. Computer simulation techniques have been used to determine design parameters and can have beneficial impacts even at the masterplanning stage.

Residential density is a key issue for the development of Olympic Villages. Sustainable development principles encourage a rather compact urban form for the purpose of energy and land-resource efficiency and socio-economic vitality. Barton *et al.* (1995) believe a minimum density of 100 persons per hectare (pph) is required to enable the operation of a good bus service in an area. Thomas and Potter (1977) suggested a density of 250 to 300 pph for a residential block, so that day-to-day facilities for a settlement of 20,000 to 30,000 inhabitants could be accommodated at a pedestrian scale. This was echoed by British Planning Policy Guidance for housing development (PPG3), when it defined good practice standard as 40 dwellings per hectare (dph) or equivalent habitable rooms per hectare (hrh). For Olympic Villages, past experience and the above figures seem to indicate that 200–300 pph would be an appropriate benchmark for the award of a high credit. However, the high-rise building this could encourage is not necessarily suitable for Olympic Villages as it affords less opportunity for socialisation among athletes.

Appropriate form of development: venue scale (Indicator B-4)

The seating capacity of each Olympic venue is a crucial factor in determining the overall scale of the development, including the height and plan dimensions of each venue, the arrangement for car parking and transportation, and the impacts of development on views, vistas and skylines. In light of possible under-utilisation of Olympic venues after the Games are over, the design capacity for new and refurbished venues should be conceived as two figures: the number of permanent seats and the maximum capacity for the Olympic event. If the pitch is to be of variable size to cater for different events then variable seating schemes should be considered. Decisions on a venue's permanent seating capacity should be based on long-term realities such as the city's population, the accessibility of the venue by transport systems (excluding special Olympic provision), the local popularity of the sports, and the existence/location of similar premises of the same type. Nevertheless, as one purpose of building Olympic venues is to attract future

Indicator B-4	Score:						
Appropriate form of development: scale							
5 Δ > 0.8	**4** 0.6 < Δ ≤ 0.8	**3** 0.4 < Δ ≤ 0.6	**2** 0.2 < Δ ≤ 0.4	**1** 0 < Δ ≤ 0.2			

	Assessment criteria	Good	Medium	Poor
1	The seating capacity of the new or refurbished venue is appropriate according to the value range recommended	6	3	0
2	Temporary facilities have been incorporated into the development where possible	2	1	0
3	The surrounding areas have been studied in determining the height and massing of the new development (this is especially applied to Olympic Villages and Olympic non-sports buildings)	2	1	0
4	If the venue's height and massing have a considerable contrast with the surrounding areas, measures have been taken to enable the development to effectively merge into the ambience	2	1	0

Maximum credits:	12	Credits awarded:	
Indicator B-4		Assessment index (Δ):	

international sports events, it is reasonable for a city to develop several large-scale, 'world-class' stadiums that are for more than just the local market.

Regarding seating capacity, one reference is the venue standard set by the International Federation for each Olympic sport and endorsed by the IOC. Yet past experience shows that this figure has often been over-estimated by the ambitious IFs. A more practical proposition would be to evaluate attendance at a particular Olympic event in the past. This takes into account the fact that many on-site Olympic spectators have an interest in a specific sport and that this is a rather stable number in many cases. Other spectators could be described as 'carnival hunters', whose attendance would be affected by factors such as ticket price and availability, accommodation, travel convenience and the cultural profile of the host city. With globalisation some variations are now blurred: when Melbourne hosted the Games in the 1950s, there were fewer Olympic visitors than expected due to the remote location; the high attendance at Sydney in 2000 suggested that more recently the need for long-haul travelling has had less impact on the Olympics.

Figure 9.5 (a–z) illustrates venue capacity and actual occupation for the 26 Olympic sports from Rome to Sydney. The values are determined on an average basis irrespective of differences between events (e.g. preliminary round v. finals) and venues used for the same sport (e.g. different Olympic football grounds). They show the spectator number range for each Olympic sport. The statistics are calculated from Olympic ticketing records, specifically, the tickets available and sold for each venue at each event, which includes the seats reserved for and used by the 'Olympic family' and media representatives but excluding unusable seats due to technical or management reasons.

The diagrams show the average seating capacity and occupation fluctuations over time; for some sports, consistently high attendance can be found irrespective of the change in venue capacity, suggesting there is still potential to increase the number of seats in the future Games. For some others, a deviation between the two tendency lines can be detected when the venue capacity is too high, indicating an over-sizing of the facility and identification of a threshold level for a particular sport. Figure 9.5 enables the derivation of recommended seating capacities for the venues of each Olympic sport, which acts as the benchmark for this evaluation. The standards of the IOC's minimal venue capacity are also listed for comparison, which can be seen to be inappropriate in at least some cases.

Recommendations arising from Figure 9.5:

a   Archery is a relatively low-key Olympic event and normally accommodated within entirely temporary settings. Recommended seating capacity: 4,000 to 4,500.

b   For aquatic sports the diagram shows a consistently high attendance since 1964, suggesting the threshold value for the Olympic aquatic centre could be higher than that of the 1984 and 2000 peaks. Recommended seating capacity: 12,000 to 18,000 (including temporary seating of between 4,000 and 10,000).

c   The athletic stadium is also used for Olympic ceremonies, so its capacity could be larger than required by the sport. Empirical studies, however, suggest that stadium capacities larger than 100,000 have some spectators beyond the maximum viewing distance and also cause circulation difficulties. Recommended seating capacity: 60,000 to 100,000 (including temporary seating of between 10,000 and 50,000).

d   Badminton is relatively new to the Games and thus the sample is comparatively small; nevertheless, it still can be seen from the diagram that the IOC's standard for minimal venue capacity seems a little too high. Recommended seating capacity: 3,000 to 4,500 (including temporary seating of between 500 and 2,500).

Figure 9.5 a–d
Trends in venue capacity and attendance for individual sports compared to Olympic recommendations (for legend see page 166)

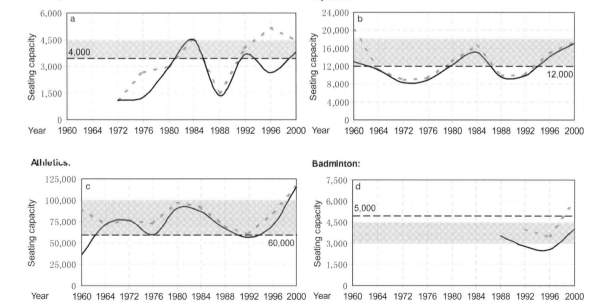

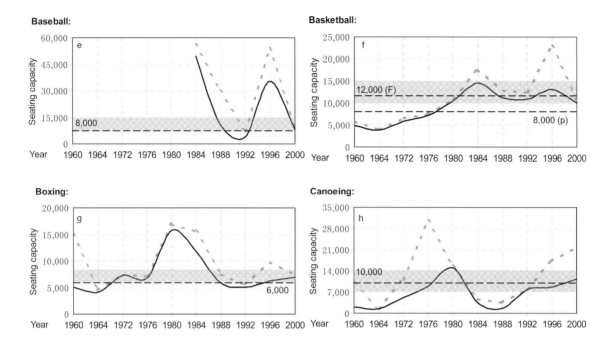

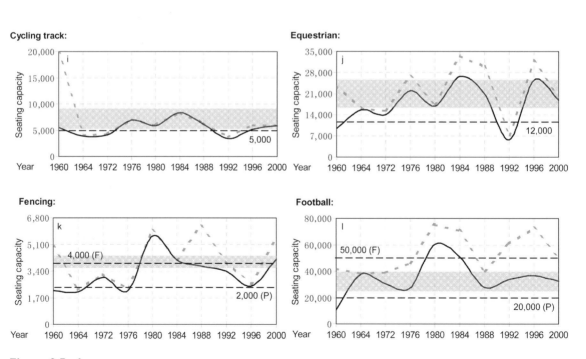

Figure 9.5e–l

Trends in venue capacity and attendance for individual sports compared to Olympic recommendations – continued (for legend see page 166)

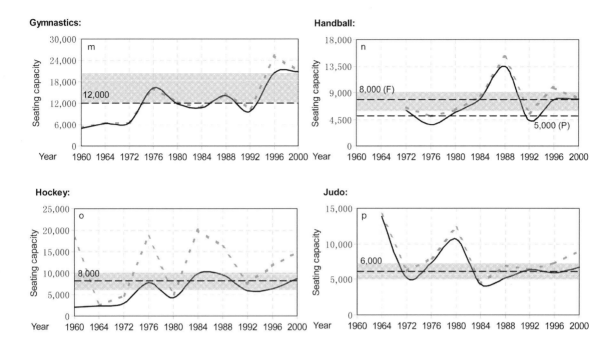

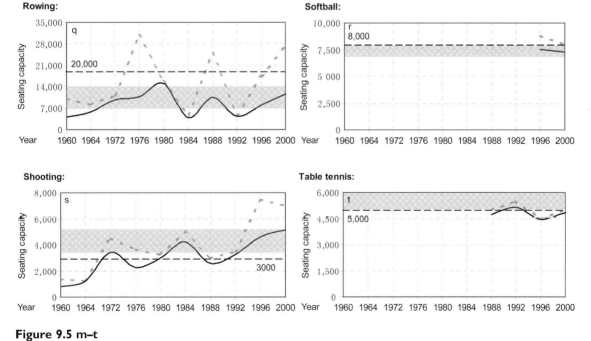

Figure 9.5 m–t

Trends in venue capacity and attendance for individual sports compared to Olympic recommendations – continued (for legend see page 166)

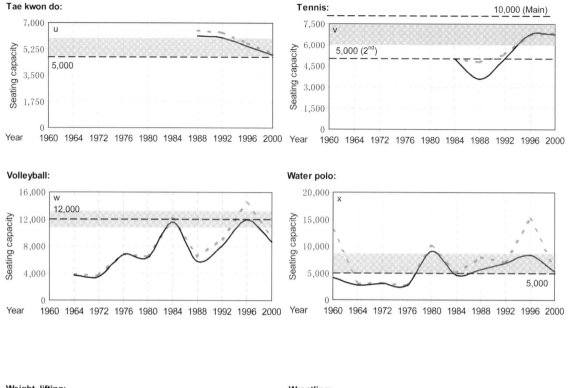

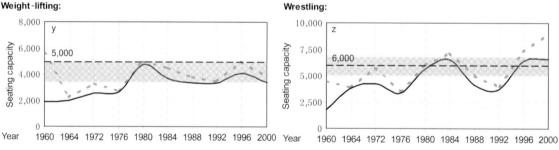

Legend for diagrams

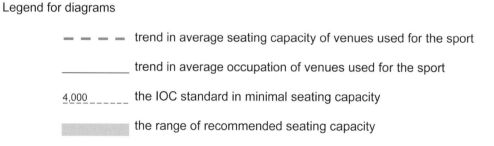

– – – – trend in average seating capacity of venues used for the sport

_____ trend in average occupation of venues used for the sport

4,000 _ _ _ _ _ _ the IOC standard in minimal seating capacity

▨▨▨ the range of recommended seating capacity

Figure 9.5 u–z
Trends in venue capacity and attendance for individual sports compared to Olympic recommendations – continued

e   Baseball varies considerably because of different levels of popularity in different parts of the world (it is a very high-profile event in the USA but less so elsewhere). Recommended seating capacity: 8,000 to 15,000 (including temporary seating of between 2,000 and 9,000); however, in North America, the figures could be enlarged.

f   Venue capacity for Olympic basketball events has increased since the 1970s, although values for 1984 and 1996 suggest 15,000 might be a threshold for an Olympic event. Recommended seating capacity: 10,000 to 15,000 (including temporary seating of between 2,000 and 7,000).

g   Although 1980 saw a leap in audience capacities for boxing, it is normally regarded as a medium-sized Olympic event; due to the dimension of boxing rings a significant number of temporary seats can be arranged. Recommended seating capacity: 6,000 to 8,000 (including temporary seating of between 3,000 and 5,000).

h   For canoeing it seems that oversized facilities were provided in 1976, 1996 and 2000; the attendance line suggests that 14,000 would be a reasonable threshold. Recommended seating capacity: 7,000 to 14,000 (including temporary seating of between 4,000 and 11,000).

i   Cycling attendance seems relatively stable over time, with potential to enlarge venue capacities up to about 9,000. Recommended seating capacity: 5,000 to 9,000 (including temporary seating of between 1,000 and 5,000).

j   Equestrian event spectator numbers are generally in line with the seating availability, although deviations in 1976, 1984 and 1996 suggest a certain degree of over-capacity. Recommended seating capacity: 16,000 to 26,000 (including temporary seating of between 8,000 and 18,000).

k   Fencing is a small-scale Olympic sport. Historically, the difference between the highest and the lowest seating capacity is only about 2,000. Except for 1980, attendance has been less than 4,500. Recommended seating capacity: 3,500 to 4,500 (including temporary seating of between 1,500 and 2,500).

l   Football attendance is very dependent on the stage in the competition and the attraction of the teams playing. This partly explains the similar average attendances for different seating capacities. Since the finals are often staged in the Olympic Stadium, the capacities for preliminary rounds can be set rather smaller. Recommended seating capacity (preliminary rounds): 25,000 to 40,000 (including temporary seating of between 5,000 and 20,000).

m   Gymnastics is a popular Olympic sport; the figures suggest 20,000 as a threshold value for the venue. Recommended seating capacity: 12,000 to 20,000 (including temporary seating of between 4,000 and 12,000).

n   Handball enjoys particular popularity in South Korea, which explains the high attendances in 1988; for other Games, attendance has been below 9,000. Recommended seating capacity: 6,000 to 9,000 (including temporary seating of between 2,000 and 5,000).

o   The IOC's standard for hockey has changed several times and can be seen in the large seating capacities for 1960, 1976, 1984 and 1988. Actual attendances suggest 10,000 may normally be the limit for hockey. Recommended seating capacity: 6,000 to 10,000 (including temporary seating of between 3,000 and 7,000).

p   Judo event capacity has fallen during recent Games with attendance of less than 7,000 since 1984. Due to the dimension of judo mats and nature of the sport it is possible to arrange temporary seating. Recommended seating capacity: 5,000 to 7,000 (including temporary seating of between 3,000 and 5,000).

q   For rowing there are deviations in 1976, 1988, 1996 and 2000, suggesting over-sizing of facilities. The diagram shows the IOC's standard is high compared to attendances; Olympic rowing often shares the same course as canoeing, therefore the latter's seating capacity range can be used as a reference. Recommended seating capacity: 7,000 to 14,000 (including temporary seating of between 4,000 and 11,000).

r   Softball is a new sport to the Olympic Games; the attendances in 1996 and 2000 can be used to set venue capacity. Recommended seating capacity: 7,000 to 8,000 (including temporary seating of between 3,000 and 4,000).

s   Venue capacity for Olympic shooting events has increased steadily since the 1960s, although considering figures for 1996 and 2000, 5,000 seems to be a sensible threshold. Recommended seating capacity: 3,500 to 5,000 (including temporary seating of between 2,000 and 3,500).

t   Table tennis is a comparatively new Olympic sport. Attendance has been relatively high since 1988 suggesting there is space to enlarge the venue capacity to 6,000 and to allow for significant numbers of temporary seats. Recommended seating capacity: 5,000 to 6,000 (including temporary seating of between 3,000 and 4,000).

u   Tae kwon do has experienced a decrease in seating capacity in recent Games, although previous attendances suggest a threshold value of 6,000. Large numbers of temporary seats can also be considered. Recommended seating capacity: 5,000 to 6,000 (including temporary seating of between 3,000 and 4,000).

v   For tennis, more recent attendance figures for preliminary rounds suggest an increase in popularity, therefore 7,500 could be an average capacity but with some variability over several courts. Recommended seating capacity: 6,000 to 7,500 (including temporary seating of between 3,000 and 4,500).

w   Volleyball (indoor) is another popular Olympic sport with high attendances and 13,000 being a venue threshold. (Note that beach volleyball is excluded due to its recent inclusion in the Olympics.) Recommended seating capacity: 11,000 to 13,000 (including temporary seating of between 5,000 and 7,000).

x   For water polo there are deviations between capacity and attendance in 1960, 1988 and 1996, suggesting a certain degree of over-sizing. Generally, attendance is less than 8,000. Recommended seating capacity: 5,000 to 8,000 (including temporary seating of between 1,000 and 4,000).

y   Weightlifting is a small-scale Olympic sport and it seems the IOC's standard for minimal venue capacity is higher than actual attendance; 5,000 can be identified as the threshold value. Recommended seating capacity: 3,500 to 5,000 (including temporary seating of between 500 and 2,000).

z   Wrestling has experienced varying attendance; these suggest 6,500 as the threshold value for an Olympic wrestling venue. As with judo, a large number of temporary seats can be added. Recommended seating capacity: 5,000 to 6,500 (including temporary seating of between 3,000 and 4,500).

In the case of Indicator B-4 (which is designed to be applied to each Olympic development site or venue) scores for all sites/venues can be averaged or it is possible to evaluate each component of the indicator if such level of detail is required; however, if different venues are considered to be of different levels of importance, the overall assessment may be adjusted and weighted for this factor. This means of averaging and weighting can also be applied to other indicators where an evaluation can be carried out for each venue separately or in combination with others.

Energy consumption (Indicators C-1 to C-5)

Energy efficiency and use of alternative sources are important both as a means for avoiding climate change/global warming and to avoid cost increases and security of supply associated with fossil fuels. Several assessment tools have developed over a period of time focusing on different impact measures and it is clearly important to evaluate energy performance of Olympic developments. This section focuses on sports venues; for other types of building, such as housing (e.g. Olympic Villages) and offices (e.g. MPC and IBC), there are well-established evaluation frameworks already available. These should be used as a matter of course according to building type and can be incorporated into other broader assessment tools as appropriate (such as BREEAM and LEED, discussed in Chapter 8). In terms of use in the evaluation system proposed here, each building that can be assessed using an established assessment tool should have such an assessment performed. Since each host country will have its own set of regulations an indication of performance might be gained by establishing the degree of improvement over existing regulations that each venue achieves. A base standard would be compliance with standards at the time the project commenced with a sliding scale indicating improvements – say, from one credit for meeting current regulations up to ten credits for creating a net zero-carbon building. No indicator is formally proposed for such scoring of buildings since it can already be undertaken; however, the issue of Olympic sports venues is somewhat different, requiring more attention.

Energy use in Olympic venues

In order to establish the energy-load profile for Olympic Stadiums, it is useful to look at each of the energy-consuming components of the venue. Figure 9.6 illustrates the types of energy use in a typical stadium: there are 11 components identified under four system headings; their application to different types of venue is illustrated in Figure 9.7,

The energy-consuming components can be summarised as follows:

* Hot water is delivered to players' changing areas, public toilet outlets, food and beverage catering facilities and private suites in high-specification stadiums. Sometimes it is also used for the space-heating network and to warm the swimming pool.
* Thermal environmental control systems include components for space heating, cooling and ventilation. In temperate climates some form of heating is required

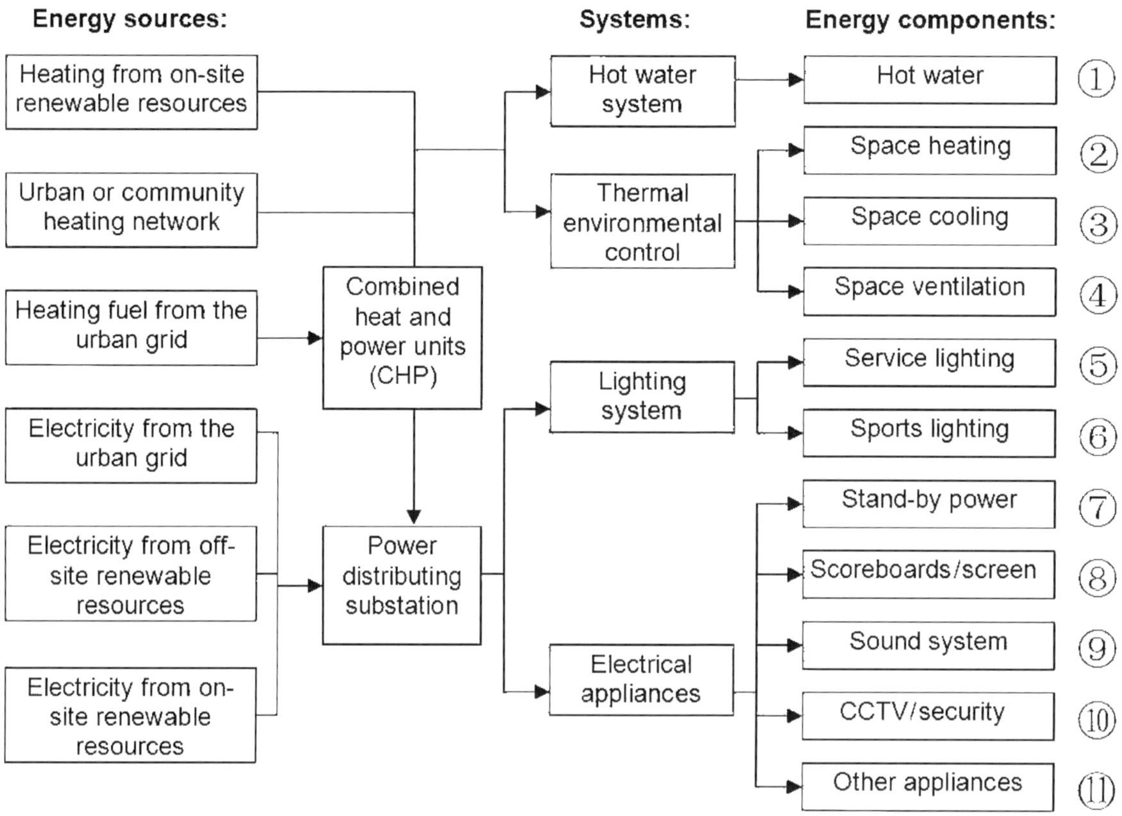

Energy sources:

Systems:

Energy components:

Heating from on-site renewable resources

Urban or community heating network

Heating fuel from the urban grid

Combined heat and power units (CHP)

Electricity from the urban grid

Electricity from off-site renewable resources

Power distributing substation

Electricity from on-site renewable resources

Hot water system

Thermal environmental control

Lighting system

Electrical appliances

Hot water ①

Space heating ②

Space cooling ③

Space ventilation ④

Service lighting ⑤

Sports lighting ⑥

Stand-by power ⑦

Scoreboards/screen ⑧

Sound system ⑨

CCTV/security ⑩

Other appliances ⑪

Figure 9.6
Energy sources and uses for a typical stadium

in all types of sports halls, aquatic premises, velodrome, shooting gallery and many of the ancillary spaces in large stadiums. Sometimes, heating is also used in the open-air stadium; for instance, heating ducts under seats and pitch. Cooling and air-conditioning systems are very large energy consumers and should only be considered in high-specification halls, large stadiums with complex ancillary spaces, and the aquatic centre where control may be needed over temperature and humidity. Simpler ventilation systems are preferred where possible as a low-energy alternative for indoor spaces.

• Lighting systems allow sporting events to be played and watched at night. They include service lighting (use in supportive and ancillary spaces in large and complex arenas); and sports lighting (floodlighting for the event area). Some Olympic sports, such as shooting, archery, rowing and canoeing, are normally arranged as daytime outdoor events; intensive lighting systems therefore may not be necessary in these venues.

• Basic electrical systems' power for scoreboards, sound systems and security apparatus are essential facilities for sports venues, either in permanent or temporary form. Other appliances may include large screens, pitch irrigation systems and motors to operate opening roofs, movable pitches and retractable seats if used. In Figure 9.7 small electrical appliances are ignored.

Type of Olympic venue	Olympic sports	Energy components										
		1	2	3	4	5	6	7	8	9	10	11
Large open-air stadiums	opening/closing ceremony, football, baseball, softball, equestrian	■	■	■		■		■	■		■	■
Medium/small open-air stadiums	hockey, tennis, volleyball beach	■				■		■	■		■	■
Temporary open-air venues/courses	archery, cycling (circus), marathon, cross country, canoe slalom, sailing	■							■		■	■
Regatta	canoeing, rowing	■						■	■		■	■
Large halls	basketball, volleyball, gymnastics (artistic, rhythmic and trampoline), handball	■	■		■	■		■	■		■	■
Medium/small halls	badminton, boxing, table tennis, wrestling, weightlifting, fencing, judo, tae kwon do	■		■	■	■		■	■			■
Aquatic complex (preferably indoors)	swimming, water polo, diving, synchronised pool events	■		■	■	■		■	■		■	■
Velodrome (preferably indoors)	cycling track	■			■	■		■	■		■	■
Shooting range (semi-indoors)	shooting	■			■		■	■	■		■	■

There are three generic criteria for the evaluation of energy use in Olympic venues: first to minimise the demand for energy by good design; second to supply much of the reduced demand from new and renewable resources; and third to fulfil the remaining requirements with efficient use of the cleanest available fuels.

Figure 9.7
Energy system components used in different types of venue

Setting energy benchmarks for Olympic venues

Building energy performance can be rated by comparison with benchmarks or standards on energy consumption so that credits can be awarded according to the level it has attained. Many evaluation frameworks adopt this simple approach but have limitations because of the narrow range of building types for which benchmarks can be defined, and also the impact of climatic variations.

The situation in Olympic venues is complicated as sports buildings are very diverse in function and settings. Open-air stadiums, indoor halls, swimming pools, ice rinks, white-water courses and shooting galleries all have very different energy demands. In theory it may be possible to define different sets of benchmark for each of the building types for the Summer Olympic sports. In practice, however, this might be unrealistic because many Olympic venues are designed as multi-functional complexes with different sports facilities and use patterns. Further, large sports complexes often encompass different forms of non-sports spaces, such as banqueting halls, entertainment lounges, hotel rooms and commercial centres. John and Sheard (2001) reported that in a major multi-purpose stadium the energy demand from those non-sports functions over the year might exceed that for large spectator events. Due to the highly integrated design it is difficult to separate the different energy loads, making comparisons very difficult.

The operation of sports venues is intermittent and dependent on activities (not always sports events) and the systems in use. Longer or more intense use will increase energy consumption, but a low figure for annual energy consumption may result from under-utilisation rather than energy-efficient design. The use of 'annual energy consumption per spectator' values as the indicator has been proposed. For example, the annual energy usage for the Melbourne Cricket Ground is approximately 4,200MWh with attendance figures of around 2.93 million; the energy index is therefore approximately 1.4kWh per person but does not include venue area.

Energy benchmarks are also sensitive to the external climate, the available building technologies and applicable regulations. It may be impossible to develop a range of universal benchmarks for use by all Olympic host cities for venue evaluation, so in this framework, energy efficiency is considered in terms of energy-saving measures utilised rather than targets. The indicator is based on lighting systems, thermal control systems and use of renewable energy.

Energy-efficient lighting systems (Indicator C-1)

Energy saving in sports venue lighting systems has three components: use of daylight where possible in both sports and non-sports spaces; use of efficient light

Indicator C-1	Score:					
Energy efficient lighting systems						
5 Δ > 0.8	**4** 0.6 < Δ ≤ 0.8	**3** 0.4 < Δ ≤ 0.6	**2** 0.2 < Δ ≤ 0.4	**1** 0 < Δ ≤ 0.2		
Assessment criteria				Good	Medium	Poor
1	Daylight penetration to the venue's perimeter spaces is maximised by optimising the window-wall ratio and shading device of the facade			2	1	0
2	Clearstory, light pipes or roof glazing system are used wherever possible to light even spaces			2	1	0
3	Translucent canopy is used wherever possible for spectator areas (open-air venue)			2	1	0
4	Light shelves, light wells or atria are introduced to bring daylight into spaces buried deeper			2	1	0
5	Internal surface is decorated by using bright colour and high albedos materials and textures to reflect as much light as possible			2	1	0
6	The level of illuminance matches the requirements of the sport event and the venue's capacity			2	1	0
7	Multi-level switching system is introduced to control the lighting efficiently for different purpose, individual courts can be lit independently			2	1	0
8	Automatic control devices such as photocells and movement sensors are introduced to modulate the lighting switching and levels in frequently used spaces			2	1	0
9	Energy-efficient light fittings are used with carefully distribution			4	2	0
Maximum credits:	20	**Credits awarded:**				
Indicator C-1		**Assessment index (Δ):**				

fittings and rationalisation of illumination levels; and optimising distribution, maintenance and control systems including different switching levels.

Naturally-lit spaces save energy and often create a more pleasant visual ambience for athletes and spectators; daylight is also necessary for pitch turf growth. For open-air stadiums, a translucent canopy can be used over spectator areas and to fade pitch shadows for a softer contrast; for indoor arenas, a skylight can reduce the artificial lighting required. The use of natural light should be taken into account at design concept stage and may impact on the building structure. External fenestration can be optimised for daylight penetration, and devices such as light shelves, light wells and atria can be used to bring daylight into more concealed areas.

The level of illuminance required for a sports event often determines the selection of light fittings and hence the energy load. Since many sports involve observing a fast-moving object, such as in ball games, the event area normally requires an illuminance level from 300 to 1,500 lux. The minimum lighting requirements depend on the sport types and the standard of play because of the different speeds, distances and colour contrasts involved. The smaller the object and the faster it moves the higher the illumination required; also at higher standard events, higher illumination levels may be expected. The venue size is a further consideration because the lighting level may depend upon the needs of spectators sitting furthest from the action. Lighting requirements for professional television coverage are generally higher than even the best visual standard due to camera contrast

Table 9.4 Minimum lighting requirements (lux) for some Olympic sports

Sports	International (televised)		Inferior competition (spectator < 5,000)		Club competition (no spectators)		Training/recreational (schools)	
	Horizontal	Vertical	Horizontal	Vertical	Horizontal	Vertical	Horizontal	Vertical
Archery (target)	750	1,000	750	750	750	750	500	750
Archery (shooting zone)	300	300	200	200	200	200	200	200
Aquatic sports	1,500	1,500	750	750	500	500	300	300
Athletics	500	500	300	300	100	100	100	100
Baseball	1,500	1,000	1,000	700	500	400	300	250
Badminton	1,200	1,200	750	750	500	500	300	300
Basketball	1,200	1,200	750	750	500	500	300	300
Boxing	500	200	300	200	100	100	100	100
Cycling	500	500	300	300	100	100	100	100
Football	1,000	800	500	400	300	250	200	150
Gymnastics	1,200	1,200	500	500	300	300	200	200
Handball	500	300	300	200	150	100	150	100
Hockey	500	500	300	300	250	250	200	200
Shooting	1,000	1,500	500	1,000	100	500	100	300
Table tennis	1,500	1,500	750	750	500	500	400	400
Tennis	1,000	1,000	750	750	400	400	300	300
Volleyball	1,000	500	500	300	300	200	200	150
Wrestling	500	200	300	200	100	100	100	100

(Horizontal = horizontal illuminance; Vertical = vertical illuminance)

limitations. As a result, a single sport may have several illuminance scenarios: training (without spectators); competition (with or without spectators); and important competitions with television coverage. Although Olympic venues should be designed to satisfy the highest standard of performance as well as the greatest spectator capacity, it will be more energy efficient to have several switching levels to allow different illumination for different kinds of activity. Moveable and individually switched lights may also allow adaptation of one arena for different events. Table 9.4 summarises typical lighting levels for a variety of Olympic sports.

Energy efficiency of light fittings is generally considered in terms of luminance efficacy (lumens per watt) and lamp control-gear loss (watts). Although energy-efficient fittings should be considered as the priority, other factors such as maximum illuminance, lifespan (hours) and cost, should be well balanced.

Energy-efficient thermal control systems (Indicators C-2 and C-3)

Generally, thermal comfort requirements for sports venues are less stringent than those for offices and homes because adaptation is more feasible when watching sport or other events. A typical preferred temperature in an office building may be 20°C to 22°C, whereas between 16°C and 26°C or wider may be found

Indicator C-2	Score:			
Energy efficient heating systems				
5 Δ > 0.8 **4** 0.6 < Δ ≤ 0.8 **3** 0.4 < Δ ≤ 0.6 **2** 0.2 < Δ ≤ 0.4 **1** 0 < Δ ≤ 0.2				

Assessment criteria		Good	Medium	Poor
1	The orientation, landscaping, site planning and building morphology of the venue have been carefully conceived to maximise the solar gains in the winter season	2	1	0
2	Venue is designed with compact form and high volume to surface ratio to reduce fabric losses	2	1	0
3	Building components exceed the requirements of insulation value in local building regulations; and appropriate insulation has been applied to avoid cold bridges in the building fabric	4	2	0
4	Earth shelter or other forms of thermal mass are used to reduce fluctuations of internal air temperatures and also as passive heating sources	2	1	0
5	Wind shield, airtight windows and airtight detail junctions are used to reduce the air infiltration	2	1	0
6	High efficient heating system is considered, including high efficient boilers, ground heating system, heat recovery and storage techniques etc.	2	1	0
7	Efficient control to heating system is established based on the use of venue spaces and the level of occupancy	2	1	0
8	If the heating system is directly supplied by the district heating network, high insulation is applied to the water pipes so that heat loss can be minimised during the distribution	2	1	0
Maximum credits:	18	**Credits awarded:**		
Indicator C-2		**Assessment index (Δ):**		

Indicator C-3	Score:						
Energy efficient cooling and ventilation systems							
5 $\Delta > 0.8$	**4** $0.6 < \Delta \leq 0.8$	**3** $0.4 < \Delta \leq 0.6$	**2** $0.2 < \Delta \leq 0.4$	**1** $0 < \Delta \leq 0.2$			

Assessment criteria		Good	Medium	Poor
1	Bioclimatic design features such as green belt, green space and natural water are introduced to improve the microclimate around the venue site	2	1	0
2	Shading device is used to avoid over heating from solar radiation	2	1	0
3	Light colour and materials with high albedos are selected for the venue's external walls	2	1	0
4	Earth shelter or other forms of thermal mass are used as part of passive cooling strategy to reduce fluctuations of internal air temperatures	2	1	0
5	The potential of natural ventilation is harnessed by appropriating the venue's shape, layout, orientation and openings and/or through the application of special structures like wind towers, solar chimneys, atria and ductworks etc.	4	2	0
6	Other passive cooling techniques such as night cooling, desiccant cooling, buried earth pipes, chilled ceiling and heat sinks etc. are explored in the scheme wherever possible	2	1	0
7	If mechanical cooling is inevitable, high efficient HAVC system is conceived, e.g. to use extract fans rather than artificial cooling as the first consideration; to use high efficient air conditioners or heat pumps that combine the use of natural cooling resources such as river, ground water or sewage	2	1	0
8	Innovative HVAC scheme is considered to match the character of sports venues (e.g. large space, flexible range in thermal comfort and intermittent running pattern etc.)	2	1	0
9	Efficient control to HVAC system is established based on the use of venue space and the level of occupancy	2	1	0
Maximum credits:	20	**Credits awarded:**		
Indicator C-3		**Assessment index (Δ):**		

acceptable for stadiums. Except for a few sports, most Olympic events have no specified requirements for thermal conditions from their International Federations. This means a flexible approach can be applied with respect to environmental standards; it also means less energy needs to be invested in heating, cooling and ventilation in sports buildings than many other building types. Even so, some forms of thermal modulation are essential in Olympic venues to ensure a minimum acceptable level of comfort.

There are three aids to improved energy efficiency: first, use of passive heating and cooling technologies to minimise the demands on HVAC systems; second, use of energy-efficient appliances and distribution in essential HVAC systems; finally, use of efficient and effective controls.

Passive thermal control techniques provide a means to achieve acceptable comfort in designated spaces by natural or low-energy means, such as prevention or encouragement of solar (heat) gains; modulation of heat storage capacity of buildings; and use of heat dissipation. For Olympic venues, the highest demand with large spectator numbers may occur in summer rather than winter, therefore passive cooling and ventilation techniques deserve more attention. The overall

Indicator C-4	Score:					
Use of new and renewable energy resources						
5 Δ > 0.8	**4** 0.6 < Δ ≤ 0.8	**3** 0.4 < Δ ≤ 0.6	**2** 0.2 < Δ ≤ 0.4	**1** 0 < Δ ≤ 0.2		

	Assessment criteria	Good	Medium	Poor
1	The potential of the Olympic site to use new and renewable energy has been studied	2	1	0
2	What percentage of electricity consumed by the venue is produced from an on-site renewable scheme (e.g. wind turbines, PV panel, geothermal etc.) **Good**: 25% and above; **Medium**: 10%–24%; **Poor**: 9% and below	2	1	0
3	In the rest of the electricity load apart from above, what percentage is produced from an off-site renewable scheme (e.g. purchasing green power from the energy market) **Good**: 60% and above; **Medium**: 30%–59%; **Poor**: 29% and below	2	1	0
4	What percentage of hot water consumed by the venue is produced from an on-site renewable scheme (e.g. solar collector, geothermal pump etc.) **Good**: 40% and above; **Medium**: 20%–39%; **Poor**: 19% and below	2	1	0
Maximum credits:	8	**Credits awarded:**		
Indicator C-4		**Assessment index (Δ):**		

Indicator C-5	Score:					
Other energy saving initiatives						
5 Δ > 0.8	**4** 0.6 < Δ ≤ 0.8	**3** 0.4 < Δ ≤ 0.6	**2** 0.2 < Δ ≤ 0.4	**1** 0 < Δ ≤ 0.2		

	Assessment criteria	Good	Medium	Poor
1	Sports equipment with high efficiency ratings are used in the venue	2	1	0
2	For aquatic centre, covers are utilised when pool is not in use to retain heat	2	1	0
3	Well matched and integrated Combined Heat and Power (CHP) plant is used to produce heat and electricity	6	3	0
4	Hot water for venue toilets assessed and minimised; time-control fittings are used (e.g. push-button showers)	2	1	0
5	Measures introduced to minimise electricity distribution losses	2	1	0
6	Innovations to reduce the overall energy demand from venue operation have been considered (e.g. photo-luminous way-finding system)	2	1	0
7	Energy monitoring and management system has been established for the venue	2	1	0
8	Greenhouse gas emissions from all energy used at the venue is assessed and reported upon, on a regular basis	2	1	0
Maximum credits:	20	**Credits awarded:**		
Indicator C-5		**Assessment index (Δ):**		

Water conservation (Indicator D-1)

Water is a scarce resource in many parts of the world and deserves conservation in new developments; and Olympic venues could be designed as demonstration projects. In addition, adverse impacts of Olympic development on local water resources should be minimised by considering several issues: the selection of

Indicator D-1	Score:			
Water conservation				
5 Δ > 0.8 **4** 0.6 < Δ ≤ 0.8 **3** 0.4 < Δ ≤ 0.6 **2** 0.2 < Δ ≤ 0.4 **1** 0 < Δ ≤ 0.2				

	Assessment criteria	Good	Medium	Poor
1	Local water resources surveyed and assessed before planning the development	2	1	0
2	Selection of Olympic sites minimises impacts on existing watersheds, watercourses and ground water levels	2	1	0
3	Sustainable drainage systems used on the site to control surface water run-off	4	2	0
4	Passive treatment systems introduced to deal with surface water from venue operation and construction process (e.g. detention ponds and reed beds etc.)	2	1	0
5	Potable water and grey water are designed as separate systems at the venue	2	1	0
6	Rainwater is collected from roofs and run-off points and stored around the venue or fed into the greywater system after treatment	4	2	0
6	Greywater is recycled for non-potable uses	2	1	0
7	Percentage of water usage in the venue from rainwater and recycled grey water: **Good**: 30% and above; **Medium**: 10%–29%; **Poor**: 9% and below	2	1	0
8	Leak detectors used in venue water systems	2	1	0
9	Low flush, vacuum toilets used at the venue; aerated taps installed; automatic control systems used to urinal cleaning etc.	4	2	0
10	Suitable planting and vegetation encouraged around the development site and drought resistant turf selected to reduce the need for irrigation	2	1	0
11	Water metering is used around the venue, and the consumption monitored and evaluated on a periodic basis	2	1	0

Maximum credits:	30	Credits awarded:	
Indicator D-1		Assessment index (Δ):	

Olympic sites should avoid impinging on existing watersheds; watercourse and ground water levels should be protected; sustainable drainage systems should be specified and permeable paving used for hardstanding areas to facilitate water infiltration into the soil and to filter pollutants. Surface run-off occurring during normal operation, but particularly during the building process, should be treated before entering the public drainage network to avoid the contamination of water resources. This can be achieved partly by exploiting detention ponds and reed beds.

Large sports venues consume substantial amounts of water at times of peak spectator attendance – for drinking, toilet flushing and pitch irrigation (the aquatic centre must be considered separately however). Demands for potable water can be reduced by separating supply systems and establishing rainwater collection and grey-water recycling systems for non-potable purposes. The large areas of roofs and canopies of Olympic venues can be used as collecting and run-off platforms.

Water consumption can be further reduced by using water-saving fittings such as aerated spray taps; leak detectors; low-flush, chemical or vacuum toilets; automatic control systems to minimise the use of water (such as push-button taps); and infrared detectors to control urinal flushing. Planting and vegetation can be useful to hold water on site, drought-resistant turf can be selected to minimise the need for irrigation, and water features can be introduced to the site not only to enhance the microclimate and encourage wildlife, but also to be used as rainwater and grey-water storage and settling ponds.

Materials and structures for sustainable Olympic venues (Indicator E-1)

Use of sustainable materials and structures in Olympic developments can not only reduce depletion of natural resources and other negative environmental consequences but also provide a strong exemplar to designers. The extraction, processing, manufacture, transport and installation of building products all involve use of resources, energy and water, and can contribute to pollution and environmental

Indicator E-1	Score:			
Materials and structures for sustainable Olympic venues				
5 Δ > 0.08	**4** 0.6 < Δ < 0.8	**3** 0.4 < Δ ≤ 0.6	**2** 0.2 < Δ ≤ 0.4	**1** 0 < Δ ≤ 0.2

	Assessment criteria	Good	Medium	Poor
	Use of materials and structures with low embodied impact			
1	Venue structure is lightweight to avoid large resource use	4	2	0
2	Prefabricated components with pre-stressing and post-tensioning techniques are used in engineering of the development to save materials	2	1	0
3	Local or national 'green material guide' developed/used for materials selection	2	1	0
4	Venue designed to maximise the use of natural materials and materials with low embodied environmental impacts	4	2	0
5	Venue designed to avoid the use of toxic or ozone depleting materials, or volatile organic compounds	2	1	0
6	Venue designed to maximise the use of local produced materials	2	1	0
7	Timber and renewable organic products are from verifiable sustainable sources	2	1	0
8	Life Cycle Assessment (LCA) carried out to examine venue environmental impact	2	1	0
	Encouraging reuse and recycling of materials			
9	Evidence that availability of local recyclable materials has been surveyed and considered in the design of the venue	2	1	0
10	Building products containing recycled materials selected as priority	2	1	0
11	Venue designed for disassembly, including cladding materials and finishes	2	1	0
12	Venue design considers local modular systems	2	1	0
13	Materials selected for high durability to enable reuse	2	1	0
14	Waste management system established on construction sites with wastes recycled on site wherever possible	2	1	0
15	Collection points and facilities for reusable materials from day-to-day operation integrated into the layout of the venue to encourage recycling over the longer term	4	2	0
	Efficient site management			
16	Material quantities estimated appropriately to avoid over purchase	2	1	0
17	Site storage well organised to minimise damage or loss of materials	2	1	0
18	Off-cuts of materials collected for use on-site rather than disposed of as waste	2	1	0
Maximum credits:	40	**Credits awarded:**		
Indicator E-1		**Assessment index (Δ):**		

impacts. Careful selection of materials and construction elements reduces the overall 'embodied impact' of the building. A number of evaluation schemes are available to aid the selection and specification process. Building materials and structures also affect the architectural spaces they form and consequently the operational and energy demands of those spaces in the long term. Further, materials selection affects durability and the potential for disassembly, reuse and recycling. Each of the above issues is highly interlinked and the selection and assessment of the source of materials used in the construction of buildings should be carried out on the basis of life-cycle analysis/evaluation and environmental impact.

Overview of materials and structures for Olympic venues

Sports venues have been built of every conceivable material since their inception. The stands and shelter of the Greek hippodrome were built in timber; the Roman amphitheatres were built in marble and stone; the early Olympic Stadiums in Stockholm, Paris and Amsterdam were massive brick structures. After the Second World War stadiums evolved with concrete as the main component, reaching a climax in the 1960s and 1970s with the development of the Rome sports centre for the 1960 Games (pre-cast concrete) and the Montreal Olympic complex for the 1976 Games (*in situ* concrete).

From the 1980s, metal-based lightweight structures began to dominate stadium construction, showcased by recent Olympic projects in Sydney, Athens and Beijing. The materials used in modern Olympic venues can be divided into five categories, as shown in Table 9.5. Among them, the materials used for building structure stand out as important for reduction of the overall embodied environmental impacts of the venue. The selection of structural materials is closely connected with the selection of the venue's structural forms. In the case of partially or totally roofed stadiums, the roof is often the dominant component in the whole system. Using the roof form as an indicator, modern stadiums can be classified into eight principle

Table 9.5 Materials usage in Olympic venues

Material categories	Detailed information
Finishes and detailing materials	Finishes are those materials used to clad the structure for decoration purposes. Detailing includes doors, windows, rails and balustrades, etc.
Playing-surface materials	The playing surface in Olympic venues is determined by the International Federation of each Olympic sport. It includes a wide range from natural grass and timber to synthetic materials
Equipment materials	These refer to the service systems and apparatuses in venues, such as sanitary fittings, ventilation systems and water pipes, etc.
Structural materials	These are used to build up the main frame of the venue, including the roofs, seating tiers, foundations, and enclosure and partition structures.
Overlay materials	These are used to structure the temporary overlays such as lighting towers, giant scoreboard or screens, temporary stands and timing equipment, etc.

forms, which are listed in Table 9.6. Although the list is not exclusive and there are other variations or combinations, it can be used as a reference for stadium structure classification.

Post and beam and air-supported roof options are generally considered outdated and have been almost abandoned for use because of their weaknesses. Shell

Table 9.6 Summary of structure forms of the Olympic Stadium

Structure forms	Detailed information
Post and beam structure	The roof is carried by beams and trusses which in turn are supported by a row of columns parallel to the pitch. It is simple and economically sound, but the columns can obstruct spectators' sightlines.
Goal-post structure	An improved version of post and beam structures with posts only at the two ends of the stand to form a goal shape. The roof is supported by a single girder spanned the entire length of the stand. It has been widely used for medium- and small-sized stadiums for it is column-free and comparatively cheap. Yet there are difficulties to smoothly joint the adjacent stands in the corner.
Cantilever structure	The roof is fixed at one end while the other end is left to hang free without any support. This is one of the most commonly used structures with the advantages of providing the spectators with unobstructed views, suitable for continuous seating bowl and aesthetic opportunities. It has a relatively high cost.
Concrete shell structure	Shell has the ability to transfer the vertical forces acting upon its surface to the horizontal direction. It is the geometric shape rather than the firmness of the material providing the strength and stability to the system; it therefore has the potential to save materials use. A shell is unlikely to provide a translucent roof.
Compression and tension ring structure	This is a doughnut-shaped structure consisting of an inner tension ring, an outer compression ring, and radial connecters between them. The structure can be very light and at the same time span deeply enough to cover all stand areas; its strength is derived from the mechanical principles and system coherency. The advantage is that it can be applied to an existing seating bowl without additional reinforcement to the old foundations. But the nature of this structure means it can be used only with circular- or oval-shaped venues.
Tension structures	This 3-D structure retains its integrity under tension, which equally distributes and balances the forces of compression and tension using elastic cables and rigid struts. The support comes from the entire structure as opposed to its individual components. Tension structures provide the opportunity to use soft materials such as membrane and glass fibre fabric to replace the traditional rigid materials of the roof covering. Yet it is an expensive solution and relies on sophisticated mathematical calculation and engineering designs to achieve success
Space frame structures	This is a 3-D shaped grid structure normally constructed of steel. It is best used when spanning equally in two directions so that the proportion of the stadium should be roughly square. Recent cases indicated that space frame structures tend to be an expensive solution.
Air-supported roof structure	This system is composed of a membrane (polyester) that covers the whole stadium and is supported by positive internal pressure provided by fans. Although it can be used to create a giant enclosed space with relatively low cost and less materials, it needs significant energy to run the fans to keep the roof up.

structures are the only applications largely made of concrete while cantilever structures can be either steel or concrete in their framework. The remainder are lightweight steel-framed structures incorporating light roof coverings. This reveals the trend for stadium structural development in recent decades: the physically lightweight, mechanically advanced, materially efficient and visually translucent structure has gradually overwhelmed and replaced the heavyweight, opaque and massive structures that relied on the thickness and firmness of the materials. The development of Olympic venues has been at the forefront of this trend.

Materials and structures with low embodied environmental impacts

Many countries produce guides to green or ecological materials based on their embodied environmental impacts. By such means, those materials consuming less energy, water and other resources, and causing less environmental pollution during the procurement and manufacturing process, can be differentiated from their counterparts. Those associated with toxic, ozone-depleting or other hazardous substances can also be identified. However, it is very difficult to provide a precise value for a material's embodied impact because there are many variations affecting material life cycles from exploitation to distribution, including local variations in sourcing, transport and use. Therefore any materials' guide can only reflect a generic validity within a certain geographical area.

When considering major structural components, timber and other renewable organic products are often the most environmentally sound; but they must be verifiably procured from sustainable sources rather than, say, tropical rainforest. Steel frames tend to have a slightly higher embodied energy than similar concrete structures; but it should also be noted that concrete has a wide range of composition ratios for cement and aggregates (generally, the higher ratio of cement the less environmentally friendly the concrete would be). This could impact on assessment of long-span structures such as in an Olympic Stadium where high-strength concrete is necessary. Concrete has advantages of plasticity, natural fireproofing and low maintenance cost, but disadvantages of appearance, weight, site processing time, and difficulties in quality control. Due to concrete curing requirements, winter construction in some cold climates may also be compromised without use of special processes. This raises problems especially when construction time is limited, such as the case of Montreal. To some extent the deficiencies of *in situ* concrete processing can be remedied by pre-cast techniques; and by use of pre-stressing and post-tensioning techniques, materials use could be reduced. Concrete is not a mainstream material for the development of lightweight structures however.

Steel is particularly useful for long-span technology for its high strength-to-weight ratio through the development of structural hollow sections. Examples of use of steel in stadium design include: the Shanghai stadium, which has a massive tubular-steel cantilever roof of 73m extending towards the pitch; the triangular girder at Ibrox, Glasgow has a 145m span forming a goalpost structure; and the trussed arch in Stadium Australia spans more than 300m. This makes steel an obvious choice for roof structures. Steel frames also provide the opportunities for translucent covering to aid requirements for filming and broadcasting. For seating bowls, steel can also challenge concrete in some respects: a steel terrace has a smaller profile for beam and column, which makes the space beneath larger and more flexible in use. Parts of a steel terrace can also be designed as either moveable or demountable elements so that the stadium can be quickly shifted between different seating schemes. Furthermore, steel components can be accurately prefabricated and quickly assembled on site, and may be disassembled afterwards for reuse.

As with other materials, steel has its drawbacks: it is expensive in some parts of the world and has weakness in fire, but overall steel structures have advantages over concrete in aesthetic features, construction times, spatial flexibility, recycling potential and long-span techniques. Steel provides great possibilities for the development of lightweight structures that can save on quantities of materials overall, and hence reduce the embodied environmental impact of a venue.

Materials and structures for sustainable venues

The strategy for using materials and structures in Olympic-venue development can be summarised as follows: lightweight structures and associated materials should be considered at the outset; timber and steel frames can be generally regarded as superior to those of mass concrete in terms of environmental impact and functionality; materials with low embodied impact in the whole life cycle should be selected wherever possible; and materials associated with harmful substances should be replaced by other alternatives. A local green materials guide can be a useful reference to support decision-making for materials and construction choices for Olympic venues.

The use of new materials can be minimised by reusing and recycling existing building products either in their original functions or in innovative ways. Timber products and many standard building components can be reused directly; concrete and bricks can be crushed on site to form aggregate or hardcore; glass, plastics, ferrous and nonferrous metals can be recycled. To benefit this process, venues should be designed for easy disassembly, for instance using screws instead of adherents, and bolts rather than welds to join components. A venue's dimension should be based on modular systems so that building components can be easily replaced if necessary.

Efficient site management can minimise material waste during construction. This should include suitable estimation of material quantities to avoid over-purchasing, rationalisation of site storage and recycling on site. For the longer term, a material's durability should be taken into account so that the need for replacement can be reduced during maintenance and refurbishment.

Olympic transport issues (Indicator F-I)

Transport is a major user of fossil fuels and responsible for a range of environmental and socio-economic impacts. The positioning of Olympic venues in relation to transport infrastructures has a strong influence on how fully they will be used during and particularly after the Games, and also on the amount of energy consumed to transport people and goods between the venues and the rest of the city.

design of the venue, its orientation, landscaping, surroundings and building morphology, will also impact on its passive performance. The ratio of volume to exposed surface area can be used as an indicator of the rate at which a building gains or loses heat; a high volume-to-surface ratio implies a slow heating-up in summer and heat loss during winter. Thermal loads can also be modified by the venue's orientation, site planning of shading devices, and the colour and texture of the external surface. Bioclimatic design features around a venue can adjust wind penetration in winter and enhance cooling in summer. The use of water features can also have a beneficial effect on the microclimate of an area in hot seasons by reducing the ambient air temperature through evaporation. The modulation of heat flows can be achieved by increasing fabric thermal mass/capacity of the exposed surfaces of the venue; thermal insulation reduces heat transfer between internal and external environments; and these together reduce excessive temperature swing. Earth-shelter technology, which has been tested in several large sports facilities in recent years with promising results, may also be used. Shields and canopies can protect spectators from wind and rain; wind towers, solar chimneys, stairwells and ductworks can be arranged to harness cross-ventilation and buoyancy effects; and buried pipes can be used to moderate temperatures.

Passive thermal techniques can be used alone or in combination, and a number of computer simulation programmes have been developed as tools to aid the design process. Energy-saving measures also include the use of efficient appliances, innovative HVAC schemes (such as that used in the Sydney Aquatic centre to create a comfort envelope around each spectator rather than the entire space), heat recovery, energy storage techniques and efficient control systems.

Application of new and renewable energy sources, and other energy-saving initiatives (Indicators C-4 and C-5)

Features attracting credits under these criteria are described below. Venues should be supplied where possible using renewable energy sources such as: solar thermal collectors, wind turbines, hydropower, tidal power, photovoltaics, biomass, geothermal and even potentially nuclear power. Some sources may be local to the venue, others more remote. Stadiums and arenas have large areas of roof or canopy, which have potential for on-site installation of various forms of solar collectors; areas of Olympic parkland with low density, non-residential development might incorporate small-scale wind turbines; and geothermal pumps have been exploited in recent Olympic projects in Athens and Beijing. Apart from directly connected renewables, alternative energy sources can be accessed by purchasing 'green' power from the market through the grid.

Other energy-saving initiatives include: use of sports equipment with high efficiency ratings; co-generation systems for heat and electricity; reduction of hot water distribution in public toilets (experience shows that hot-water taps in public toilets in sports venues are rarely used); and minimising distribution losses in the electricity supply system. In addition, innovative products sometimes contribute to energy saving; for example, in Sydney's Super Dome, photo-luminous material was used to produce an energy-free way-finding system through absorbing and reflecting ambient light.

Indicator F-1	Score:			
Olympic transport issues				
5 Δ > 0.8　　**4** 0.6 < Δ ≤ 0.8　**3** 0.4 < Δ ≤ 0.6　**2** 0.2 < Δ ≤ 0.4　**1** 0 < Δ ≤ 0.2				

Assessment criteria		Good	Medium	Poor
Accessibility of Olympic venues by normal means of transportation				
1	Olympic development positioning meets the requirements of the local Transport Plan	2	1	0
2	The development is well connected with existing or new developed transport infrastructures, including urban road network and/or light rail routes	2	1	0
3	The existing or planning transport infrastructures have adequate capacity to serve the Olympic precinct and its further development	2	1	0
4	Traffic Assessment has been carried out for the Olympic site as part of the design document	2	1	0
Minimisation of the use of private vehicles				
5	Regular public commuting services/routes are specified for the transport corridors for Olympic sites. Good practice principles used for tram, train and underground; satisfactory practice for shuttle or mini bus services	6	3	0
6	Sites and particularly gateways to new development are arranged within walking distance of fixed public transport nodes	2	1	0
7	Essential shelters for stops and interchanges are provided along the service route	4	2	0
8	Real time information systems are installed in public transport nodes and at stops in proximity to the Olympic site	2	1	0
9	Areas and capacities of parking around Olympic site are minimised according to local regulations or standards; restrictions apply only if adequate public transport provided	2	1	0
10	Percentage of car parks at the Olympic site designed to be flexible in use (e.g. as multi-functional area for amenity or retail) **Good**: 20% and above; **Medium:** 10%–20%; **Poor:** 10% and below	2	1	0
11	Network of safe pedestrian routes set-up throughout the site and linking major venues	2	1	0
12	Network of safe cycling routes set-up throughout the site and linking major venues	2	1	0
13	Safe crossing points (and facilities such as bridges, subways, control lights, etc.) are installed across major roads around the site	2	1	0
14	User friendly signpost system provided for pedestrians and cyclists	4	2	0
15	Adequate bicycle storage planned for each major facility and strategic point	2	1	0
Management of the traffic during Olympic period and in long-term				
16	Traffic management and information systems provided as part of planning initiatives to ensure smooth transport operation during Olympics	2	1	0
17	Mixed-use development planned around Olympic venues and Villages	2	1	0
Maximum credits:	42　　**Credits awarded:**			
Indicator F-1	**Assessment index (Δ):**			

The assessment here focuses on several aspects of which the primary is the accessibility of Olympic venues by normal means of transportation (as opposed to special services only operated during the Olympic period). This requires that the development of Olympic facilities is in line with the existing or proposed urban transport infrastructures, such as road networks, junctions and interchanges, underground train extensions, light-rail routes and water transport. It is important to ensure that the urban transport system is not only well-connected with Olympic facilities but also has adequate capacity to serve the city's development in the longer term. The planning of Olympic clusters and the consequent transport connections should be consistent with the city's Transport Plan.

Olympic developments have the potential to be used as travel generators for public transit and therefore the second concern is to examine the strategy to minimise the use of private vehicles in accessing Olympic facilities. Regular public commuter services (shuttle bus, tram, underground, train, ferry, etc.) should be defined within the transport corridor articulating all the Olympic sites. Most of the footprint and gateways of the new developments should be within walking distance (less than 1km) of a fixed public-transport node. The provision of essential ancillaries such as bus stop shelters and real time information boards will further improve the viability of the public transport service.

Other aspects of the strategy should involve controlling parking capacity in each Olympic site to discourage car trips, while at the same time providing a welcoming and safe environment for pedestrians and cyclists throughout the site, including separated pedestrian and cycling routes, safe crossing points and bicycle storage.

For the longer term, transport in and out of new Olympic quarters may be reduced by promoting mixed development through planning residential, commercial, retail and social amenities in proximity to the sports complexes and the Olympic Villages. The local strategic plan for land allocation, development density and civic services should reflect this point. Yet during the Olympic period, overwhelming traffic between Olympic sites and other parts of the city is inevitable; Olympic traffic management and information systems should be introduced to aid smooth traffic circulation.

Post-Olympic usage (Indicator G-1)

The after-use of Olympic facilities is a crucial issue for sustainable Olympic development and should be planned from the outset. Historically, many Olympic venues

Indicator G-1	Score:			
Improving post-Olympic utilisation of venues				
5 $\Delta > 0.8$　　**4** $0.6 < \Delta \leq 0.8$　**3** $0.4 < \Delta \leq 0.6$　**2** $0.2 < \Delta \leq 0.4$　**1** $0 < \Delta \leq 0.2$				

	Assessment criteria	Good	Medium	Poor
1	Study of existing and potential users of the development carried out to guide the decisions on design parameters such as scale, seating capacity, function, etc.	2	1	0
2	Clear post-Olympic usage plan and management strategy defined for the venue	2	1	0
3	Venue designed as a multi-functional facility. **Good**: 5 functions or more; **Medium**: 2-4 functions; **Poor**: single-function venue	4	2	0
4	Permanent seating capacity at the venue is moderated according to longer-term local needs, and temporary additions used to fulfil the Olympic demands	2	1	0
5	Venue is designed for high adaptability and transformability	2	1	0
6	The Olympic Village is designed with diversity in suite form, size and layout; or can achieve this diversity easily in post-Olympic redevelopment	2	1	0
Maximum credits:	14	**Credits awarded:**		
Indicator G-1		**Assessment index (Δ):**		

have experienced under-utilisation after the Games were over, showing differences in the need for sports facilities between the local community and the Olympic organisation. The modern Olympics require the finest venues for around 28 Summer Olympic Sports and 300 breakdown events; yet not all the sports and events are likely to be widely practised in the host city and some sports and venue types will be novelties to the local market. Although the Olympics have the potential to promote new sports among local communities, the effect is not guaranteed and it may require a long time to generate stable user groups. For large stadiums of Olympic standard, their financial viability is unlikely to be achieved by catering for sporadic high-profile events or amateur competitions, rather they rely on the regular use and management by professional clubs. The viability of the clubs and their league competitions will largely depend on the local interest in the sport and in many cases, the lack of local enthusiasm and participation can turn an Olympic venue into a 'white elephant' after the Games.

Another scenario is that some sports have a degree of popularity in the host city and an active user group, but the existing facilities do not satisfy the requirements of the Olympic events in terms of scale and/or specification. New venues may then be constructed by the organising committee but on a scale that exceeds future demand potential. This is also linked to another reason for the under-utilisation of more general Olympic venues: the venue may be too large to cater for local events, and, as mentioned previously, some organisers prefer to use smaller settings to create the right ambience rather than a half-empty large arena, even if the costs are similar. The cost will also be important if Olympic venues are more expensive to lease because of their high standards of fit-out, as is location if Olympic venues are in relatively remote areas with inconvenient access.

Some measures can however be taken to promote the post-Olympic usage of venues. The first is to draft the development brief of any new venues (as well as large extensions to existing ones) on the basis of a thorough study of existing and potential user groups of the venue in the local region. Each major development should define a clear post-Games use plan and management strategy. If some sports assets can be foreseen to have only modest future local demand, temporary settings should be considered. The second is to fully utilise existing facilities wherever possible as the redevelopment of an old venue is a better solution than the launch of a new one in economic and environmental terms (this item has already been covered by indicator A-2).

The third is to exploit the versatility of each venue. Table 9.7 summarises the potential sports and non-sports adaptation functions that can be used in each type of Olympic venue. Many venues can be designed as multi-functional spaces with the careful arrangement of their dimensions, interior layouts, flooring materials, moveable partitions, and stands.

The fourth option is to keep the permanent seating capacity, architectural scale and specification of the new development as low as necessary, and to use temporary overlays to fulfil the Olympic demands. This item has been covered by indicator B-4.

The final strategy is to improve the adaptability and transformability of the venues for new functions in the future. New urban development should also be designed considering changes that may occur. Simple building forms with easily modifiable

Table 9.7 Function adaptation potential for each type of Olympic venue

Sports and functions that can be adapted to use space	Archery field	Athletics stadium	Regatta course	Badminton court	Baseball & softball diamond	Basketball court	Boxing hall	White water course	Cycling Velodrome	Equestrian ground	Fencing hall	Football stadium	Gymnastics hall	Handball court	Hockey field	Judo hall	Weightlifting hall	Wrestling hall	Aquatic centre	Tae kwon do hall	Tennis court	Table tennis hall	Sailing port/course	Shooting range	Volleyball court	Beach volleyball ground
Options for sports event or training																										
Archery	●	●			●					●																
Athletics		●			●					●		●			●											
Rowing/canoeing			●																				●			
Badminton				●		●	●		●		●		●	●								●			●	
Baseball		●			●					●																
Basketball				●		●	●		●				●	●								●			●	
Boxing				●		●	●		●		●		●	●		●	●	●		●		●			●	
Canoe slalom								●																		
Cycling									●																	
Equestrian		●			●					●		●														
Fencing				●		●	●		●		●		●	●		●	●	●		●		●				
Football		●			●					●		●														
Gymnastics		●		●	●	●	●		●	●	●		●	●	●							●			●	
Handball				●		●	●		●				●	●								●			●	
Hockey		●			●					●		●			●											
Judo				●		●	●		●		●		●	●		●	●	●		●		●			●	
Sailing																							●			
Shooting		●								●														●		
Swimming																			●							
Softball		●								●																
Tae kwon do		●		●		●	●		●		●		●	●		●	●	●		●		●			●	
Tennis		●			●					●		●			●						●					
Table tennis				●		●	●		●				●	●								●			●	
Volleyball				●		●	●		●				●	●								●			●	
Volleyball beach		●			●					●					●											●
Weightlifting		●		●	●	●	●		●		●		●	●		●	●	●		●	●	●			●	
Wrestling		●		●	●	●	●		●		●		●	●		●	●	●		●	●	●			●	
Options for non-sports events																										
Natural amenity	●		●					●															●			●
Open-air exhibition		●			●					●		●			●						●					
Indoor exhibition				●		●	●		●		●		●	●		●	●	●		●		●			●	
Performance show		●		●	●	●	●		●	●	●	●	●	●		●	●			●		●			●	●
Banquet				●		●	●		●		●		●	●								●			●	
Conference				●		●	●		●		●		●	●		●	●			●		●			●	
Concert		●		●	●	●	●		●	●	●	●	●	●						●	●	●			●	●
Ceremonial gathering		●		●	●	●	●		●		●	●	●	●						●	●	●				
Fairground		●			●					●		●														
Special market		●	●	●						●		●														
Aquatic amusement			●					●											●					●		

layouts and façades would allow the greatest degree of flexibility for redevelopment, with the main structure largely unchanged. The location and arrangement of service units are important for the success of a building's transformation as the expense involved in relocating water supplies, sewers, drains, gas pipes, electricity ducts and telephone lines is often prohibitively high.

For Olympic Villages, the after-use is generally less problematic. If the village is planned to be transformed into social or commercial housing, diversity in suite form, size and tenure, provision of amenities such as shops, restaurants and bars may improve the occupation rate. Flexible arrangement of the load-bearing structure and easily movable partitions will help to change athlete dormitories into family houses.

Functionality of Olympic venues (Indicator H-1)

The issues in this category of assessment are more straightforward. Olympic venues clearly need to function well in serving the Olympic sports extravaganza and provide a healthy, pleasant and comfortable environment for athletes and

Indicator H-1	Score:			
Improving the functionality of Olympic venues				
5 $\Delta > 0.8$ **4** $0.6 < \Delta \leq 0.8$ **3** $0.4 < \Delta \leq 0.6$ **2** $0.2 < \Delta \leq 0.4$ **1** $0 < \Delta \leq 0.2$				
Assessment criteria		Good	Medium	Poor
1	The design of the venue conforms to the technical requirements of the relevant IF	2	1	0
2	Planting and decoration are used to enhance the aesthetic features and hence pleasant ambience of the interior and exterior spaces	2	1	0
(for open-air venues–indoor venues ignore the following 3 criteria)				
3	Protection provided for spectators and athletes from excessive solar radiation	2	1	0
4	Protection provided for spectators and athletes from excessive wind and rain	2	1	0
5	Protection provided for spectators and athletes from excessive ambient noise	2	1	0
(for indoor venues–open-air venues ignore the following 3 criteria)				
6	Efficient passive or active heating and cooling systems integrated into venue to provide comfort	2	1	0
7	Natural or mechanical ventilation systems provide adequate fresh air	2	1	0
8	Excessive moisture removal strategy for venues (particularly aquatic centre)	2	1	0
9	Venue designed for easy cleaning and maintenance when in daily use	2	1	0
10	Finishing materials selected to avoid VOCs and particulates	2	1	0
11	Natural and artificial lighting systems well coordinated in the venue	2	1	0
12	Measures have been taken to control or eliminate glare	2	1	0
13	Acoustic design delivers a pleasant and practical acoustic environment to the venue	2	1	0
14	Reverberation time of venue spaces can be changed to meet needs of various events	2	1	0
15	Audibility of the broadcasting in the venue space is satisfied	2	1	0
16	Noise level and intensity meet the local standard for relevant sports facilities	2	1	0
Maximum credits:	26	**Credits awarded:**		
Indicator H-1		**Assessment index (Δ):**		

spectators. The architectural settings should conform to the technical requirements of the International Federation of each Olympic sport in terms of spatial dimensions, enclosure materials, indoor air quality, visual environment, thermal standards and acoustics. In cases where design features are not specified by the IF's technical manual, the general well-being of athletes and spectators should be taken into account when defining the environmental standards to be met.

For outdoor settings, protection should be provided from excessive solar radiation, wind, rain and urban noise through good design. For indoor venues, adequate heating, cooling and air ventilation, either in passive or artificial forms, should be included to control the fluctuation of internal temperature, air movement and humidity to an acceptable level (based on local standards). Moisture-removal is particularly important for aquatic sports centres because the moisture may cause condensation and promote the growth of micro-organisms that may cause health hazards.

Luminance requirements for the playing area of some sports venues have already been discussed, however, adequate illumination should also be provided for non-sports space. An important factor in lighting design for Olympic venues is to control the glare; not only does it affect the visual comfort of the occupants but it can impact on athletic performance. Control can be achieved by regulating the contrast between the light sources and the adjacent background, by maintaining the light sources outside the observer's line of sight, and by screening the light sources with louvres or using deep reflectors.

Although sports venues sometimes need a certain atmosphere to attract on-site spectators and television viewers, excessive noise may be a distraction and impact on participant performance. Furthermore, announcements must be heard over the background noise of the crowd but also allow commentators to speak without causing distraction; this requires appropriate acoustic design of the venue space through consideration of shape, dimensions, fabric, materials and by placement of reflectors and absorbers. Such techniques can be used to reduce noise transmission, control reverberation time for various frequencies, avoid flutter echo and ensure that desirable sound can be evenly dispersed within the space. Intrusive internally generated noise (such as from HVAC plant) should be minimised if it cannot be eliminated. For multi-functional sports venues that may be used as performance spaces after the Games, the audio and acoustic design is particularly important.

Environmental impacts (Indicator I-1)

All major developments have impacts on their natural surrounding habitats and the wildlife they support. General environmental impacts of Olympic urban development such as the contribution to global warming, ozone depletion and air and water pollution have been discussed in previous sections. In this section, the focus is on issues of local scale, the ecological value and natural attributes of the development site.

Construction does not necessarily reduce the ecological value of a site; it can be used to enhance it. If a site with low ecological value, e.g. a brownfield site or previously derelict land is used, damage to the existing local ecology can be

Indicator I-1	Score:			
Delivering positive environmental impacts through Olympic development				
5 Δ > 0.8	**4** 0.6 < Δ ≤ 0.8	**3** 0.4 < Δ ≤ 0.6	**2** 0.2 < Δ ≤ 0.4	**1** 0 < Δ ≤ 0.2

Assessment criteria		Good	Medium	Poor
1	A site with low ecological value has been selected for the development	2	1	0
2	Ecological survey and evaluation of the site carried out before design and planning	2	1	0
3	Wildlife corridor or network established or reinforced in the development site	2	1	0
4	Ecological value of the site enhanced through landscaping techniques and addition of new environmental features to the site	2	1	0
5	Soil erosion and loss minimised during the construction process, e.g. application of covers to exposed plots	2	1	0
6	Classification and management system for waste and refuse established on site	2	1	0
Maximum credits:	12	**Credits awarded:**		
Indicator I-1		**Assessment index (Δ):**		

minimised or even reversed. Landscaping and horticultural techniques can be employed to create a viable natural asset as well as improving the visual attractiveness. New environmental features such as ponds and woods can be added to introduce new ecosystems, and wildlife corridors can be considered at the masterplanning stage.

Special care should be exercised during the construction process to avoid erosion and loss of surface soil. Wastes generated from the construction process (and later from venue operation) should be collected, classified and treated to keep the site tidy and to avoid contamination of air, water and soil.

Weighting factors

The weighting of each indicator in this framework has been determined using AHP (a multi-criteria decision-making approach proposed by Saaty 1980, 1994, 1999). It is a powerful and widely accepted model for solving complex evaluation problems, to develop priorities for alternatives, and the criteria used to judge them. The fundamental principle of the mathematical process is to use paired comparison to determine the relative importance, or weight, of the alternatives in terms of each criterion involved in a given objective-making scenario. The alternatives can be of different dimensions and measurement units, either in quantitative or qualitative forms.

In this evaluation, the alternatives are the nine issue categories used above and the process is used to identify the importance of each category in contributing to the overall objective of sustainable Olympic development. The sub-weight for each indicator within a category can be deduced in the same way. The general criteria is that the categories or issues with global impacts are more important than those with local impacts; those involving strategic planning at a holistic level are more important than those for individual venue development; and those closely linked with architectural and design features are more important than those focusing on

Table 9.8 Weighting factors for each indicator

A:	6.0	B:	8.0	C:	20.0	D:	6.0	E:	12.0	F:	4.0	G:	9.0	H:	2.0	I:	3.0
A-1:	2.0	B-1:	4.0	C-1:	4.0	D-1:	6.0	E-1:	12.0	F-1:	4.0	G-1:	9.0	H-1:	2.0	I-1:	3.0
A-2:	1.0	B-2:	1.0	C-2:	4.0												
A-3:	2.0	B-3:	2.0	C-3:	4.0												
A-4	1.0	B-4	1.0	C-4:	4.0												
				C-5:	4.0												

institutional or management approaches. Due to the limitation of this chapter, the detailed calculation process is omitted here but is derived from norms and acceptable data sources.

The final results after the normalisation are given in Table 9.8. The consistency of each judgement matrix has been examined and figures listed here are used as default weightings within the framework. They are subject to calibration and adjustment to suit the unique conditions applicable to each city; for instance, in evaluating Olympic urban developments in Beijing, the weighting for water conservation may need to be increased to encourage initiatives in a city with a level of water shortage; whereas for Athens, the post-Olympic usage might be given more weight to highlight the challenge faced by a small host city in utilisation of Olympic facilities after the event.

Summary

In this chapter an evaluation framework for Olympic sustainable development has been defined and presented. The intention has been to explain the indicators, assessment criteria, benchmarks and weightings for each issue included in the evaluation. The indicators that have been developed produce an outcome with a scoring potential of between 70 and 350 (the ratio of 1 to 5 reflecting the range possible for each indicator).

An environmental performance index (EPI) can be derived based on this range to assess the overall sustainability of existing Olympic development or of a proposed scheme. A range of performances outcomes could be defined if the following minima are achieved: 150 for 'pass'; 200 for 'good'; 250 for 'very good'; and 300 for 'excellent'. These boundaries could be varied according to external factors. The overall rationale is to provide a mechanism for encouraging improvements of the various components of development in order to achieve a higher score through application of the evaluation and also to aid decision makers in prioritising effort and resources.

As with other evaluation frameworks, an independent overview with adjudication will be needed to support the validity of the framework as a whole. A potential problem lies in obtaining accurate and suitable input data upon which judgements are made, but as the basis of the analysis in criteria and benchmark settings has been empirical information and historical records from previous Games, it suggests such data ought to be available for the study and assessment of future Games.

In the application of this approach, decision makers will imprint their own interpretations on the data based on their knowledge and expertise, which may result in biased outcomes that may not perfectly reflect the opinions of all the stakeholders involved. It is crucial therefore in the evaluation to elicit quantitative judgement from qualitative information where possible, but with the diversity of Olympic cities there will be a need for calibration to suit the local conditions. The framework has been designed to include flexibility and adaptability; it is enabled for further adjustment, and leaves scope for modifying embodied benchmark values.

The London 2012 Olympics

Introduction

This chapter consists of two main components: first a description of the preparations for the London 2012 Games and the emphasis being placed on sustainability by the organisers; and second an example of use of a section of the evaluation procedure developed in the preceding chapter to examine Beijing and London schemes.

In 2000, the organisers of the Sydney Games produced what has been generally regarded as the greenest Olympics to date, and marked a step change not only in outcomes but also in attitudes towards environmental concerns (Pitts, 2004). Athens initially attempted to follow in a similar vein in 2004, although the expectations for advances in excess of Sydney's performance were not met. Some commentators have expressed concern over the Athens legacy, too (Warner, 2008), where some venues are now rather unused and unloved.

In 2008 the Games in Beijing, though following a number of underlying sustainability themes, produced a rather different immediate legacy with much media attention concerned with the grand scale of both the events and the premises used, as well as their cost. Funding provided was at unprecedented levels, in excess of £20 billion, and reflected the substantial support of the national government and the resources of the most populous nation on the planet. The Beijing Olympic Park was also on a grand scale, especially with the inclusion of almost 700ha of forest at its northern extreme; this area alone being approximately three times that of what is to be the main site in London. The longer term impacts in Beijing cannot yet be fully judged though the terms 'sustainable' and 'sustainability' were not often used by commentators in describing the event. In fact a sustainability evaluation procedure was used and there may be a number of good long-term urban legacies, which may become more evident and of interest, and also hopefully open to scrutiny, in the future.

The 2012 edition of the Summer Olympic Games is being held in London and from the outset the organisers were concerned with sustainable development and sustainability as important themes of the Games. The candidature file for London's bid focused on sport, health and, crucially, environment; organisers had completed full environmental impact assessments for its venues early, putting it ahead of all the other candidates. In the aftermath of the Beijing event, organisers have been keen to point out both the differences that the London Games will exhibit and its focus on different legacy themes. Both the Olympic Development Authority and the Local Organising Committee for the Games have appointed teams to address sustainability issues, and these teams work alongside each other and with oversight from third parties such as the Commission for a Sustainable London 2012. The challenge for any Games organisers is substantial, and as has been oft quoted: in the case of London it is like building something twice the size of Heathrow airport's terminal 5 in half the time. The whole Olympic Park extends over 246ha and includes most of the new facilities but with a number of temporary elements where long-term legacy use could not be assured. The plans also utilise some existing sites – particularly those for more specialist sports outside the park area. In this chapter information available concerning the development and future plans will be reviewed, together with some discussion of issues raised by commentators.

Winning the bid

As has been referred to elsewhere, the process of winning a bid to stage an Olympic Games can be one that takes several decades; a period during which development continues to take place in a host city. No city can afford to either wait until a successful bid occurs before making preparations or suspend development just because of an unsuccessful outcome. The smoothness with which a city moves from candidate status to being host city may be an indicator of its preparedness and how easily the bid document can be transformed into reality.

The case of London's successful bid for the 2012 Games, and its background history, has proved a fruitful area for discussion by a number of authors. At the time of the award in 2005, the favourite to host the 2012 Games was Paris, and it has been suggested that because success was somewhat unexpected, it may have led to some interesting consequences. Initially there may have been some laxity in collating detailed and complete costs for the event, leading to a subsequent, somewhat troubling, substantial and well-publicised inflation when all factors were included (rising from approximately £2.5 billion to over £9 billion). Further, there was a focus on principles of culture, multi-ethnicity and inclusiveness as part of a more general marketing strategy for London; a strategy that was being pursued even without the Games. The primary Games site chosen (the Lower Lea Valley) was one ripe and needy for regeneration and also an area with only a small population likely to be displaced or object to the proposals, thus lessening any pre-award negative comments. This situation has been described previously (Gold and Gold, 2008). Nevertheless it has been clear in the transformation of the city's status that it is attempting to continue with the main facets of the bid and to generate an outcome that will have its own distinct characteristics – a number of which are in sustainability-related areas.

Sustainable development themes and objectives

The Sustainable Development Strategy was released for London in early 2007 (ODA, 2007); it has five principal themes: climate change; waste; biodiversity and ecology; inclusion; and healthy living. These five themes are resolved into 12 interlinked development objectives within the strategy:

- Minimisation of carbon emissions from the venues and the Olympic Park.
- Provision of opportunities for efficient use, recycling and reuse of water.
- Protection and enhancement of biodiversity and ecology for the Olympic sites.
- Minimisation of adverse impacts for land, water, noise and air quality.
- Provision of healthy lifestyle opportunities around the Olympic Park and venues.
- Prioritisation of walking, cycling and public transport for access to, and movement within, the site.
- Accessibility with emphasis on principles of inclusive design.
- Identification, sourcing and use of environmentally and socially responsible materials.
- Reduction of materials wastage through good design and maximisation of reuse and recycling of materials from demolition, remediation and construction activities.
- Support for local communities in creating mixed-use public space, housing and other facilities, suited to the area and adaptable for future climate.
- Creation of new business and employment opportunities.
- Involvement, communication and consultation with stakeholders and local communities around the Olympic Park and venues.

These are each important objectives, but taken together have potential to showcase London as the most sustainable Games thus far. A further document, *The London 2012 Sustainability Plan – Towards a one planet 2012* (London 2012, 2007) was issued in late 2007 (to be updated annually). It brings together all aspects of the preparations and staging of the Games and aspires to the concept of 'One Planet Living' (living within the means of the planet) and also proposes carbon-footprinting studies. In order to help enforce the development to be in line with policies, compliance with 40 key performance indicators has been, and will continue to be, built into any contracts awarded for the building and staging of the Games. A 'gateway' process has been proposed to function at each stage of design to ensure compliance.

The main actions to support the themes above have been designed around enhancing developments in the Lower Lea Valley, a few kilometres to the east of Central London, though there are also several individual external sites. In the sections below, attention is first paid to the main objectives.

Carbon emissions

The phrase 'lean, mean and green' has been used by the London ODA to indicate its approach to reducing carbon emissions and therefore its consequent impact on global climate change. The Games are to be a 'low-carbon' event rather than a 'zero-carbon' event. Design of energy-efficient venues has been proposed, which should maximise passive heating and cooling opportunities while also using optimal controls and monitoring systems. Energy is planned to be supplied from efficient combined cooling, heating and power centres, which can also be flexible in fuel choice (using both biomass/woodchip and natural gas, as well as having potential for post-Games change). System capacities have been designed for heating at 100MW, cooling at 15MW and electricity at 15MW. Further renewable energy sources are also to be used, including two 2.2 MW wind turbines.

Aspirations were for an approximate 50 per cent reduction in emissions as a whole in post-Games use, arising from lower demand (15 per cent), improved efficiency (17 per cent), and use of renewables (20 per cent). The organisers are also putting in place a strategy for enabling reductions in subsequent Games. The 15 per cent improvement over standards in venue energy use should be complemented by 25 per cent improvement in the Olympic Village, which will be designed to host 17,000 occupants. Buildings in the Olympic Village have been set a target of Level 4 in the Code for Sustainable Homes rating scheme with consequently limited carbon emissions. It is possible that the standards may be enhanced as the project progresses. There is also the commitment in the Sustainable Development Strategy to design for future climate through requiring design teams to submit information using the London Climate Change Adaptation Checklist.

Water

Water is a scarce resource in many parts of the world. Even in locations such as the UK there can be shortages due to imbalances between supply and demand for potable water at particular times of the year. Reduction in water use depends upon improvements in technology, but also on changes in behaviour. The aim in the London scheme is to reduce demand by implementing new management techniques and water-saving technologies, with 40 per cent reduction in Games venues usage and 20 per cent reduction in residential use. Alternative sources of water are also planned for non-potable needs with the feasibility of rainwater harvesting under consideration. Education programmes are to be put in place for building users to aid demand reduction. There are also efforts to reduce water use during construction as well as to address issues of groundwater contamination.

Biodiversity and ecology

The Lower Lea Valley has some heavily polluted zones comprising as it does of previously used (brownfield) land and a number of waterways. Ecological management has been planned and is being implemented to deal with construction activities as well as to provide a remediated final product. Both organisers and designers associated with the Games express enthusiasm for revitalising the waterways and making them a positive feature of the Games event and including development of new habitat types. Projects are planned to improve 3,000m of river/stream courses, 3,500m of riverbank and 3,800m of canals. Over 110ha of new Olympic parkland are also proposed with new wetland areas created. In locations with existing habitats in key construction zones, flora and fauna will be preserved or relocated; and post-Games restoration is also planned. Strategies for the main site to act as both an ecological corridor and also to provide recreational opportunities are described. Adverse impacts during construction, Games use and in the post-Games period are each mentioned in the strategy as necessitating attention.

Land, water, air and noise

As well as minimising negative impacts of the Games venue construction and wider development on land, water and air, and consideration for noise, there is also a stated strategy to optimise any positive impacts too. Remediation of land and improvements to watercourses are aimed for; internal air quality and external air pollution are each dealt with in the published strategy. Sustainable urban drainage schemes (SUDS) are prescribed where possible, and planning for floods arising from 1 in 100-year event scenarios is also considered. Since some of the main features of the Lower Lea Valley site are the existing, largely derelict waterways, a number of proposals deal specifically with this aspect of the development.

Health and well-being

The strategy here includes providing health and safety for workers during construction and Games operation as well as providing a legacy that encourages a healthy lifestyle with areas for outdoor pursuits in an area currently lacking them. Occupational health is a further theme being developed and proposed restrictions on car parking are meant to encourage healthier modes of movement and transport.

Transport and movement

There is much encouragement within the strategies being developed for alternatives to the private car, indeed there are no provisions planned for private vehicle access and parking except for disabled users. It has been proposed that tickets to attend Games events should also include public transport to reach the site. The compact nature of the main site certainly aids in the above-mentioned aspirations. During the construction period there are aims to use train and waterway transport to bring materials to the site rather than road vehicles, with potential to reduce fuel use, pollution and congestion. There is an aspiration for 50 per cent of materials by weight to be moved by sustainable means (ODA, 2007). Concern has also been given to on-site facilities for workers to reduce movement and transport. Cycle parking places (approximately 5,000) will be provided in and around the main site for use by visitors, and pedestrian routes will be defined not only for security but also for safety. For spectator/visitor transport to the site much is planned: ten rail links using three main 'gateway' stations capable of operation at frequent intervals and with a capacity of 240,000 passengers per hour.

Accessibility

Principles have been adopted to make the Games sites highly accessible through use of inclusive design and the setting of benchmarks and production of exemplars. The aim is set out to make the places designed for the Games to be safe and easily accessed and useable in flexible ways. There is further focus on convenience and encouragement for use by all 'regardless of age, gender, mobility, ethnicity or circumstances' (ODA, 2007). Special attention is of course given to access for the disabled and extends beyond the basic site venues to transport to and from the Games.

Materials

Four areas are addressed in the documentation produced: responsible sourcing; embodied impacts; healthy materials; and 'secondary' materials. In the case of responsible sourcing, the supply-chain documentation must show compliance with legal requirements and to be from sustainable sources as defined by third-party schemes. Embodied impacts are dealt with through the Building Research Establishment's *Green Guide to Specification* (Anderson et al., 2002). The strategy document expressed requirements for A- and B-rated products; this categorisation might be considered somewhat lax as defined by the third edition of the guide but, as the guide is being rewritten and redefined, changes may evolve. The term 'healthy materials' implies use of safer alternatives where these exist, and 'secondary materials' refers to encouragement to reuse and recycle materials in the construction of facilities.

Wastes

A number of initiatives have been signalled in the waste strategy that address not only the important construction period but also the Games period itself. The target is for 90 per cent of demolition materials to be reused or recycled on site and for no use of landfill disposal during the Games (70 per cent reused, recycled or composted). Responsible sourcing, reducing embodied impacts and promoting use of healthy alternative materials are all encouraged by the Games procurement processes. Materials from Games' temporary facilities, overlays and items only used at the Games, should be fed through 'asset recovery' systems and into reprocessing or reuse. There are also efforts to 'design-out' waste production. Since there are to be a number of temporary facilities and services developed only for use during the Games period, much effort has been directed at planning for their post-Games use, and how any wastes that would be otherwise produced can be minimised.

Local communities

Since the main Olympic site is surrounded by some of the most deprived communities in London, this is an important objective area, particularly to inspire long-term legacies. One impact of the Games will be to provide new housing, facilities and mixed-use development that will not only deliver regeneration in the area of the Lower Lea Valley, but also be sufficiently robust as to match the needs of future climates. Those specific facilities that are only needed to allow operation of the Games in 2012 are planned to be removable; and many of the new features, such as numerous bridges over various waterways, should support the functioning of the new communities. These new communities are expected to link in to those already existing and for the main Games legacies to be suited to the local needs. Safety and techniques to reduce risk of crime are included in design principles through engagement with *Secured by Design* (ACPO, 2004). Further, the main Olympic Village should be constructed to match the *Building for Life* standard (CABE, 2008).

The involvement with local communities and derived outcomes that are reflected in the final design and development of the Games plan is crucial to achieving many sustainable outcomes. Particular infrastructural items that have roles for the future of the area have already been identified and it is to be hoped that they will not be diminished or lost along the way to the 2012 Games.

Business and employment

Along with community issues, the development of businesses and employment opportunities is also very important for the longer term sustainability of the area, although the wording in the strategy document refers to local, regional and national opportunities for business and employment. However, policies and masterplans for Games legacies are aimed to encourage local skills development and local employment. Changes to original plans have also been introduced to avoid some of the existing businesses having to relocate from the Olympic Park area. Besides direct venue construction there are also intended to be business opportunities through involvement in the supply chain and also through working towards employment during the Games and through use of facilities post-Games. The London Employment and Skills Taskforce and the Local Employment and Training Framework have both been established to help deliver local employment benefits. It is also planned to provide 139,000m^2 of new retail space and 185,000m^2 of new office space.

Involvement and inclusion

This theme embraces several elements that are aimed to encourage people to make the most from the Games and also to lower barriers to participation. The involvement of those less often engaged in sports and culture is a particular target, whether the differences are based on gender, disability, cultural or economic backgrounds. Plans target a number of themes including: incorporation of inclusive design to enable access for all; encouragement for jobs for local people; community engagement activities; and promotion of excellence in design.

Commission for a Sustainable London 2012

In order to provide independent review of the progress of the London Games programme, the Commission for a Sustainable London 2012 was set up in 2007. It is the first body of its type in Olympic history. The Commission reports directly to the Olympic Board and is able to comment and also to assure confidence that the aims can be achieved. It is comprised of commissioners with specialist interests and knowledge in aligned disciplines but not directly involved in the Games procurement; it makes regular published reports and these are further scrutinised by the media. At the time of writing it had already made a number of key recommendations in its publications, several associated with sustainability-reporting procedures that should be used to manage the programme-wide approach (CSL, 2008).

The aim of having the Commission must be to both ensure that the development and running of the Games conforms as far as is practicable to the initial intention to deliver a sustainable Games, and also to help ensure the post-Games legacies meet as closely as possible the impressive aspirational intent. Its role is not only to work to an annual cycle but also to provide ongoing scrutiny. It is clear from the reports so far issued that this body intends to pursue its goals with some vigour.

Sustainable Strategy development

As the preparations for the London Games progress so does the detail of the Sustainable Development Strategy. This reveals more clearly how certain objectives might be met but also allows more public scrutiny and criticism of the development. Some pertinent issues will be described below.

A bespoke version of the Building Research Establishment's Environmental Assessment Method (BREEAM) is also to be developed, although at the time of writing no details were available. Typically, BREEAM addresses such issues as energy use and carbon emissions; water use; health and well-being; management; transport; materials; pollution; land use and ecology. Although for a number of building types benchmarks exist against which performance might be judged, such data are not so readily available for all Olympic venue types.

Some criticism has been levelled at the original plans for energy efficiency as being rather un-ambitious; the case is that they were overtaken by events. Initially the plan was to have venues, and particularly residential development, meeting standards in excess of Building Regulations compliance. However, after the initiation of the Games planning, the UK Government signalled its desire to create national energy standards that would lead to zero-carbon homes by 2016, and indeed significant step improvements well before that date. Further existing plans and commitments extending over parts of the site indicate rather low targets of renewable-energy use that may cause conflicts in delivering certain overall objectives. This left the London proposals to be seen as somewhat underwhelming, but also reinforces the predicament faced by Olympic planners because the cycle of Games bidding and eventual development lasts over a significantly longer timescale than many other activities. Organisers have attempted to deal with criticism by explaining the constraints of the cycle of development and the tight timetable for design and construction. Further criticism has followed the revelation that the enormous amounts of funding being drawn in by the Games may have the effect of reducing sports development funds for other areas in London and elsewhere; for instance some funding from the UK Lottery seems to have been diverted in this fashion.

Stadiums and venues

One of the most complex and controversial aspects of most Olympic Games has been the design, construction and most importantly post-Games use of the venues required for the events taking place (often overlooked in advance). As has been discussed in earlier chapters, the complexity of design can cause both cost over-runs as well as construction difficulties and on more than one occasion, the potential to cause cancellation of the Games due to lack of time. It would seem that the London event organisers have attempted to avoid such problems, though perhaps at the expense of the venue's appearance being less striking than those of several previous host cities.

Information on the design of the main Olympic Stadium was released in late 2007; it is to have a Games capacity of 80,000 spectators but with the upper layers comprising 55,000 seats removable after the Games. The reason for this is to avoid some of the legacy issues associated with previous Games, in that the stadium may be simply too large to be viable as a sports venue. There has been speculation that the demountable portion of the stadium could be sold-on to a future Games venue as a means of enhancing sustainability. The field of play will be sunk into the ground along with lower-level seating; the roof will be of a cable-supported type flowing around the whole perimeter and providing cover for about two-thirds of the spectators. The location will mean the stadium is surrounded on three sides by water. Service facilities (such as for merchandising and catering) are to be designed to occupy 'pods', thus offering flexibility, particularly post-Games. A flexible 'curtain' will wrap around the exterior of the stadium to provide protection from the elements. Though predicted to cost about £500 million, the design when unveiled was treated with a certain amount of criticism, possibly prompted by the comparison with the spectacular Bird's Nest Stadium in Beijing that was being completed at the time.

The aquatic centre (architect Zaha Hadid) has received more favourable design criticism though the budget for it has increased substantially. It will be a landmark building being positioned close to the south-east entrance to the Olympic park; together with an adjacent bridge the total cost has been predicted to reach approximately £300 million. The centre is also being designed for flexibility in post-Games use with approximately 3,500 permanent spectators' seats with 17,000 temporary seats for the Games. After the Games, the centre is intended to provide a venue for both community use (for residents of Stratford) and for elite sports development.

The velodrome is being designed by Hopkins Architects with a seating capacity of 6,000; it will form part of a velo-park with post-Games additions to provide facilities for local use, such as a mountain-bike circuit. The basketball arena will seat 12,000 spectators and is being designed in such a way that components may be removed after the Games for use elsewhere. Another venue that will be moved after the Games is the hockey centre, which will be located in the north-west area of the main site with seating for 20,000. Other venues on the main site are still in the process of development, such as the handball centre.

There are several venues/sports removed from the main site for the London Games:

- Broxbourne (canoe/kayak slalom course) 30km north of the main Olympic site;
- Earls Court (volleyball centre) situated in central London;
- ExCel (boxing, fencing, judo, table tennis, tae kwon do, weightlifting, wrestling, etc. accommodated in four halls) site is an exhibition centre in the London Docklands area;
- North Greenwich Arena (gymnastics), formerly the Millennium Dome on the Greenwich peninsula, a further arena for sports such as badminton is planned adjacent to the site;
- Greenwich Park (equestrian events) located on the south bank of the River Thames close to the Docklands area;
- Horse Guards Parade (beach volleyball) located in central London;
- Weymouth and Portland Harbour (sailing regatta) situated some distance away from London on the south coast of the UK;

- Eton Dorney (rowing and flat-water canoe/kayak) situated to the west of London;
- Lords Cricket Ground (archery) in central London;
- Wimbledon (tennis) situated in south-west London, the existing facilities are in process of upgrading;
- Royal Artillery barracks (shooting events) adjacent to Woolwich Common in south London;
- various football grounds where rounds of the soccer competition might take place, and a number of other outdoor venues.

Olympic Village

The Olympic Village is being designed with sustainability in mind. The original proposals were for accommodation for over 17,000 athletes and officials in approximately 4,000 four-bed apartments. The site of the Village is within the Olympic park allowing for walking to many venues. As is usual, communal facilities are also being provided. The designs have received a certain amount of criticism, as previously mentioned, due to the fact that national standards are likely to be in advance of Olympic ones by the time of the event. The proposals are also under revision however, apparently due to finance issues, and it has been reported that five athletes will be sharing each apartment in order to reduce the number required (Booth, 2008). After the Games the apartments will be converted into housing for sale and rent as part of the Stratford City Regeneration Project, though there are concerns over the strength of the property market. It is perhaps too early in the cycle of development to ascertain how successful the Village will be in meeting aspirations.

Sustainable urban development and the Olympic legacy

The organisers of the London Games have actively pursued a policy focused on sustainability; however, the need to deliver the Games venues and environment within limited physical, financial and particularly time constraints necessarily means something of a top-down approach. There has also been a substantial emphasis on 'legacy', which appears to be operating in a more successful way than at some recent previous Games. The spatial planning is evolving with more use of existing facilities and slightly more clustering.

Investigations should now be in place into a number of issues and questions along with research to gather information 'on the ground' to establish if the top-down planning is resulting in not only the physical impacts suggested, but also those on perception and actions within the local communities directly and indirectly involved. Such information could then be linked to a longer-term understanding of urban development and legacy impacts from other Games. Following the success of the Beijing Games in terms of creating a spectacular impact on the senses and the notion that those Games raised the bar in terms of expectations of facilities, the London bid looked somewhat lacking. It will not be possible to lavish the same funding on the London event, all the more reason therefore to ensure that the specified ideals and focus on longer-term legacies is adhered to.

Commentary on London proposals

At the point of writing, a start has been made on delivering many of the components of the Sustainable Development Strategy but it is too early to know if they will all come to fruition in the ways described. A review of previous Games events shows that numerous problems and difficulties can be expected along the way, leading to some compromises; however, in the case of London there does seem an underlying will to achieve as much as is possible. Several features of the procurement process are designed to support and enable the delivery of a sustainable event: the embedding of sustainability in systems and processes; the relationship established with the supply chain; the setting of challenging and aspirational standards; and the sharing of best practice.

There are still a number of reasons to be cautious, however, not least of which are the likely final costs of developing the venues and hosting the Games, which may reduce the organisers' abilities to deliver all components of the strategy. This is exacerbated by the so-called 'credit-crunch' that beleaguered international finance markets in the run-up to the Games. There are also reasons to be optimistic: the strategy and commitments are well-documented and in the public realm; the organisers respond actively to criticisms; the plan shows clear benefits in the re-development of a run-down area, which would be required regardless of the Games; public opinion has shifted with much more concern for sustainability and more willingness to embrace the costs of achieving it; and finally that sustainable solutions should in the longer term be the more cost-effective solutions.

Testing the evaluation framework

A part of the evaluation framework elaborated in Chapter 9 is now tested by using it to study the Olympic urban scheme of the two latest host cities: Beijing and London. An exact evaluation of the host cities, incorporating all indicators in the system, is not the purpose of the text since the evaluation method should be interpreted at local level and with local inputs and weightings. Rather this test is a demonstration of how factors could be interpreted and evaluated.

As with any assessment method, the framework needs to be tested for its effectiveness and validity. However, it is not possible with this methodology to carry out a validation as might be done for energy assessment (which might involve comparing measured values with predictions). The nature of host cities is complex, and to a significant degree the concept of sustainable development is ambiguous, multi-dimensional and generally not easily measured. In other words, there is no alternative method to measure the real effect of an Olympic scheme; this real effect can only be fully understood many years later after the Games are over, which is why this framework has been built upon the study of historical experiences and lessons.

Mitchell et al. (1995) summarised eight criteria commonly used to assess the value of sustainability indicators. They suggested that indicators should:

- be relevant to the issues of concern and scientifically defensible;
- be sensitive to change across space and across social groups;

- be sensitive to change overtime;
- be supported by consistent data;
- be understandable and, if appropriate, resonant;
- be measurable;
- be expressed in a way that makes sense;
- permit the identification of targets and trends that allow progress towards or away from sustainability to be determined.

These criteria can be used to test this Olympic framework.

In this section, a study is made to evaluate and compare certain development features of the Beijing and London Olympic schemes. Since the London scheme has not been finalised at the time of writing and since there are still gaps in information available for the Beijing event, the method does not deliver a final verdict but rather illustrates its use. Indicator B-1 has been chosen to run the test and the following points (arising from the above criteria) are examined during the case study:

- whether the framework can identify the distinctions between different Olympic urban schemes, and quantify the result for a meaningful comparison;
- whether the framework can evaluate the deficiencies of the Olympic urban scheme, and direct improvements;
- whether the criteria in the indicator sets are coherent with each other;
- how easy or difficult it is to find information to complete the evaluation process;
- whether the framework can be generalised to all host cities without losing sense;
- any other restrictions or limitations of the framework.

Initial comparison of London and Beijing

Table 10.1 compares some basic urban features of Beijing and London. Figures 10.1 and 10.2 schematically show the urban form and Olympic site planning of these two cities. Beijing and London share some similarities in urban form: both have a circular central mass that expands from their ancient cores; they have an urban road network that encompasses multiple ring roads orbiting the inner city, and radiating connections articulating the inner city with their outskirts; they both adopt a green-belt system to circumscribe the urban sprawl; and they each have a vast heritage of listed architecture and historic blocks that need to be preserved during urban development.

On the other hand these two cities also have many differences. From Table 10.1 it can be seen that Beijing's central agglomeration is one third smaller than that of London whereas the population is almost double, resulting in a much higher central city density and development pressure. While Beijing is more compact than London, it has a severe shortage of urban green and open spaces. Beijing's urban parkland per capita is about $10m^2$ per person, much lower than London ($25m^2$ per person) and many other European cities. In addition, Beijing's road network density and underground line length, although in a leading position among Chinese cities, have fallen behind the needs of its population size and rapid economic growth.

Table 10.1 Urban features of Beijing and London

Urban features	Beijing	London
Location	On the north-western margin of the North China Plain, at 116° E and 40° N	On the Thames River floodplain in the south-east of England, at 0° W and 53° N
Climate	Warm temperate continental monsoonal climate, with four distinctive seasons. Hot and dry during the Olympic period.	Cool temperature marine climate, summers are warm but not hot, winters are cool. Olympic period is generally pleasant.
Area (built-up agglomeration)	1,085km^2	1,578km^2
Area (administrative)	16,808km^2	11,230km^2
Population (great metropolitan)	10,849,000 (2005)	7,615,000 (2005)
Central city density	13,697 people/km^2	7,299 people/km^2
Central city road network density	4.64km/km^2	> 9km/km^2
Underground & light rail length	200km (2008)	433km (2008)
City property	The capital of China; political, cultural, educational and commercial centre of the Asian Pacific Rim; important gateway to north-east Asia	The capital of the UK and England; political, cultural, educational, finance and commercial centre of the world; the primary gateway to west Europe
Urbanisation phase	Rapid urbanisation period	Urban regeneration period
Urban economy (2004)	Light industry and business service dominated, GDP: 75.9 billion USD	Financial, cultural and business service dominated, GDP: 236.2 billion USD

Over the past half century, Beijing has experienced rapid urban expansion (built area expanding more than 300 per cent) and a population increase from 1.56 million in the 1950s to nearly 11 million in the late 1990s. This sevenfold increase within 50 years – faster than many industrialised cities during their peaks of urbanisation – has placed huge demands on housing and civic infrastructures (Sit, 1996). From 1953 to 1978, Beijing also experienced a hasty growth of new industrial areas in its western and south-eastern suburbs; these initiatives, especially the development of many polluting and water-intensive industries, left Beijing with a series of environmental problems and infrastructural discrepancies.

During the last two decades, Beijing authorities have focused on investment in commerce and tourism to boost service industries; a process accelerated by the staging of the Asian Games in 1990 and preparations for the 2008 Olympics. In order to release the development pressure from the saturated inner-city, and to constrain the unbridled sprawl of its central mass, Beijing planned a number of self-sufficient peripheral settlements outside the greenbelt to disperse the population and jobs. This strategy has been followed since the city's 1958 General Plan,

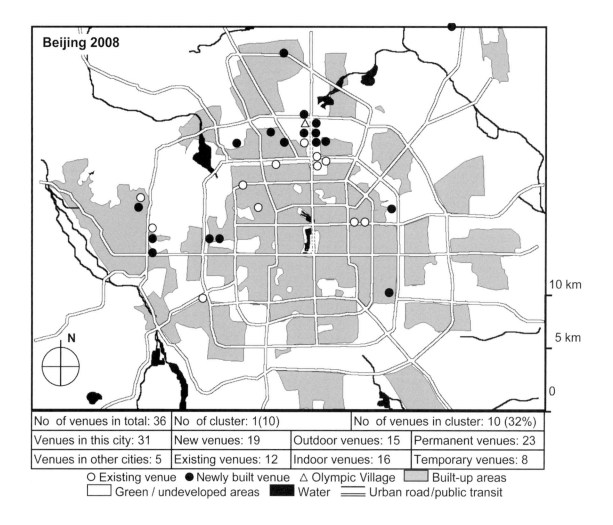

No of venues in total: 36	No of cluster: 1(10)		No of venues in cluster: 10 (32%)	
Venues in this city: 31	New venues: 19	Outdoor venues: 15	Permanent venues: 23	
Venues in other cities: 5	Existing venues: 12	Indoor venues: 16	Temporary venues: 8	

O Existing venue ● Newly built venue △ Olympic Village ▭ Built-up areas
▭ Green / undeveloped areas ■ Water ═ Urban road/public transit

Figure 10.1
Schematic drawing of the Olympic site planning for Beijing 2008

and continuing through the later urban plans of 1982, 1991 and 2004 (Beijing Municipality, 1982, 1991, 2004).

London has also undergone major changes over recent decades, driven in the main by economic globalisation, the decline of manufacturing industry and the boom of financial and business activities interlinked with advances in technology. According to a recent study, London has reinforced its status as the economic power in Europe in terms of the annual gross domestic product (GDP) value (Lyne, 2002). The growth of income and wealth raises demands for leisure and service activities, but also increases social and economic polarisation.

Arising from earlier decentralisation of economic activities, London's population declined from a peak of over eight million in 1939 to 6.8 million in 1983 (GLA, 2002). This trend has been reversed in more recent times and a steady population renaissance has been evident since the 1990s, projecting increasing demands for housing and local service facilities. Traditionally, east London was more industrial

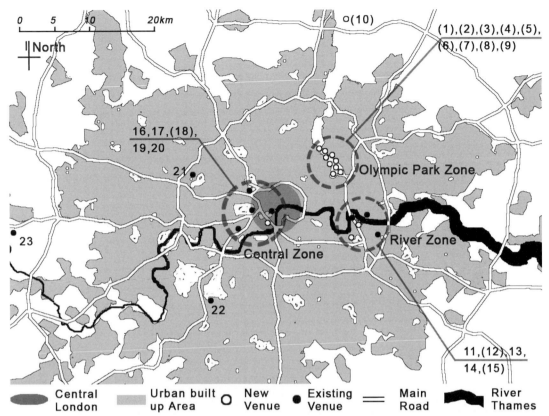

0   5   10   20km

North

○(10)

(1),(2),(3),(4),(5),
(6),(7),(8),(9)

16,17,(18),
19,20

21

23

Olympic Park Zone

Central Zone

River Zone

22

11,(12),13,
14,(15)

| Central London | Urban built up Area | ○ New Venue | ● Existing Venue | — Main Road | River Thames |

13 new venues: (1) Aquatics Centre (2) Basketball Arena (3) Olympic Stadium (4) Handball Arena (5) Hockey Centre (6) VeloPark (Velodrome and BMX circuit) (7) Fencing Hall (8) Olympic Media & Press Centre (9) Olympic village (10) Broxbourne Canoe Slalom (12) Greenwich Arena (15) Greenwich Park (Equestrian Ground) (18) Horse Guard Parade

17 existing venues (10 in great London area): 11 The Dome (O₂) 13 Excel 14 Royal Artillery barracks 16 Lord's Cricket Ground 17 Earls Court 19 Regent park (for road cycling) 20 Hyde Park (for Triathlon) 21 New Wembley Stadium 22 Wimbledon Tennis Centre 23 Eton Dorney (for Flatwater Canoe/Kayak)

in character but with twentieth-century industrial decline, many boroughs and the docklands area suffered a range of environmental and social decay, and required effective regeneration. As in many bustling cities, London has also experienced considerable surface-traffic congestion in its central zones and its underground system required upgrading.

Beijing and London conceived their Olympic urban-scale development schemes with different motivations and facing different problems. Beijing planned 31 competition venues and 58 training grounds, 20 of them as newly built facilities and 11 renovated sites. Its Olympic planning created a 'periphery clustering' model, with the existing and refurbished venues scattered in the west and north-west part of the city. Most of the key sports facilities, Athletes' Village and media centres were accommodated in the large Olympic park on the northern edge of the city's central mass. The underpinning idea was to exploit Beijing's existing sports premises developed for the 1990 Asian Games with the Olympic cluster elements tactically

Figure 10.2
Schematic drawing of the Olympic site planning for London 2012

located adjacent to the 'Asian Games Park'. In a symbolic sense, Beijing's north–south axis is also reinforced, as the series of key Olympic buildings, including the national stadium, national arena, national aquatic centre and national exhibition centre, sit on the northern end of a ritualistic route aligned with the Imperial Palace (Forbidden City) and the Tiananmen Gate in the heart of Beijing.

In Beijing's 1991 General Plan (published before the first Olympic bid), the city's further development orientation was actually identified to be towards the southeast. This occurred not only because Beijing's north and west were flanked by mountains acting as development barriers, but also because it supported regional combination with another large city in that direction: Tian-Jin (Beijing Municipality, 1991). However, Beijing's Olympic plan did not follow this option and was northwards focused. This change came about in order to help develop the Olympic bid because the urban environment, sports amenities and civic infrastructure in the north of the city were considered superior to those in the long-neglected south.

Criticisms were made that Beijing's Olympic plan would further aggravate city development imbalance and social inequity. Nevertheless, this deficiency is partly compensated for by the city's ambitious plan to extend the underground and light-rail network. Beijing planned to extend its underground by 87.1km, making the total length of the network over 200km. Although this project was budgeted for in the Olympic urban package, only a portion of these lines were designed to serve the Olympic precinct, the remainder stretch to other parts of the city, especially to the south, in support of transit-orientated development.

This evaluation relates to London's initial plans as a means of proving the concept rather than arriving at a final evaluation. This in any case would need to include information for all indicators. In the original proposals one could speculatively identify 28 competition venues (plus 50 training grounds), 11 to be new and 17 renovated. The evolution of the plans now appears to make greater use of existing facilities, which is to be welcomed. The basic Olympic planning matches the 'inner-city poly-clustering' model, with existing and renovated venues being clustered in three zones. Most of the new venues and the Olympic Village are to be located on two concentrated sites in east London, with a third 'cluster' just west of the central zone might now be identified. The primary site is at Lower Lea Valley (only seven minutes by train from the city centre at Kings Cross station); here the Olympic Stadium, Olympic arena, Olympic aquatic centre and other key premises are located. Most of London's Olympic venues are to be accessible through the city's public transport network. The Lower Lea Valley Olympic park will be particularly well-served by the 225km/hr 'Olympic Javelin' shuttle service.

The Mayor of London's plan for the city, adopted in 2004 (before London won the Olympic bid), identified 28 'opportunity areas' as the priorities for a spatial and economic regeneration by 2016 (GLA, 2004). Most of the areas were in east London and Lower Lea Valley is one of the most frequently mentioned sites. From this point of view, London's Olympic plan is more consistent with the city's long-term development strategy than was the case in Beijing.

Improving the green landscape is also one of the selling points of London's bid; the development of the Olympic park will transform 200ha of degraded land into a new sports legacy park, forming part of the extension of the Lea Valley Regional Park system, stretching from the edge of London right down to the River Thames.

Figure 10.3
Construction site for London 2012 Games

Test of framework indicator

Indicator B-1 (contribution of overall Olympic masterplanning to a sustainable urban form) was chosen to examine the functioning of the evaluation framework. This indicator incorporates a significant number of criteria and therefore provides an opportunity to examine a number of issues.

The various components and evaluations are shown in the boxes in Table 10.2. They demonstrate how the indicator B-1 is used to evaluate the effect of the Olympic masterplanning in Beijing and London against the objective to pursue a more sustainable urban form.

Table 10.2 Evaluation of masterplanning for Beijing and London (Indicator B-1)

Criterion 1: In favour of urban containment policy	
Beijing: not applicable. Beijing's main Olympic site involves peripheral expansion. The extension of the urban underground network will also trigger an organised sprawl. Yet the 1,085ha Olympic-related parkland may strengthen the northern part of the greenbelt, and since Beijing's inner-city density has already been very high and the mid-term strategy is to disperse the population to the satellite settlements, the overall Olympic urban concept is acceptable.	**London:** supported. London's main site involves inner-city land modification and brownfield redevelopment. The Lower Lea Valley area is only 13km east from the London centre. Other main projects also located within London's second ring road. In particular, Olympic urban development will help to attract investment and follow-up development to east London, and provide a vehicle for inward urban regeneration.
Sub-credits awarded: 0	**Sub-credits awarded: 2**

Criterion 2: Optimisation of urban density

Beijing: not supported. In some parts of Beijing the urban density is too high to enable adequate quality of life. Beijing's Olympic precinct and the village park have been planned at around 35–40 DPH, much lower than traditional local density values. Although the point is to demonstrate a low-rise, medium-density experiment for the city's housing market, there is potential to raise the ratio by 20%.

London: supported. London is a relatively compact city in the UK. According to PPG3, a good practice for development density is 40–60 DPH. London's Olympic Village and the development in Lower Lea Valley have been conceived to follow this principle. The village will provide 3,000+ housing units after the Games. It can be foreseen that Olympic intervention would raise the urban density in East London.

Sub-credits awarded: 0

Sub-credits awarded: 2

Criterion 3: Rectification of dispersed urban form

Beijing: supported. In recent years, with the city's rapid growth, Beijing's satellite settlements have consistently expanded and blended with each other, forming a low-density semi-urban ring outside the greenbelt. Beijing's Olympic plan rectifies this problem in two aspects: one is to encourage a range of high-density development corridors through the erection of 11 new urban transit lines; the other is to reinforce the Olympic precinct as one of the city's north sub-centres. It is expected that Beijing will be transformed from an even sprawling form to a cruciform fabric based on the arterial lines in the post-Olympic period.

London: supported. The early decentralisation policy implemented in post-war London has left some negative consequences. On one hand the greenbelt cannot prevent 'overspill' town development across the outer metropolitan area; on the other hand the out-of-city developments further weaken the strength of the inner-city. London's Olympic plan will help to attract the investment back to the inner-city, especially Lea Valley and the Thames Gateway. This will also help to promote a 'poly-centric' urban form in east London that has been advocated in the Mayor of London's plan for the city.

Sub-credits awarded: 4

Sub-credits awarded: 4

Criterion 4: Definition of centres for community

Beijing: supported. Beijing's chief Olympic site includes six new multi-functional venues, a thematic park and various urban amenities, which are strong enough in spatial and economic sense to form a centre for the local community. The adjacent 'Asian Games Village' is also a commercial centre in north Beijing. This combination will reinforce the centric feature of the site.

London: supported. London's chief Olympic site includes nine new multi-functional venues, transport hub, a thematic park and other urban amenities, which is strong enough in spatial and economic sense to form a centre in Lower Lea Valley area with Stratford City. This centre, together with Canary Wharf CBD, Greenwich town centre and City Airport area, will contribute a poly-centric urban form in east London.

Sub-credits awarded: 4

Sub-credits awarded: 4

Criterion 5: Encouragement of mixed-use development

Beijing: supported. Beijing's main Olympic precinct includes the development of housing projects and a variety of other facilities, including leisure, office and commercial premises. The balance of employment, dwelling areas and public service was specified in the development brief. Other new Olympic venues are mainly built as student sports centres in university campus areas, which can also be used by the local community.

London: supported. Encouragement of mixed-use development is a basic theme in London's Olympic bid together with other sustainable development commitments. The regeneration plan for the Lea Valley should result in 7,000 jobs, 3,600 housing units and substantial service infrastructure left to the community. Also the public–private partnership is a maturing mechanism to support mixed development for marketing profit.

Sub-credits awarded: 2

Sub-credits awarded: 2

Criterion 6: Brownfield development potential

Beijing: not supported. Beijing's main Olympic site sits on the edge of the city's central mass. The 405ha Olympic Park was established on semi-rural land and the 700ha 'forest park' is zoned from the greenbelt. The amount of brownfield is rather low in overall land usage. The potential for brownfield recycling is also moderate for proposed follow-up development in the precinct.

London: strongly supported. Lea Valley and nearby areas contain many degraded brownfield sites of an industrial character. The development of London's Olympic park has a strong blend of land modification and brownfield redevelopment. As many 'opportunity areas' have been identified in east London, the potential of brownfield transformation around the Olympic precinct is high.

Sub-credits awarded: 0

Sub-credits awarded: 2

Criterion 7: Public transportation triggering

Beijing: strongly supported. Beijing's Olympic package includes an ambitious plan to extend its current transport network, including 11 new underground and light-rail lines with total length of 87.1km, the No. 5 ring road (93km) and various urban arterial motorways (140km). Olympic urban development will effectively improve the city's transport capacity.

London: partly supported. London's Olympic plan will trigger some public transport improvement in the east London area, including the establishment of the 'Olympic Javelin' line connecting Kings Cross station and Kent, and the extension of DLR and Jubilee line. In addition, waterborne transport will be enhanced on the River Thames and canals in Lea Valley.

Sub-credits awarded: 2

Sub-credits awarded: 1

Criterion 8: Transit-orientated development promotion

Beijing: supported. This is attached to Beijing's major plan to extend the city's public transit system and urban road network. Some schemes have been released to encourage a few high-density corridors to be developed in the post-Olympic period.

London: partly supported. With more public transport hubs envisaged in east London, transit-orientated development will be promoted in the area. The main focus in London's Olympic plan is to upgrade the existing transport infrastructure and focus of the local sites, transit-orientated development promotion may be less prominent elsewhere.

Sub-credits awarded: 2

Sub-credits awarded: 1

Criterion 9: Inner-city renaissance

Beijing: partly supported. Generally speaking Beijing has not experienced an obvious decline in terms of urban economy and population since it was selected as the capital of the nation. Yet the environmental conditions have become degraded in recent decades. Olympic plans included the clearance of some pollution sources throughout the city. Also the Games promoted a cultural renewal. Yet these impacts are rather indirect, and the southern part of the city has received less benefit.

London: strongly supported. London's Olympic urban development will stimulate environmental, economic and social renaissance in the Lea Valley area, the Thames Gateway and nearby industrialised precincts in east London. It is planned that inner London will increase in population and jobs in the coming decades, and Olympic urban development will further strengthen this trend.

Sub-credits awarded: 2

Sub-credits awarded: 4

Criterion 10: Urban green/open space enhancement

Beijing: strongly supported. Beijing's Olympic plan includes the development of a 405ha thematic park, 700ha 'forest parkland' and 50ha of other public green spaces. The greenbelt will also be reinforced through the transformation of some neglected land in the semi-rural ring into managed woodlands.

London: strongly supported. London's Olympic plan includes the development of a 200ha thematic park, which will form part of the Lea Valley Parkland, one of the largest urban parks in Europe. Lea Valley used to be one of the main green wedges in London's landscape system.

Sub-credits awarded: 2

Sub-credits awarded: 2

Criterion 11: Urban run-down area revitalisation

Beijing: not supported. Beijing's run-down areas are mainly in the south part of the city. Olympic urban development does not involve run-down area regeneration. Furthermore, there is a risk that the current development imbalance would be intensified in the post-Games period.

London: strongly supported. London's Olympic plan is based on the revitalisation of declining areas in east London, particularly Lower Lea Valley and nearby precincts that have been identified in the city's long-term plan.

Sub-credits awarded: 0

Sub-credits awarded: 4

Criterion 12: Energy efficient and CHP/DH system promotion

Beijing: supported. Beijing has a tradition of using district heating systems in its residential quarters owing much to the early soviet influence. New and renewable energy appliances were used in the Olympic park, and the Athletes' Village including CHP systems. It is not possible to be sure about the efficiency of the systems.

London: supported. The London proposals focus significant attention on energy and power provision using high efficiency systems and sources of renewable energy. Energy centres are being provided with options to change fuels source. The development is themed 'low-carbon' rather than zero-carbon.

Sub-credits awarded: 2

Sub-credits awarded: 2

Criterion 13: New urban landmark creation

Beijing: strongly supported. Beijing's north–south urban axis has long been regarded as the most important cultural vein of the city, which strings the city's key monuments together. The Olympic park and the key venues have been arranged on the north end of this axis to consummate this invisible line, and also form an essential part of the new urban landmark.

London: partly supported. Perhaps the River Thames is the cultural vein of London. London's Olympic complex will provide a unique landmark to east London, and together with the Millennium Dome – Maritime Greenwich – the Thames Barrier help form east London's new urban identity. Closer to the event as full design proposals are released further credit may be awarded.

Sub-credits awarded: 2

Sub-credits awarded: 1

Criterion 14: Coherence with the IOC's planning policy

Beijing: supported. Beijing's Olympic plan is consistent with the IOC's 'site concentration' policy: 32% of venues (and all main sites) are clustered in the Olympic park and most of the rest within 25 minutes' driving distance from the Olympic Village. All of the permanent venues have been defined with post-Games usage.

London: supported. London's Olympic plan is consistent with the IOC's 'site concentration' policy: 45% of venues are clustered in the Olympic park and most of the rest are in 20 minutes by train from the Olympic Village. All of the permanent venues have been defined with the post-Games usage.

Sub-credits awarded: 2

Sub-credits awarded: 2

Criterion 15: Implementation feasibility

Beijing: supported. Due to the peripheral location, the disturbance to many citizen's daily life during the site construction was low and the project was completed well on time.

London: partly supported. The construction process may raise some urban disturbance and displacement, though no general problem has been identified at present; potential to award a second credit exists.

Sub-credits awarded: 2

Sub-credits awarded: 1

Summary of the evaluation process outcomes for indicator B-1

Contribution of overall Olympic masterplanning to a sustainable urban form:

Beijing

> Total credits available for this process for Beijing: 38
> Total credits awarded to Beijing in this process: 26
> Assessment index (Δ): 0.684
> Overall score for Beijing in evaluation of this indicator: 4 ($0.6 < \Delta \leq 0.8$)

London

> Total credits available for this process for London: 38
> Total credits awarded to London in this process: 34
> Assessment index (Δ): 0.895
> Overall score for London in evaluating this indicator: 5 ($\Delta > 0.8$)

Commentary on the evaluation test

In the exercise, the performance of London's Olympic urban plan appears superior to that of Beijing. Beijing's plan has benefits in the following areas: triggering new public transport infrastructures, and hence transit-orientated development in some defined corridors; and promoting large open spaces and parklands, and creating strong symbolic urban landmarks. Its weakness lies in the relatively low development density and potential for urban sprawl, brownfield recycling potential, and remediation of run-down or poor urban areas. If Beijing's plan had included some of its development (not necessarily the main Olympic site) in its less-developed southern outskirts, this would have promoted the city's overall development balance and the revitalisation of its problematic industrial quarters. By comparison, London's plan has strong benefits in using brownfield sites, regenerating its degraded areas, and hastening inner-city renaissance. It has no obvious weakness but gets less credit for public transport triggers, urban landmark creation and implementation feasibility; in these areas the performance of London's Olympic intervention is believed less prominent than those of the Beijing plan. In each case it should be noted that though some criticisms have been made under the B-1 indicator, there may be compensating credits under other indicators not shown here.

Based on this exercise, those questions posed earlier now can be answered: the framework is able to identify the distinctions between different Olympic urban schemes, and qualify their performance for meaningful comparison. Through the evaluation the weaknesses embodied in each Olympic plan can be identified and therefore provide opportunity for consideration and possible amendment in appropriate decision-making activities. The indicators are generally consistent with each other throughout the evaluation.

Several additional observations can be made. First, the implementation of the evaluation process relies on awareness and knowledge of substantial data and background information of the Olympic urban scheme as well as the host city. Any missing information, as might be the case early in the planning stages, could cause problems in making any judgement. Second, during the credit-awarding process, the assessor's personal interpretation is inevitably involved, particularly for those diagnoses based on qualitative criteria. These two points suggest that the framework would be better manipulated by an evaluation team rather than an individual, in order to have broader consensus and more convincing outcomes. Third, the very different urban plans for Beijing and London achieve relatively close scores. This may suggest that the overall scoring gradation may need to be adjusted to ensure the differences between two schemes can be effectively compared. Fourth, not all the criteria are clearly applicable to every host city (for instance criterion I could have been excluded from the Beijing assessment). There is a need to transform the generic framework into a more local version to suit the situations of individual locations. And finally, once the framework has been applied to a number of schemes the outputs may help to develop the procedures better to distinguish, and hence score, performance against the criteria.

CHAPTER 11

Conclusions and recommendations

Summary

The aim of this final chapter is to draw together some analysis of the major findings and proposals developed in the preceding chapters, and to suggest the remaining gaps in knowledge that need to be addressed in the future.

The principal aim of this study was to investigate the summer Olympic events, and their host cities, and to carry out analysis to aid in the development of more sustainable future Games. An output of this research has been an attempt to define an integrating evaluation framework that can be used to guide Olympic urban development. Any such analysis should benchmark and assess the numerous interwoven elements of the planning and design process.

Key influences have been identified. First, the major factors that shape the use of energy and other finite resources in large Olympic projects during their procurement and operation. Second, the influence of Olympic site integration on the host city's spatial form, land patterns, resource efficiency, transport infrastructures, ecological footprints, and economic and social cohesion. Finally, the imperatives of the Olympic Movement as any potential innovation made to Olympic urban development should not compromise its fundamental function, thus safeguarding a successful Olympic celebration.

This naturally led to the explorations of the background to the Games and their inception in Part 1 of the text (Chapters 1 and 2). The scope of Olympic urban development was identified to have different levels and forms of infrastructure based on connections with the Games. 'Direct-Olympic-related' development embodies major facilities in staging the event, which need to be examined at both individual project level and urban level for their environmental consequences. The 'indirect-Olympic-related' development, by comparison, has much to do with the macro-scale impact of Olympic intervention on the host city's general built environment; this should be evaluated at the strategic planning level for its interactions with the city's long-term plan. The influence of the International Olympic Committee and its leaders in shaping Olympic urban settings was noted. In particular, De Coubertin's concept in creating a 'Modern Olympia' still inspires the spatial arrangement of Olympic facilities at the present time. The IOC's commitment to leave positive environmental legacies supports sustainable development principles being integrated into the decision-making process for Olympic urban issues.

In Part 2 (Chapters 3 to 6), a range of driving forces behind the evolutionary course of Olympic urban design, sports venues and the Olympic Villages were discussed. First, the forms of Olympic impacts on urban design and development were examined and the main phases explained. Six typical urban models of Olympic integration were identified, each having various advantages and disadvantages in triggering urban transformation, and in impacts on spatial deficiencies and development pressures. The potential for Olympic urban intervention to address local environmental issues involved discussion of positive and negative impacts derived from historical review. The development of Olympic venues from simply equipped, open-air sports grounds to an increasing array of highly specified, micro-climatically controlled complexes was further considered. The increase in Olympic sports and required premises raises the question of venue flexibility and versatility. The recognition of the continuing trend towards enclosure also led to the investigation of structure and canopy forms, and also the requirements of modern media and television broadcasts with impacts on lighting design and roof material selection. A review of the transformation in standards of the Olympic Villages from austere pre-competition lodges to full-service urban quarters was also carried out. Research findings revealed that the development of Olympic Villages (and hence the selection of the main Olympic precinct) should be in line with the host city's urbanisation strategy. The identification of various issues helped to cast light on the understanding of the dynamics between Olympic architecture and its environmental imprints, and to lead to appropriate responses through design considerations. The range of impacts in economic, social and environmental fields completed this part of the text, by which point substantial data had been accumulated upon which evaluations might be based to aid sustainable design and development.

Part 3 (Chapters 7 to 11) dealt more specifically with contemporary positions and future developments. The wide-ranging infrastructure requirements to host a Games – enshrined in the major Olympic documents and codes – were considered. Notable points included those for venue selection, the issue of 'site concentration' and 'easy accessibility'. Key principles were identified that would be reflected by the evaluation criteria of the later framework. The IOC and IFs also recommend a range of design parameters for Olympic facilities, for instance: the number of venues for each sport; the seating capacity and floor space; and other technical specifications. These data provide useful references in setting up the benchmarks for some indicators used, although the study found that some needed to be revised according to empirical evidence.

Contemporary sustainable development and evaluation techniques for the built environment were examined and consensus with respect to environmental sustainability discussed, along with implications for Olympic urban intervention. A Symptom – Driving force – Response – Olympic Initiatives (SDROI) analytical process was suggested to identify the issues of concern in the evaluation framework. The input information came from an examination of environmental symptoms that can exist in Olympic host cities and which are subject to influence through Olympic urban development. Through this process, the upper hierarchy of the framework and essential evaluation components were conceived. The evaluation framework was developed and justified in some detail in Chapter 9. It is composed of 19 indicators grouped into nine themes; each indicator encompasses multiple assessment criteria, scoring benchmarks and provides a default weighting factor to enable the evaluation. A performance index could be set up based on the evaluation score.

A review of proposals for the London 2012 Games was carried out considering the specific emphasis on sustainable development. A test of one of the evaluation indicators was also performed by comparing possible inputs for London and for Beijing. This suggests that the evaluation methods are workable and can be developed further.

Conclusions

The first conclusion to this study is that the potential of Olympic design to redress the deficiencies of a host city's built environment and to contribute to long-term sustainable development has been demonstrated through examination of historical records and theoretical analysis. The implementation is not the same for each location, however, and should be considered according to the circumstances of each host city. The environmental performance and impacts of Olympic schemes can be evaluated, compared and improved by using assessment techniques, which can enable more sustainable Olympic design and development, at urban scale but also in connection with individual venues and the Olympic Village.

The text has established a framework that can be used to evaluate the inter-related parameters embodied in Olympic urban schemes in terms of environmental credentials and impacts. It has used evidence from previous Games and from the wider field of sustainable development to define a range of basic indicators and criteria, linked to assessment methods, scoring benchmarks and weighting coefficients. The data and values incorporated may need to be expanded, calibrated and corrected over time and particularly with the evolution of the Olympic Games, societal issues and knowledge of sustainable development. Nevertheless, it does provide a basis and starting point on which any further study can be built.

Another contribution of this work is the compilation, in a systematic manner, of a database of previous Olympic development information concerned with design parameters, planning concepts, technical regulations, environmental impacts, after-use options, and various experiences and lessons from previous Olympic urban preparations. These data may form the basis for further study and development. The continuing work of the IOC should also be incorporated; it now collects together its sustainability-focused material on its website (IOC, 2008).

There are several topic areas for which evidence allows a degree of inference and extrapolation, too. The current enthusiasm for creating ever more spectacular Games should be moderated, particularly if cities other than major capitals are to be able to bid in the future. Smaller cities do not have the resources nor the need for multiple large-scale sports venues in the post-Games period. Two options suggest themselves – first that temporary settings and reusable structures should be encouraged; and second that perhaps the IOC might review its emphasis on single cities acting as hosts in favour of a more regional approach. In the case of large cities, although the hosting of a Games can act as a focus for regeneration and development, the shortened timescale and pressures that result once a Games has been awarded can be counter-productive. A more sustainable outcome for a city may well be easier to achieve without the Games intervention. Efforts and policies should be supported to avoid the acquisition and monopolisation of finance and resources by the Games activities that are to the detriment of other local areas. Large cities will still wish to bid for the Games, however, so the main themes that could be stressed are: to be less lavish and more focused, and particularly realistic about spectator numbers; to determine those sports with real long-term legacies and encourage more temporary structures for others; and to ensure that a city already has a plan for sustainable urban design and development within which the Games operates effectively and efficiently.

Future developments

For the future, promotion of knowledge transfer is important and there is a need to transform the content of the evaluation framework into design guidelines or a development checklist. The outcomes could also be used in examining and potentially amending the Olympic rules or expectations (through the IOC and the International Federations) in order to steer infrastructural preparation for future Games. Data collection and knowledge accumulation from future Olympic urban activities, particularly the issues related to environmental techniques and urban sustainability, is also to be encouraged. Experience has shown that studies can be disrupted by inadequate information and data fragmentation. Since examination of environmental and sustainability issues through an Olympic host city is a relatively new area, appropriate mechanisms or channels for data acquisition, compilation and dissemination are required. This could be in a form similar to the IOC's Olympic Observers Programme or Olympic Study Commission but should involve built-environment professionals to maximise the benefit for all those who engage with planning and design.

As the Olympic Games can be seen as one extreme of a wide spectrum of mega-events, a better understanding of the impacts of Olympic Games on major world cities may also be of value for other large-scale events (world championships, intercontinental games and national fairs) both in large but also smaller cities. Research would add to the understanding of mega-event orientated urban development and enrich the findings of this study.

Finally, this book has provided an overview of the current state of knowledge with regard to the evaluation of Olympic urban design and development for environmental sustainability. It cannot be exhaustive as the potential spectrum of activity that falls in the subject is enormous, and in the future it will probably be necessary to invoke corporate efforts and mechanisms through which the complexity of the subject can be understood and developed. Such efforts may be associated with national or international evaluation schemes or with the IOC itself. In pursuing the goal of understanding the subject and developing a response, the authors have concluded that there are no right or wrong answers to producing methods and processes of evaluation. What is important is to continue to develop better techniques that are able to reveal the potential problems, to direct actions, and to indicate progress. Each and every evaluation method that has been systematically conceived and developed is useful and adds to knowledge that is refined from previous wisdom, and provides a step in the cycle of refinement.

Figure 11.1
The Bird's Nest Stadium for the Beijing Olympics under construction

It is hoped that the information presented here has the potential to create such a step and has some potential to improve understanding and the creation of sustainable development in future Olympic Games.

References

Aalborg Charter (1994) *Charter of European Cities and Towns Towards Sustainability*. Approved by European Conference on Sustainable Cities and Towns, 27 May 1994, Aalborg.

Abad, J. (1996) *Olympic Village, City and Organisation of the Olympic Games. The Experience of Barcelona'92*. In: Proceedings of the International Symposium on Olympic Villages, November, Lausanne, International Olympic Committee, p.16.

Abelson, P., Joyeux, R., Milunovich, G. and Chung, D. (2005) *House Prices in Australia: 1970 to 2003, Facts and Explanations*, Sydney, Macquarie University.

Abitare (1983) 'Melbourne 1956'. *Magazine of Abitare l'Olimpiadi*, 9 November, p.76.

ACOG (1996) *Official Report of the Games of the XXVI Olympiad, Atlanta 1996* (three volumes). Atlanta, Atlanta Committee for the Olympic Games.

ACPO (2004) *Secured by Design Principles*, Association of Chief Police Officers Crime Prevention Initiative. Available online www.securedbydesign.com/pdfs/SBD-principles. pdf (accessed 21 September 2008).

Amis, D. (2005) *Urban Renewal, Gentrification and the Impact on the Working Class in London*. The Independent Working Class Association. Available online www.iwca.info/cutedge/gentrification.D.Amis.2005.05.pdf (accessed 7 July 2005).

Anderson, J., Shiers, D. and Sinclair, M. (2002) *The Green Guide to Specification*, Building Research Establishment, Oxford, Wiley/Blackwell.

Andranovich, G., Burbank, M. and Heying, C. (2001) 'Olympic Cities: Lessons Learned from Mega-event Politics'. *Journal of Urban Affairs*, (23) (2): 113–31.

ASOIF (2003) *Technical Rules on Venues for Summer Olympic Sports* [Internet] The official website of the Association of Summer Olympic International Federations. Available online www.asoif.com (accessed 12 October 2008).

ATHENS 2004 (2004) *Unforgettable Games, Dream Games* [Internet] The official website of the ATHENS 2004 Olympic Games – Games of the XXVIII Olympiad. Available online www.athens2004.com/en (accessed 6 October 2004).

Atkinson, R. (2002) 'Does Gentrification Help or Harm Urban Neighbourhoods? An Assessment of the Evidence Base in the Context for the New Urban Agenda'. *CNR Paper 5*, Glasgow, ESRC Centre for Neighbourhoods Research.

Bailey, R. (1993) 'What the Games did to Melbourne'. *Sydney Morning Herald*, 12 August.

Baker, N. (1989) 'The Games that almost Weren't: London 1948'. *Olympika*. Centre for Olympic Studies, Western Ontario University.

Balderstone, S. (2001) *Agenda 21 and IOC requirements*. (Speech record) In: Proceedings of the International Conference on Olympic Games and Architecture – the future for host cities, May, Lausanne, International Olympic Committee, pp. 1–6.

Bale, J. (1994) *Landscape of Modern Sport*, Leicester, Leicester University Press.

Banister, D. (1992) Energy use, transport and settlement patterns. In: Breheny, M. (ed.), *Sustainable development and urban form*, London, Pion, pp. 160–81.

Barton, H., Davis, G. and Guise, R. (1995) *Sustainable Settlements: a Guide for Planners, Designers and Developers*, London, Local Government Management Board.

BBC (2005) *Buying the Games* [Internet] BBC Panorama Website. Available online http://news.bbc.co.uk/1/hi/programmes/panorama/4649677.stm (accessed 13 October 2008).

Beck, R., Kolankievvicz, L. and Camarota, S. (2003) *Outsmarting Smart Growth, Population Growth, Immigration and the Problem of Sprawl.* Washington DC, Centre for Immigration Studies.

Beijing Municipality (1982) *General Plan of Beijing (Draft).* Unpublished Chinese Internal Official Document, Beijing Town Planning Commission, Chinese text.

Beijing Municipality (1991) *General Plan of Beijing (1991–2010).* [Internet] Beijing Development and Reform Committee, Chinese text. Available online www.bjpc.gov.cn/fzgh/csztgh/200508/t130.htm (accessed 11 November 2005).

Beijing Municipality (2004) *General Plan of Beijing (2004–2020).* Beijing Development and Reform Committee, Chinese text. Available online www.bjpc.gov.cn/fzgh/csztgh/ght/200508/t249.htm (accessed 13 November 2005).

Bentivegna, V. (1997) Limitations in environmental evaluations. In: Brandon, P., Lombardi, P. and Bentivegna, V. (eds) *Evaluation of the built environment for sustainability*, London, E. & F.N. Spon, pp. 25–38.

Berlioux, M. (1991) *Olympica*, Paris, Flammarion.

BIADR (2002) *Olympic Games and Sports Buildings.* Beijing Institute of Architectural Design and Research, Chinese text. Tian-Jin, Tian-Jin University Press.

Booth, R. (2008) 'Athletes Forced to Cosy Up as £250m Shortfall Hits London's Olympic Village'. *The Guardian*, 6 September.

Bosselmann, P., Dake, K., Fountain, M., Kraus, L., Lin, K. and Harris, A. (1988) *Sun, wind and comfort: a field study of thermal comfort in San Francisco.* Centre for Environmental Design Research, Berkeley, CA, University of California, September, Working Paper 627.

Brandizzi, G. (1989) 'Architecture and the Games'. *Spaziosport*, special number dedicated to the Seoul Olympic Games 1988, 7 (3): 180.

Brandon, P. (1998) Managing sustainability: endurance through change. In: *Proceedings of the CIB World Conference*, 25–26 March, Gavle.

Brandon, P., Lombardi, P. and Bentivegna, V. (1997) *Evaluation of the Built Environment for Sustainability*, London, E. & F.N. Spon.

Brandon, P. and Lombardi, P. (2005) *Evaluating Sustainable Development in the Built Environment*, Oxford, Blackwell.

Breheny, M. (1992) *Sustainable Development and Urban Form*, London, Pion Limited.

Breheny, M. (1996) Centrists, decentrists and compromisers. In: Jenks, M., Burton, E. and Williams, K. (eds) *The compact city: a sustainable urban form?* London, E. & F.N. Spon.

Breheny, M. (2001) 'The Compact City: an Introduction'. *Built environment*, 18 (4): 214–46.

Brownhill, D. and Rao, S. (2002) *A Sustainable Checklist for Developments: a Common Framework for Developers and Local Authorities.* Garston, Building Research Establishment.

Brundage, A. (1968) Presidents/Avery Brundage, Correspondence: 1952–72. IOC Historical Archives, Lausanne, Olympic Museum.

Brunet, F. (1993) *Economy of the 1992 Barcelona Olympic Games.* Lausanne, International Olympic Committee.

CABE (2008) *Building for Life – Evaluating Housing Proposals Step by Step.* Commission for Architecture and the Built Environment. Available online www.buildingforlife.org/AssetLibrary/11349.pdf (accessed 21 September 2008).

Cable, C. (1982) *Architecture of the Olympics, 1960–1980.* Monticello, Vance Bibliographies.

Cardinali, G. (1983) 'Report on Mexico City 15 Years after 1968'. *Magazine of Abitare l'Olimpiadi*, 9 November: 92.

Cashman, R. (1999) Greatest peacetime event. In: Cashman, R. and Hughes, A. (eds) *Staging the Olympics, the event and its impact*, Sydney, University of New South Wales Press.

Cashman, R. (2003) *Impact of the Games on Olympic host cities*, Barcelona, Centre d'Estudis Olímpics i de l'Esport (UAB), Universitat Autonoma de Barcelona.

CEC (1990) *Green Paper on the Urban Environment*, Brussels, Commission of European Communities.

Chalkey, B.S. and Essex, S.J. (2000) *The Olympic Games: Catalyst of Urban Change*, University of Plymouth. Available online www.geog.plym.ac.uk/research/groups/Olympic_games.html (accessed 6 April 2002).

CIRIA (1998) *Remedial Treatment for Contaminated Land*, Volume IV: *Classification and selection of remedial methods*. CIRIA Special Publications 104, London, Construction Industry Research and Information Association.

CLG (2008) 'Eco-towns Prospectus', Department for Communities and Local Government. Available online www.communities.gov.uk/publications/housing/ecotownsprospectus (accessed 8 May 2008).

COHRE (2006) *Forced Evictions, Violation of Human Rights, Global Survey 10*. Geneva, the Centre on Housing Rights and Evictions.

COJO'76 (1976) *Official Report of the Games of the XXI Olympiad, Montreal 1976* (three volumes). Ottawa, Montreal Olympic Organising Committee.

Colombo, M. (1984) 'Urban Designs of the Los Angeles Olympics'. *Domus*, 656, Dec.: 154–5.

Conde, Y. (1993) 'Real-estate Barcelona After the Olympics'. *Lotus International* 77: 129–30.

CONI (1960) *Official Report of the Games of the XVII Olympiad, Rome 1960* (two volumes). Rome, Italian National Olympic Committee.

Constanza, R. (1991) *Ecological Economics*. New York, Columbia University Press.

COOB'92 (1992) *Official Report of the Games of the XXV Olympiad, Barcelona 1992* (four volumes). Barcelona, Comitè Organitzador Olimpic Barcelona'92, S.A.

CSL (2008) *A Measure of Performance – Reporting Review August 2008*. Commission for a Sustainable London 2012. Available online www.cslondon.org/documents/A_measure_of_performance.pdf (accessed 17 September 2008).

Curwell, S., Hamilton, A. and Cooper, I. (1998) 'The Bequest Network: Towards Sustainable Urban Development'. *Building Research and Information*, 26 (1): 56–65.

Deakin, M., Curwell, S. and Lombardi, P. (2001) 'BEQUEST: Sustainability Assessment, the Framework and Directory of Methods'. *International Journal of Life Cycle Assessment*, 6 (6): 370–90.

Deakin, M., Curwell, S. and Lombardi, P. (2002) 'Sustainable Urban Development: the Framework and Directory of Assessment Methods'. *Journal of Environmental Assessment Policy and Management*, 4 (2): 171–97.

De Coubertin, P. (1896) The modern Olympic Games. In: Athens 1896 OCOG (ed.) *Official Report of the Games of the I Olympiad, Athens 1896* (one volume). Athens, Organising Committee for the Games of the I Olympiad Athens 1896.

De Coubertin, P. (1906) 'Olympie' (Olympia). *Revue Pour Les Français*, April: 135–9.

De Coubertin, P. (1907) 'Olympic Competitions in Painting, Sculpture and Architecture for 1908'. *Revue Olympique*, October: 343–5.

De Coubertin, P. (1908) *Lettre circulaire aux membres du CIO* (Circular letter to the IOC members). March, Lausanne, IOC archives.

De Coubertin, P. (1909a) 'Le Cadre, Une Olympie Moderne' (The Setting, a Modern Olympia). *Revue Olympique*, October: 153–6.

De Coubertin, P. (1909b) Arts, letters and sports. In: De Coubertin, P. (ed.) *A twenty-one year campaign*, Paris, Hachette, pp. 192–200.

De Coubertin, P. (1909c) 'L'Administration' (Administration). *Revue Olympique*, November: 167–70.

De Jesus, G. (2004) 'A City and Olympic Mega Event: Geography, Who for?' (Internet) *Lecturas EF y Desportes*, 78, November. Available online www.efdeportes.com/efd78/geo.htm (accessed 22 November 2005).

Dubi, C. (2003) Olympic Games management: from the candidature to the final evaluation, an integrated management approach. In: *Proceedings of the International Symposium on the legacy of the Olympic Games, 1984–2000*, 14–16 November, Lausanne, International Olympic Committee.

EPA (2001) *Our Built and Natural Environment: a Technical Review of the Indicators Between Land Use, Transportation, and Environmental Quality*, Washington DC, Environment Protection Agency.

Espy, R. (1979) *The Politics of the Olympic Games*, Berkeley, CA, University of California Press.

Essex, S. and Chalkey, B. (1999) 'Urban development through hosting international events: a history of the Olympic Games'. *Planning Perspectives*, 14: 369–94.

Essex, S. and Chalkey, B. (2002) The infrastructural legacy of the Summer and Winter Olympic Games, a comparative analysis. In: *Proceedings of the International Symposium on the Legacy of the Olympic Games, 1984–2000*, 14–16 November, Lausanne, International Olympic Committee, pp. 94–101.

Essex, S. and Chalkey, B. (2003) *Urban Transformation for Hosting the Olympic Games: University Lecture on the Olympics*, Barcelona, Centre d'Estudis Olimpics (UAB). Available online http://olympicstudies.uab.es/lectures/web/pdf/essex.pdf (accessed 17 May 2005).

Ewing, R., Pendall, R. and Chen, D. (2000) *Measuring Sprawl and its Impact, the Character and Consequences of Metropolitan Expansion*, Washington DC, Smart Growth America.

Felli, G. (2002) IOC requirements and view of Sydney needs for the future – Olympic venue review (Speech record). In: *Proceedings of the International Conference on Architecture and International Sporting Events*, May, Lausanne, International Olympic Committee, pp. 15–19.

Felli, G. (2003) Interview with the author on 23 July, Lausanne, Olympic Studies Centre.

Frenckell, E. (1949) 'Olympic Village of Helsinki 1952'. *Olympic Revue*, 15, April: 30–1.

Fu, L. (2002) 'The Olympic Games' impact on host's tourism, procedure and performance'. Unpublished thesis of the IOC Olympic Study Centre Postgraduate Research Grant 2002, Lausanne, Olympic Studies Centre library.

GLA (2002) *Planning for London's Growth*, London, Greater London Authority.

GLA (2004) *Mayor of London. The London Plan: Spatial Development Strategy for Greater London*, London, Greater London Authority.

Gold, J.R. and Gold, M.M. (2008) 'Olympic Cities: Regeneration, City Rebranding and Changing Urban Agendas', *Geography Compass*, 2/1: 300–18.

Gordon, B.F. (1983) *Olympic Architecture, Building for the Summer Olympic Games*, New York, John Wiley & Sons.

Gratton, R. (1999) The media. In: Cashman, R. and Hughes, A. (eds) *Staging the Olympics, the event and its impact*, Sydney, University of New South Wales Press.

Greene, S. (2003) 'Stages Cities: Mega-events, Slum Clearance and Global Capital'. *Yale Human Rights & Development Law Journal*, 6: 161–87.

Guttmann, A. (1992) *The Olympics: a History of the Modern Games*, Chicago, IL, University of Illinois Press.

Hall, C.M. (1987) 'The Effects of Hallmark Events on Cities'. *Journey of Travel Research*, 26 (2): 44–5.

Hall, C.M. (1992) *Hallmark Tourist Events: Impacts, Management and Planning*, London, Belhaven.

Hamilton, K. (2000) The rent race: Sydney's new Olympic sport. In: *Housing crisis in the Olympic city: special report on homelessness.* (Internet) University of Technology Sydney. Available online www.reportage.uts.edu.au/stories/2000/jun00/rent.html (accessed 21 December 2002).

Harrison, G. (1973) 'Housing Rule Pliable'. *The Montreal Star*, 17 September.

Hart, M. (1999) *Guide to Sustainable Community Indicators* (2nd edn), North Andover, MA: Sustainable Measures.

HBOS (2007) 'House prices in East End rise after Olympic win'. *Halifax and Bank of Scotland Research Bulletin*, 2 February 2007. Available online www.hbosplc.com/media/pressreleases/articles/halifax/2007–02–02–01-halifax.asp (accessed 3 March 2007).

Henry, B. (1948) *An Approved History of the Olympic Games*, New York, G.F. Putnam's Sons.

Hiller, H.H. (2003) Toward a science of Olympic outcomes: the urban legacy. In: *Proceedings of the International Symposium on the Legacy of the Olympic Games, 1984–2000*, 14–16 November, Lausanne, International Olympic Committee, pp. 102–9.

Hough, M. (1984) *City Form and Natural Process: Towards a New Urban Vernacular*, London, Croom Helm.

Huang, A. and Xu, Y. (2005) 'The redevelopment of Beijing: Does poor still afford to live here?' *China News Week*, 31 March. Available online http://news.xinhuanet.com/overseas/2005–03/31/content_2767488.htm (accessed 13 October 2008).

Huberty, E. and Wange, W.B. (1976) *Die Olympischen Spiele, Montreal Innsbruk*, Munich, Lingen Verlag.

IOC (1957) *Information for Cities which Desire to Stage the Olympic Games*, Lausanne, International Olympic Committee.

IOC (1975) *Olympic Rules*, Lausanne, International Olympic Committee.

IOC (1992) *Manual for Cities Bidding for the Olympic Games*, Lausanne, International Olympic Committee.

IOC (1993) *Environmental Guidelines for Summer Olympic Games*, Lausanne, International Olympic Committee.

IOC (1994) *IOC Olympic Village Guidelines*, Lausanne, International Olympic Committee.

IOC (1999a) *Building a Positive Environmental Legacy through the Olympic Games*, Commission on Sport and the Environment, Lausanne, International Olympic Committee.

IOC (1999b) *Olympic Movement's Agenda 21*, Lausanne, International Olympic Committee.

IOC (1999c) *Manual for Candidate Cities for the Games of the XXIX Olympiad 2008*, Lausanne, International Olympic Committee.

IOC (2001) *Report of the IOC Evaluation Commission for the Games of the XXIX Olympiad in 2008*, Lausanne, International Olympic Committee.

IOC (2002) *Olympic Games Study Commission Interim Report to 114th IOC Session* (Mexico City), Lausanne, International Olympic Committee.

IOC (2003) *Manual for Candidate Cities for the Games of the XXX Olympiad 2012*, Lausanne, International Olympic Committee.

IOC (2004) *IOC Report of Candidature Acceptance Group of 2012 Games*, Lausanne, International Olympic Committee, pp. 36–7.

IOC (2005) *Manual on Sport and the Environment* (2nd edn), Lausanne, International Olympic Committee.

IOC (2007) *Olympic Charter*, June 2007, Lausanne, International Olympic Committee.

IOC (2008) *Promotion of Sustainable Development.* Available online www.olympic.org/uk/organisation/missions/environment_uk.asp (accessed 13 October 2008).

IPCC (2007) *Fourth Assessment Report: Climate Change 2007*, Geneva, Intergovernmental Panel on Climate Change (IPCC).

IUCN, UNCP and WWF (1991) *Caring for the Earth Second Report on World Conservation and Development*. International Union for the Conservation of Nature and Natural Resources (IUCN), United Nations Environmental Programme (UNEP) and the World Wide Fund for Nature (WWF). London, Earthscan.

Jenks, M. and Burgess, R. (2000) *Sustainable Urban Form for Developing Countries*, London, E. & F.N. Spon.

Jenks, M., Burton, E. and Williams, K. (1996) *The Compact City: a Sustainable Urban Form?* London, E. & F.N. Spon.

Jennings, A. and Simpson, V. (1992) *The Lords of the Rings*, London, Associated Press.

Jewell, B. and Kilgour, K. (2000) Sharing the spirit: the impact of the Sydney 2000 Olympics on human rights in Australia. In: Taylor, T. (ed.) *How you play the game*. Sydney, University of Technology.

John, G. and Sheard, R. (2001) *Stadia: a Design and Development Guide* (3rd edn), Oxford, Architectural Press.

Killanin, L. (1973) *Presidents/Lord Killanin, Correspondence: 1972–1980*, IOC Historical Archives, Lausanne, Olympic Museum.

Kim, H. (1998) South Korea, experiences of evictions in Seoul. In: Azuela, A., Duhau, E. and Ortiz, E. (eds) *Evictions and the right to housing: experience from Canada, Chile, the Dominican Republic, South Africa, and South Korea*, Ottawa, IDRC publications.

Kwaak, Y. (1988) 'Urban Development and Olympic Facilities'. *Spaziosport*, special number dedicated to the Seoul Olympic Games, 1988.

LAOOC (1985) *Official Report of the Games of the XXIII Olympiad, Los Angeles 1984* (two volumes), Los Angeles, CA, Los Angeles Olympic Organising Committee.

Le Devoir (1973) 'Les Architectes' Opposent an Village Olympique Unique'. *Le Devoir*, 4 June, Montreal.

Leiper, N. (1997) A town like Elis? The Olympic impacts on tourism in Sydney. In: *Proceedings of the Australian tourism and hospitality research conference*, Sydney, 6–9 July.

Leiper, N. and Hall, M. (1993) *The 2000 Olympics and Australia's tourism industries*. Paper for the House of Representatives Committee, Canberra.

LOCOG (1948) *Official Report of the Games of the XIV Olympiad, London 1948* (one volume). London, London Organising Committee for the Olympic Games 1948.

Lomas, K., Eppel, H., Cook, M. and Mardaljevic, J. (1997) *Ventilation and thermal performance of design options for Stadium Australia*. Proceedings of International Conference on Building Simulation, Prague. Vol. 1, pp. 135–42.

Lombardi, P. and Brandon, P. (1997) Towards a multi-modal framework for evaluating the built environment quality in sustainable planning. In: Brandon, P., Lombardi, P. and Bentivegna, V. (eds) *Evaluation of the built environment for sustainability*, London, E. & F.N. Spon.

London 2012 (2007) *Towards a one planet 2012 – London 2012 Sustainability Plan*. Available online www.london2012.com/documents/locog-publications/london-2012-sustainability-plan.pdf (accessed 13 October 2008).

Lucas, C. (1904) *The Olympic Games, 1904*, Saint Louis, MO, Woodard & Tiernan.

Lyne, J. (2002) 'London, Frankfurt Ranked Top European Cities for Wealth Generation'. *The Site Selection*, 27 May.

McKay, M. and Plumb, C. (2001) *Reaching Beyond the Gold, the Impact of the Olympic Games on Real Estate Markets*, Global Insight 1, Chicago, IL, Jones Lang LaSalle Inc.

McKay, M. and Plumb, C. (2003) *Crossing the Line: World Winning Cities and the 2012 Games*, Chicago, IL, Jones Lang LaSalle Inc.

Maennig, W. (1997) Olympische spiele und wirtschaft. Weitverbreitete mi_verständnisse und achtzehn (Gegen-) Thesen. In: Grupe, O. (ed.) *Olympischer Sport*. Munich, Schorndorf.

Malouf, A. (1980) *Report of the Commission of Inquiry into the Cost of the 21st Olympiad.* Vol. 2, Canadian Commission of Inquiry into the Cost of the 21st Olympiad, Montreal. p. 58.

Meinel, K. (2001) Sustainability: management issues for the design: the involvement of the future manager of a new competition facility during the planning and design phase. In: *Proceedings of the International Conference on Architecture and International Sporting Events*, May, Lausanne, International Olympic Committee, pp. 67–73.

Melhuish, C. (1999) 'Iconic Architecture at the End of the Millennium – International Projects for the Millennium: A closer look at the Sydney Olympics, Expo-2000 Hanover and La Tour de la Terre'. *Architectural Design*, 142, November: 64–5.

Millet, L. (1996) Olympic Village after the Games. In: *Proceedings of the International Symposium on Olympic Villages*, November, Lausanne, International Olympic Committee, p.123.

Mitchell, G. (1996) 'Problems and Fundamentals of Sustainable Development Indicators'. *Sustainable Development*, 4 (1): 1–11.

Mitchell, G. (1999) A geographic perspective on the development of sustainable urban regions. In: *Geographical perspectives on sustainable development*, London, Earthscan.

Mitchell, G., May, A. and McDonald, A. (1995) 'PICABUE: A Methodological Framework for the Development of Indicators of Sustainable Development'. *International Journal of Sustainable Development and World Ecology*, 2: 104–23.

Mitchell, G., May, A. and Kupiszewska, D. (1997) The development of the Leeds quantifiable city model. In: Brandon, P. *et al.* (eds), *Evaluation of sustainability in the built environment*, London, E. & F.N. Spon, pp. 39–52.

Mitchell, G., Hamilton, A. and Yli-Karjanmaa, S. (2002) 'Towards an Integrated Decision Support System for Urban Sustainability Assessment: the BEQUEST Toolkit'. *Building Research and Information*, 30 (2): 109–15.

Moore, M. (2000) 'Super Dome'. *Sydney Morning Herald*, 10 June.

Muller, N. (2000) Educational use of athletic activity. In: Muller, N. (ed.), *Pierre de Coubertin: Olympism – selected writings*, Lausanne, International Olympic Committee, p. 184.

Munoz, F. (1997) Historic evolution and urban planning typology of Olympic Village. In: *Proceedings of International Symposium on Olympic Villages*, November, Lausanne, International Olympic Committee.

NBSC (2003) *The Survey Suggests Satisfaction for Most Beijing Residents in their Housing Conditions* (Chinese text). Beijing, National Bureau of Statistics of China. Available online www.stats.gov.cn/was40/reldetail.jsp?docid=72438 (accessed 13 October 2008).

Nikolopoulou, M. (2000) *Thermal Comfort in Outdoor Urban Spaces*, Cambridge, Cambridge University Press.

Noguchi, M. and Givoni, B. (1997) Outdoor comfort as a factor in sustainable towns. In: *Proceedings of the Second International Conference for Teachers in Architecture*, Paper 3.01, Florence, Italy.

OCA (1999) *Stadium Australia*. Development fact sheet. Sydney, Olympic Co-ordination Authority.

OCA (2000) *Official Report of the Games of the XXVII Olympiad, Sydney 2000* (three volumes), Sydney, Organising Committee for the Games of the XXVII Olympiad Sydney 2000.

OCLA (1933) *Official Report of the Games of the X Olympiad, Los Angeles 1932* (one volume), Los Angeles, Olympic Committee of the Games of Los Angeles 1932 Limited.

OCOA (1896) *Official Report of the Games of the I Olympiad, Athens 1896*, Athens, Organising Committee for the Games of the I Olympiad Athens 1896.

OCOG-80 (1980) *Official Report of the Games of the XXII Olympiad, Moscow 1980* (two volumes), Moscow, Organising Committee for the Games of the XXII Olympiad Moscow 1980.

OCOM (1972) *Official Report of the Games of the XX Olympiad, Munich 1972* (three volumes), Munich, Organising Committee for the Games of the XX Olympiad Munich 1972.

ODA (2007) *Sustainable Development Strategy*, London, Olympic Development Authority. Available online www.london2012.com/documents/oda-publications/oda-sustainable-development-strategy-full-version.pdf (accessed 13 October 2008).

OKOB (1936) *Official Report of the Games of the XI Olympiad, Berlin 1936* (two volumes), Organisation Kommittee Fur Die XI Olympiade Berlin 1936. Berlin, Wihelm Limpert Press.

Ortensi, D. (1972) 'The Olympic Village and the Gigantism of the Games'. *Olympic Review*, February: 56–7.

Owens, S. (1986) *Energy, Planning and Urban Form*, London, Pion.

Panstadia (1999) 'Regeneration'. *Journal of Panstadia* [Internet] Vol. 6, June. Available online www.panstadia.com/vol6/61–083.htm (accessed 17 October 2002).

Pitts, A. (2004) *Planning and Design Strategies for Sustainability and Profit*, London, Architectural Press.

Preuss, H. (2000) *Economics of the Olympic Games, Hosting the Games 1972–2000*, Sydney, University of New South Wales Press.

Radwanski, G. (1973) 'Protest from the Joint Committee for the Preservation of Green Spaces'. *The Saturday Gazette*, 15 September.

Real Talk (1967) 'Mexico, Pre-Olympics'. *Magazine of Real Talk*, 13 November: 25.

Reth, I. (1993) 'Barcelona ein Jahr nach den Spielen'. *Frankfurter Allgemeine Zeitung*, 23 July: 35.

Richardson, H., Chang, H., Bae, C. and Baxamusa, M. (2000) Compact cities in developing countries: assessment and implications. In: Jenks, M. and Burgess, R. (eds) *Compact cities: sustainable urban forms for developing countries*, London, E. & F.N. Spon.

Roaf, S., Crichton, D. and Nicol, F. (2005) *Adapting Buildings and Cities for Climate Change*, Oxford, Architectural Press.

Robinson, A. (1990) 'Olympic Village with its Face to the Sea'. *Olympic Review*, September: 267–70.

Rudlin, D. and Falk, H. (1999) *Building the 21st Century Home, the Sustainable Urban Neighbourhood*, Oxford, Architectural Press.

Rurheiser, C. (1996) 'How Atlanta Lost the Olympics'. *New Statesman*, 125 (July 19): 28–9.

Saaty, T. (1980) *The Analytic Hierarchy Process*, New York, McGraw-Hill International.

Saaty, T. (1994) *Fundamentals of Decision Making and Priority Theory with the AHP*, Pittsburgh, RWS Publications.

Saaty, T. (1999) Fundamentals of the analytic network process. In: *Proceedings of the International Symposium Analytic Hierarchy Process (ISAHP)*, 12–14 August, Kobe, pp. 1–14.

Santamouris, M., Papanikolaou, N., Livada, I., Koronakis, I., Georgakis, C., Argiriou, A. and Assimakopoulos, D.N. (2001): 'On the Impact of Urban Climate on the Energy Consumption of Buildings'. *Solar Energy*, (70) 3: 201–16.

SAS (2001) *Olympic Games and Sports Buildings*, Tianjin, Sports Architectural Studio, Tianjin University Press.

Schmidt, H. (1971) 'The Olympic Village'. *Olympic Review*, 44: 258–61.

Schrank, D. and Lomax, T. (2005) *2005 Urban Mobility Report* (Internet]) Texas Transportation Institute (TTI) website. Available online http://tti.tamu.edu/documents/mobility_report_2005.pdf (accessed 12 May 2005).

Searle, G. (2003) The Urban Legacy of the Sydney Olympic Games. In: *Proceedings of the International Symposium on the Legacy of the Olympic Games, 1984–2000*, 14–16 November, Lausanne, International Olympic Committee, pp. 118–26.

Selman, P. (1996) *Local Sustainability: Managing and Planning Ecologically Sound Places*, London, Paul Chapman Publishing.

Sheard, R. (2001) *Sports Architecture*, London, E. & F.N. Spon.

Shen, D. and Xiong, G. (1996) 'About Urban Open Space' (Chinese text). *Journal of Urban Planning*, 10 June: 12–14.

Sit, V. (1996) *Beijing, the Nature and Planning of a Chinese Capital City*, New York, John Wiley & Sons.

Slavin, M. (2006) *London Olympic Housing Impacts*, Cape Town, Habitat International Coalition. Available online www.hic-net.org/articles.asp?PID=543 (accessed 13 October 2008).

SLOOC (1988) *Official Report of the Games of the XXIV Olympiad, Seoul 1988* (three volumes), Seoul, Seoul Olympic Organising Committee.

SOCOG (1912) *Official Report of the Games of the V Olympiad, Stockholm 1912* (one volume), Stockholm, Swedish Olympic Committee for the Olympic Games of Stockholm 1912.

Somma, P. (1993) 'Atlanta – the Olympics and Ethnic Cleaning'. *Spazio e Societa – Space & Society*, 16 (64), October: 100–9.

Sorbonne, G.R. (2000) Pierre De Coubertin's revelation. In: Muller, N. (ed.), *Pierre de Coubertin: Olympism – selected writings*, Lausanne, International Olympic Committee.

Stone, C. (2001) 'The Atlanta Experience Re-examined: the Link Between Agenda and Regime Change'. *International Journal of Urban and Regional Research*, 25: 20–34.

Stratton, R. (1986) 'La Metamorfosis de Seül'. *Revista Olímpica*, 222–3: 218–22.

Synadinos, P. (2001) 'Post-Olympic Use: a Picture of the Future'. *Olympic Review*, October: 39–41.

Tarzia, V. (2003) *European Commission Project: European Common Indicators – Towards a Local Sustainable Profile*, Milan, Ambiente Italia Research Institute.

Taylor, P., Walker, D. and Beaverstock, J. (2002) Firms and their global service networks. In: Sassen, S. (ed.), *Global networks, linked cities*, London, Routledge.

Tejero, E. (2001) From district problems to city debates. In: *Proceedings of the international conference of envisioning telecity – the urbanisation of ICT*, Berlin, Technical University of Berlin.

Thomas, D. (1999) *The Olympic Village Handbook, Architecture and Environment*, Cape Town, Derek Thomas Architect and Environmental Planner.

Thomas, R. and Potter, S. (1977) 'Landscape with Pedestrian Figures'. *Built Environment Quarterly*, (3): 286–90.

Thornley, A. (1999) *Urban Planning and Competitive Advantage: London, Sydney and Singapore*. LSE London Discussion Paper No. 2. Available online www.lse.ac.uk/Depts/london/Acrobat/LSEL_DP2.pdf (accessed 15 September 2005).

TNOC (1928) *Official Report of the Games of the IX Olympiad, Amsterdam 1928* (one volume), Amsterdam, The Netherlands Olympic Committee.

TOCOG (1964) *Official Report of the Games of the XVIII Olympiad, Tokyo 1964* (two volumes), Tokyo, Tokyo Organising Committee for the Olympic Games 1964.

Towndrow, J. (1998) 'Sydney's Sustainable Olympic Village Unveiled'. *The Architect's Journal*, 23 May.

Truno, E. (1995) Barcelona: city of sport. In: de Moragas, Miquel and Botella, Miquel (eds), *The keys to success: the social, sporting, economic and communications impact of Barcelona '92*. Barcelona, UAB, pp. 43–56.

U.N. (1998) *Cities: Statistical Administrative and Graphical Information on the Major Urban Areas of the World*, United Nations Project, Barcelona, Institute d'Estudis Metropolitans de Barcelona.

UNCED (1992) *Earth Summit: Agenda 21 – The United Nations Programme Action from Rio*, New York, United Nations Conference on Environment and Development.

UNCSD (2005) *Indicators of Sustainable Development: Guidelines and Methodologies* (Internet). The official website of the United Nations Commission for Sustainable Development. Available online www.un.org/esa/sustdev/natlinfo/indicators/isdms2001/isd-ms2001isd. htm (accessed 19 January 2005).

UNEP (2002) *Global Environment Outlook 2002 (GEO Year Report)*, Nairobi, United Nations Environment Programme (UNEP).

UNEP (2003) *Global Environment Outlook 2003 (GEO Year Report)*, Nairobi, United Nations Environment Programme (UNEP).

UNEP (2004) *Global Environment Outlook 2004 (GEO Year Report)*, Nairobi, United Nations Environment Programme (UNEP).

UNFPA (2000) *Population Issues: Briefing Kit 2000*, New York, United Nations Population Fund (UNFPA).

Varela, A.M. (2002) The path of the Olympic Games: twenty-six editions. In: *Proceedings of the International Symposium on the Legacy of the Olympic Games, 1984–2000*, 14–16 November, Lausanne, International Olympic Committee.

Wackemagel, M., McIntosh, J., Rees, W. and Woollard, R. (1993) *How Big is Our Ecological Footprint? A Handbook for Estimating a Community's Appropriated Carrying Capacity*, Vancouver, University of British Columbia.

Walker, D. (1984) 'Ephemeral Olympics: Temporary Contemporary Architecture in Los Angeles'. *Architectural Review*, 176 (1050): 48–51.

Warner, A. (2008) *Athens Sounds a Warning over London Legacy*. Available online www. bbc.co.uk/blogs/olympics/2008/06/athens_sounds_a_warning_over_l.html (accessed 15 September 2008).

WCED (1987) *Our Common Future*, World Commission on Environment and Development, Oxford, Oxford University Press.

Wilson, P. (1976) Helsinki 1952. In: Killanin, M. and Rodda, J. (eds), *The Olympic Games*, New York, Macmillan.

Wimmer, M. (1976) *Olympic Buildings*, Leipzig, Edition Leipzig.

Yi, D. (2006) 'Beijing Residents Protest the Construction of an Olympic Power Station Close to their Home' (Chinese text). *Wenweipo Newspaper*, 16 October. Available online http://paper.wenweipo.com/2006/10/16/CH0610160028.htm (accessed 13 October 2008).

Index

Figures and tables are indicated by *italic* page numbers. Individual Olympic Games are listed under the city followed by the date, e.g. Los Angeles (1932).